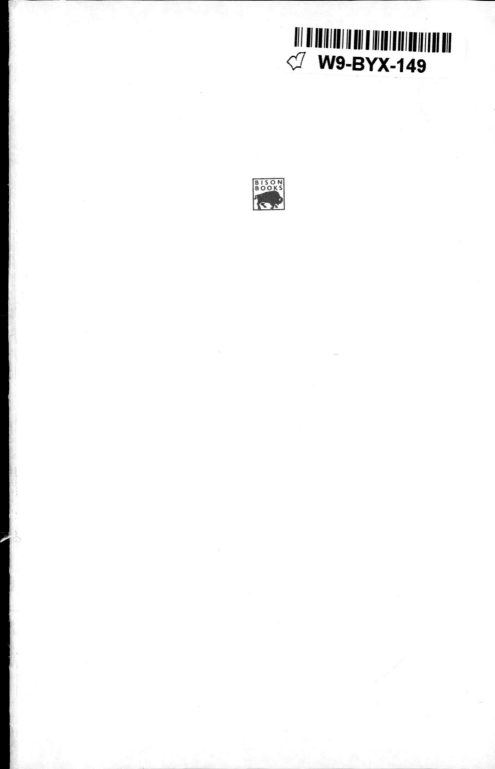

BISON
BOOKS

Books by Ralph Moody
Available in Bison Books editions

American Horses
Come on Seabiscuit!
The Dry Divide
The Fields of Home
The Home Ranch
Horse of a Different Color
Kit Carson and the Wild Frontier
Little Britches
Man of the Family
Mary Emma & Company
Riders of the Pony Express
Shaking the Nickel Bush
Stagecoach West
Wells Fargo

Horse of a
Different Color

Reminiscences of a Kansas Drover

By RALPH MOODY

University of Nebraska Press
Lincoln and London

First Bison Book printing: 1994

Library of Congress Catloging-in-Publication Data
Moody, Ralph, 1898–
Horse of a different color: reminiscenses [sic] of a Kansas drover / by Ralph
Moody.
p.   cm.
Originally published: New York: Norton, 1968.
"Bison."
ISBN 0-8032-8217-6
1. Moody, Ralph, 1898–   —Homes and haunts—Kansas.   2.
Ranchers—Kansas—Biography.   3. Ranch life—Kansas—History—20th
century.   4. Kansas—Biography.   I. Title.
CT275.M5853A3   1994
818'.5403—dc20
[B]
94-14523   CIP

Reprinted by arrangement with Edna Moody Morales and Jean S. Moody.

∞

Contents

HORSE OF A DIFFERENT COLOR

Reminiscences of a Kansas Drover

1

I Become a Drover

MY FIRST sight of Beaver Valley, lying just south of the Nebraska boundary in western Kansas, was on July 4, 1919. I'd been a Colorado ranch boy, and following my father's death in 1910 I'd worked a couple of summers for one of the leading cattle dealers there. Shortly before the outbreak of World War I my mother moved the family to Massachusetts. I was turned down for enlistment in the Army right after my nineteenth birthday, so I went away to work at carpentry in a munitions plant, where I lost more than fifty pounds during the fall of 1918. When, at the armistice, I went home, Boston specialists diagnosed my malady as diabetes, advanced to the stage where I could live no longer than six months. Our family doctor disagreed with the prognosis, put me on a strict diet, and sent me West to live outdoors in the sunshine.

I spent the winter, and the spring of 1919, in Arizona and New Mexico—riding horse falls for an outfit shooting cowboy and Indian movies, and making plaster busts of small-town bankers. I saved several hundred dollars, which I kept hidden in the cuffs of my Levi's, but lost it when my buddy and I split up in Kansas City and he took my Levi's by mistake.

Dead broke and weighing barely a hundred pounds, I hopped the night mail train for Denver, sure I could get a cowhand job from my old boss. But I was caught and kicked off the train at McCook, Nebraska, on Fourth of July morning.

Before noon I'd been hired as a harvest hand by a tenant farmer from the high divide south of Beaver Valley, and not long afterward I was fortunate enough to win the confidence of Bones Kennedy, the banker at Cedar Bluffs. Without asking my age, he lent me money after harvest to buy horses and equipment and go into the grain hauling business. By the end of the hauling season I owned thirty-seven tough mustang horses, harness for them, fourteen stout grain wagons, a good saddle, and an old Maxwell touring car that would go forty miles an hour with a little coaxing. I didn't owe a penny, had nearly three thousand dollars in the bank and a year's lease on half a section of good pasture land with a nice little home on it.

About a year before I came to the Cedar Bluffs area, Bob Wilson, who had been working for the largest livestock feeders in Kansas, moved his family there from Junction City. Except that he had some household furniture and a fairly good Buick automobile, he came as broke as I did, but Bones Kennedy set him up in the livestock buying and shipping business, and arranged for him to buy the former drover's place with no down payment.

The place was one of the finest livestock handling layouts in western Kansas. It was situated on the main road between Oberlin, Kansas, and McCook, Nebraska, and was separated from Cedar Bluffs only by the single-track branch of the CB&Q Railroad. Forty acres of rich valley land adjoined good shipping pens along the railroad siding and was surrounded on the north and east by Beaver Creek flowing at the bottom of a tree-lined gorge. Inside the bend of the creek, well protected from winter storms, were a good five-room house, barns, corrals, and a plank-fenced feed lot large enough to fatten a thousand head of stock at a time. Along the south side of the lot there were ten large sorting pens connected by stout gates and with a twenty-ton platform scale at the center.

Although Bob Wilson was an expert judge of livestock and its value, he failed as a drover because he soon earned a reputation for being tricky in his dealing and careless with the truth. There was, however, no doubt that he knew how to fatten cattle and hogs as well as any man in Kansas, so in the summer of 1919 Bones financed his going into the feeding business.

Although woefully short on experience, I started dabbling in livestock buying and shipping just before the end of the wheat-hauling season that fall. Soon afterward I worked out an arrangement with Bones for buying stock that was mortgaged to his bank. He gave me a list showing the percentage of equity each borrower had in his livestock; and I agreed to pay the farmer his equity in cash, to assume the mortgage balance, and to pay it off with interest at 10 per cent per annum when I shipped the stock to market.

I'd met Bob Wilson several times, but we'd had no business dealings, and I was never on his place until October, 1919. I was then hauling corn to the Cedar Bluffs elevator for an absentee divide landlord for whom Bones was agent, and stopped in at the bank to ask where I should deliver the nubbins.

"Deliver 'em to Bob Wilson," Bones told me, "and bring me a signed duplicate of the weight slip."

Bob, with two hired men, was weighing cattle when I drove into his dooryard. I called to him that I'd brought a load of nubbin corn from the Knapp place at Bones Kennedy's orders.

"Unload it on one of them piles," he called back, motioning toward half a dozen long corn piles outside the far end of the feed lot. To reach them I had to drive past an equal number of the worst looking haystacks imaginable. There was a ten-foot border of trampled hay around each one, and several steers were feeding at them.

The corn piles were even worse. Hogs were rooting in them, the borders were wider, and countless wagons had been driven over them in getting close enough to the piles for unloading. I drove onto one of the borders and had scooped off a dozen shovelfuls when I heard Bob shout, "Doggone you, Betty Mae! You keep away from that feed lot! One of them old sows'll chomp you up like a roastin' ear. You go play with Arvis!"

The shout was loud, but lacked any conviction that it would be obeyed.

I had the corn nearly unloaded when a little voice that sounded as if it came from under the horses called, "Hi, man!" I looked over the wagon side and saw a chubby, red cheeked little girl standing less than a foot from the lightning-fast heels of my off mustang, looking up at me with big deep-blue eyes. Afraid to make a quick move that might startle the horse, I climbed slowly down over the wheel and picked the little girl up. She snuggled against my shoulder as if she'd known me all her life, and when I asked her name she told me, "Betty Mae Wi'son, fee years old. What your name?"

"Ralph," I told her, "but they call me Bud around here." She snuggled closer and told me, "I like you, Balp."

From that moment I was hooked. I told Betty Mae I liked her too, sat her up on the wagon seat, and went back to shoveling corn. I had thrown out all but the last few ears when from the dooryard there came a musical call, "Betty Mae-eeee!"

Musical as the voice was, I recognized a note of authority in it, and so did Betty Mae. She rolled onto her stomach and started sliding off the seat. I wouldn't risk having her down behind that mustang's heels again, so caught her up and called, "She'll be right there!" Then I picked up the reins with my free hand, clucked to the team, and turned it back toward the dooryard.

As we passed the haystacks I saw a slender, dark-haired woman walking toward the scales, a baby in her arms and a pretty little girl at her side. She didn't look to be more than a year or two older than I, though Bob was at least thirty-five, but it was evident that she was his wife and thoroughly annoyed. When I pulled up at the scales she was saying, "My Lord! Anymore it seems like every time I turn my back she's off to the barns or the feed lot getting into mischief, and all you do is encourage her."

"Aw now, Marguerite," Bob answered in a half-mocking tone, "you know I don't encourage her none. Didn't you hear me holler at her a couple of times to go play with Arvis?" Then he glanced up at me and said, "This is Bud Moody, the young fella I was tellin' you about that aims to be a livestock . . ."

"No! Balp!" Betty Mae cut in.

It was just the right thing to break the tension. We all laughed, and I said, "That's right, Mrs. Wilson. The people here call me Bud, but my real name is Ralph."

"Mine's Marguerite," she told me. "That's what I like to be called, and I'm not this ornery all the time. Bob had his heart set on a boy when Betty Mae got here, and I'll swear he's still bound to make her into one. You men go on with your business; I'll try to keep her out from under your feet."

I passed Betty Mae down, and as Marguerite and the girls started toward the house Bob told me, "Come on over to the scales and I'll learn you a little something about the livestock-dealin' business."

There was plenty I needed to learn, so I tied my team and went to the scales. In the next hour I picked up several good tips, but learned more about Bob Wilson than about livestock buying. He hadn't checked the quality of the corn I brought, but signed the duplicate weight slip, crumpled the original, and threw it away. Time after time he demonstrated his ability to "guess the weight of any cow critter to within one per cent," and he bragged outrageously—apparently in an effort to show his hired men how much smarter he was than I, and to impress me with his great wealth, his independence of operation, and the fabulous profits he was making from livestock feeding.

I wasn't impressed. He claimed to have three hundred steers and half that many hogs in his lot, but I noticed a wide variation in their size, type, and condition—indicating clearly that they had been accumulated over a period of at least two months with little or no regard for quality. Since Bones had told me to deliver the nubbin corn without consulting Bob, I suspected that the off-grade stock had been acquired in the same way, and that Bob's bragging was an attempt to cover it up. At first his belittling annoyed me, but I soon realized that it was a cheap price to pay, for in order to do it he would teach me all he knew about livestock shipping and feeding.

I delivered three or four loads of nubbins a week to the Wilson place, and each time Betty Mae met me in the dooryard. She'd ride to the feed yard with me and jabber from the wagon seat as I unloaded. When I found Bob at home he was always at the scales, sharpening his guessing eye as the hired men drove steers on and off the platform. As soon as I'd unload he'd call, "Come on over here so's't I can learn you the livestock business before you lose your shirt at it." He always threw away the weight slips I brought him from the elevator, and he never failed to ridicule me when I misjudged an animal's weight. But with each session my eye became sharper, and I gained more confidence in my buying judgment. By mid-November I was shipping one or two carloads of livestock every Saturday, and making an average profit of fifty dollars a car on them.

Early on the Monday morning before Thanksgiving, Bones phoned and asked me to come to the bank right away. When I went in he told me, "A lot of poor quality hogs and cattle accumulated around here during the war, but that kind of breeding stock has to be cleared out if these farmers are to prosper. Before this week is over I aim to rid every mortgaged herd in Beaver Township of low grade stock. There's not a man on my books that wouldn't take George Miner's word for

the worth of any animal on his place, so I've got George starting out this morning to do the culling and set the amounts to
be credited against the mortgages. What I want is for you to
go with him, keep books on the stock he culls, and take care of
the rounding up and shipping. If you do a good job of it I'll
pay you fifty dollars a carload. Is that fair?"

I told him that nothing could be fairer, drove home as fast
as my old Maxwell would climb the divide, saddled my tough
little mustang mare, Kitten, and set out for the Miner place at
a canter. I knew George only by sight, but had heard a good
deal about him, for he was invariably agreed upon as arbitra-
tor when a dispute arose between Beaver Township farmers.
He was middle-aged, of medium height, slender, tight-wound,
a bit stooped, and unhurried in his movements. His farm, on
the low bench that skirted the north side of Beaver Valley,
was one of the best in Decatur County, and his herd of nearly
pure-blooded Hereford cattle was unquestionably the best.

George was waiting with a saddled horse, and I soon found
that he was as unhurried and mild in speaking as in his ac-
tions. He had evidently talked with Bones since I had, and
knew that I understood the purpose of what we were to do.
His only comment about it was that we were lucky to have
Bones as our banker, and that weeding the culls out of the
herds would do the township as much good as spring dipping
would do a lousy calf.

We started at the northeast corner of the township, working
southward onto the high divide, for it was there rather than in
the herds of the prosperous valley farmers that most of the
poor stock was to be found. When we rode into a man's place
George visited with him a few minutes, then explained the
reason for our call, saying that the value of any culled stock
would be credited against his bank loan. No man objected to
having his cattle and hogs culled, or to the value George
placed on any animal. As each was weeded out I squirted it
with a line of identification dye and entered it in a notebook
for Bones, showing description, approximate weight, and the

value George had placed on it.

There was no newspaper in Beaver Township, but none was needed, because we had a party-line telephone system and Effie Simons. Half a dozen one-to-four-party lines in Cedar Bluffs, and four rural lines—each serving from ten to fifteen ranches—covered the entire thirty-six square miles of the township. To hear all that was being said over a party line, anyone with a phone on it had only to take the receiver off the hook, so there were few private conversations. Life for the average western Kansas farmer's wife was hard, lonely, and monotonous, and when she could spare half an hour from her work her sole means of entertainment was "listening in" on the party line.

Effie Simons—in her mid-forties, wife of the mail carrier on the high divide route, garrulous, gossipy, and ample in beam and bosom with a heart to match—operated the telephone switchboard from a little ten-by-fifteen-foot central office building in Cedar Bluffs. She was not only the telephone operator, but newscaster for the township, listened in on all conversations, and handled all local advertising by making "line calls." The line-call signal was three rounds of four short rings, and at the sound of it every woman with a phone on the line dropped whatever she was doing to run and listen. Effie's enthusiasm for the subject of each line call was always reflected in her voice, and the results were usually in direct ratio to the ardor of her sales pitch.

George Miner and I had stopped at only three or four places when it became evident that Effie had put out an enthusiastic line call about the culling. There was no further need for explanations, and more often than not we found the farmer's hogs and cattle already penned up for inspection. We covered nearly a quarter of the township the first day, with George culling more than fifty cattle and a hundred hogs. He planned our route so that it would bring us to his place at sunset, and told me to meet him there at sunrise next morning.

From the buildings on the Miner place to those on the Wilson place was only three quarters of a mile by road, and little more than half that far across the fields. On my way home I stopped in at Wilson's to offer Bob twenty-five dollars for the use of his sorting pens on Saturday, found him at the house, and he asked me in. He agreed to rent me the pens, and Marguerite invited me to supper. I told her I was grateful, but would have to go home because I was on a diet and could eat only gluten bread, fish, chicken, eggs, and green vegetables. She let me go, but insisted that I bring her some gluten flour next morning and stay with them the rest of the week, rather than make the sixteen-mile ride home and back every day.

I did, and the evenings were almost like being at home with my own family again. The hired men ate and slept in the bunkhouse. Without them for an audience, Bob did less bragging, made no attempts to belittle my ability, and was jovial. Marguerite was as good a cook as my mother, and baked me gluten bread that was almost delicious, though mine always looked and tasted as if I'd made it with sawdust. Betty Mae completely stole my affection in those few nights I stayed with the Wilsons, riding piggyback on my shoulders or cuddling in my lap for a story after supper.

2

A Lesson from George Miner

By FRIDAY evening George Miner and I had covered the entire township, and with no apparent intention he had taught me more about judging livestock than I could have learned in any other way. When looking over a farmer's cattle and hogs he made no arbitrary decisions, but led the man into thinking as he did. If there was a scrawny, nondescript heifer in the herd—and in the herd of each tenant farmer on the high divide there were usually three or four of them, with a bull to match—George might say, "Was you to keep that roan heifer over the winter, Joe, I reckon you'd be owin' yourself money. If she ain't farrow, she'll drop an awful small calf come spring, don't you think? And from the looks of that bag and them little short tits, I wouldn't misdoubt that about four quarts to the milkin' would be as much as she'd ever give.

"Now you take that spotted one over there; she ain't got too bad of a bag on her, but don't you figure she's too weedy in the legs and ga'nt in the belly to ever make a good milk cow? I might be all wrong, but it always appeared to me like a good milk cow ought to have belly enough to hold a big load of grass and water—along with a good sized calf—elseways she

ain't got much to draw on when it come to fillin' a milk
bucket. Don't I recollect of you buyin' this bull of yours at the
auction when old man Peterson died, a couple of years before
the war commenced?"

"Yeah, that's the same one, George. You sure have got a
right good memory."

"I wouldn't bank much on it, Joe, but I kind of recollect
takin' note of him at that auction and gettin' the notion into
my head that his kinfolks was like as not the first cattle to be
fetched into this part of the country. My father used to tell
about 'em; Longhorns from Texas; drove up here over the
Chisholm Trail in the 1870's; some of 'em close onto six foot
high at the shoulder hump and no more'n eighteen inches
wide acrost the hips. He used to say a Longhorn cow wouldn't
give milk enough to fill a tin cup, and it was so poor it would
take four days for cream to rise on it. Used to say Longhorn
beef was tougher'n boot leather, the longer you chewed a
piece of it the bigger it got, and a man would like to strangle
if he tried to swaller it. In the eighties they begun fetchin' in
Shorthorn bulls from England to improve the herds, but a lot
of that blood got spread out so thin it didn't do much good.

"Now you understand, Joe, I couldn't say this bull of yours
come down from that early stock, but I wouldn't misdoubt it
from them wide horns of his, and that roan color. Anyways,
he's kind of gettin' on in years, and you could lose him out-
right if he was to get blowed down in a blizzard come winter.
Did ever you take note of them Holstein cattle Bud Austin
fetched home from the Kansas City stock show a few years
back? They ain't purebreds, exceptin' the bull, but they're
awful nice milk cows; bags the size of a wash tub, and some of
'em will give up to thirty quarts of milk a day. Last time I
talked to Bud he was sayin' he had three or four comin'-two-
year-old bulls in that herd that he'd like to get rid of, and I
don't reckon he'd expect to get all outdoors for one of 'em.

"If you want me to cull out old Roany here, and few of
these weedy heifers he's sired, you'd have a pretty good little

credit comin' on your notes at the bank, and I wouldn't doubt me none that Bones would leave you have a new loan for enough to get one of them Bud Austin bulls . . . and maybe a heifer or two. Seems like older cows—like them yon-der—generally always drop stronger calves when they're bred to a young bull, and one of them little fellas of Bud's would be in fine shape for next breedin' season if you was to put him into your herd this fall. The nice part about a Holstein bull for a mixed-breed milk herd is that his heifer calves most gener-ally turn out to be good milkers—that is, if the cows that bear 'em are worth their keep—and his bull calves have a big enough frame on 'em to make pretty fair beef steers."

If he was looking at hogs he'd point out that this or that one looked to be a little short on size and long on years, or he might say, "It's surprisin's, ain't it, the way these corn-country hogs run mostly to lard and fatback after they've been inbred a few generations. It used to be a fat hog was a good hog, but anymore it seems like they're goin' out of style, along with whiskers and Congress boots and the likes. Mostly the packin'-house buyers down to Kansas City and Omaha want bacon hogs—long in the back and slim in the gut, with a lot of lean streaks mixed in amongst the fat—and the way the market is now they'll pay up to three cents a pound more for them kind of hogs than what they will for fat ones.

"Did ever you take a look at Russie Redfern's Berkshires? If that brood boar of his ain't six foot long he won't miss it but a few inches, and he's no bigger 'round the belly than that little sow yonder, but the hams and shoulders on him are square as boxes. I have a notion Russie'd sell a whole litter of pigs by that boar, and out of a right good Berkshire sow, for what Bones would allow you on your boar and a couple of these wore-out old brood sows. Mix a litter like that in with the best of your young sows, Bill, and it wouldn't be scarcely no time at all till you'd have one of the best hog herds on this divide."

One of the valley farmers had a rather large herd of mixed cows and steers, with a massive-shouldered bull that weighed well over a ton and looked to be more Durham than anything else. The whole herd was in good flesh, and I judged that some of the better steers would scale above eight hundred pounds, though others that looked older wouldn't go more than six hundred. The herd had been corralled before we arrived, and the farmer showed it to us with evident pride. The cattle were unusually docile, and as we walked among them George asked, "How many of 'em you milkin', Harry?"

"Ninteen," Harry answered, "and there ain't a poor milker amongst 'em. They've been turning out close onto sixty-five pounds of butter a week all fall."

"Mmm hmmm," George hummed. "Been feedin' 'em any grain?"

"None to speak of, George. Only a load or two of frostbit corn now and again."

"Well, by jiggers, they sure are in nice flesh, Harry. I don't see one amongst 'em that I could rightly cull."

Harry bristled. "What do you mean rightly cull?" he demanded.

George didn't seem to have noticed the anger in the farmer's voice, but asked mildly, "Do you recollect that team of bay trotters I used to have before the war, Harry?"

Harry's anger subsided as quickly as it had risen, and he answered warmly, "I sure do, George. That was a mighty fine team of road horses. How fast could they make a round trip between your place and McCook?"

The sun was warm, but there was a cold breeze from the north. Instead of answering the question immediately George began climbing over the corral fence. As we followed he told Harry, "Never did make a round trip without givin' 'em a feed of grain and a couple or three hours' rest on the McCook end of the trip, but they could leg it either way in two hours and a half. By jiggers, there's a raw edge to that breeze, and it must be my hide ain't as thick as what it used to be when I was younger."

He eased the seat of his jeans to the ground, leaned his back against the warm south side of the water tank, tipped his Stetson forward to shade his eyes from the afternoon sun, drew up his knees, rested his elbows on them, and went on, "Yep, that was a pretty fair team of trotters. A man couldn't hardly cull 'em, but I'd ought to of got rid of 'em three or four years sooner'n I did. They cost me a heap of money along toward the last."

We'd squatted on our heels facing George, and Harry looked as puzzled as I felt. "How the heck could they cost you money along towards the end?" he asked. "You didn't have no vet bills on 'em, did you?"

"Nary a dime," George told him, "but to have 'em in good shape for the road they had to be stable kept, and it took about a ton of alfalfa hay and eight bushels of oats a month to feed 'em. Of course in them days grain and hay was cheaper'n what they are now but, near as I could reckon, the feed for that team cost me leastways twenty-five dollars a month, and drivin' 'em to McCook on Saturdays took the whole day's time. I ain't no Barney Oldfield at drivin' an automobile you understand, but with the Oakland I can easy make the round trip to McCook in two hours, and it don't cost me over four dollars a month for gas and oil. It seems like nowadays new ways of doin' things come along so fast a farmer can't hardly keep up with 'em, but if he don't it can sure cost him a lot of money."

Harry seemed a bit confused, and said, "I guess I ain't follerin' you too good, George. How do you mean?"

"Well, it used to be, back before the war commenced, a valley farmer could do right good with a mixed herd of cattle; one with some Jersey and Guernsey blood mixed in with his beef stock, so's't he'd have milkers enough that the butter'd square the grocery bill. When he come to sell his steers it didn't make much difference what their color was, or if them out of his milk cows was a trifle on the runty side, and them out of his beef stock was built kind of like a buffalo bull —most of their weight up front, and spindlin' off to a little of nothin' in the hind end. But it seems like the style in cattle has changed. Anymore the buyers for them big packin' houses down to Kansas City and Omaha will pay close onto twice as much for a carload of fat steers if they're all of one breed and one age and one size than what they'll give for a mixed-color carload of the same weight. To top the market every steer in a car lot has to be a match for every other one; not over two years old, and danged near square—back as flat and level as a table top, close onto as wide acrost the hips and shoulders as what they are deep in the belly, with legs no longer'n their heads."

"That don't make sense," Harry broke in irritably. "Packin' houses buy cattle to slaughter, not for the show ring, and if a steer's good and fat the color of his hide or the shape of him or whether he's a two-year-old or a four-year-old don't make no difference in the quality of the beef."

George turned his face up just enough that his eyes showed under the brim of his Stetson, fired a thread-fine squirt of tobacco juice at a corn cob between his feet, and said, "Didn't make sense to me neither, Harry, till I got to studyin' on it some. Of course, the color of a critter's hide don't make no difference in the beef, exceptin' that it marks him as a certain breed or mixture of 'em. Now you take a Jersey steer; he'll need four summers on pasture and winters on hay 'fore he's big enough to put into a feed lot, and it'll take leastways four months to put a two-hundred-pound gain on him. But with all that feedin', the beef out of him won't be no better'n if it was out of a two-year-old Hereford that never seen an ear o' corn . . . and there won't be as much of it neither.

"Or you take a steer out of a pretty good mixed-breed cow that's been bred to a heavy-shouldered twenty-five-hundred-pound bull—one that's mostly Durham, with a little Longhorn and Shorthorn and one thing another throwed in. Given three or four years on good pasture and hay he'd ought to weigh close onto eight hundred pounds, and four months on corn ought to put another three hundred on him, but he'll have bone enough to carry a ton, guts as heavy as his sire's, and when he's dressed out the forequarters'll weigh close onto double what the hinds do. Bones and guts ain't worth much to a packin' house. No matter how fat that kind of a steer is the meat out of him is bound to be on the tough side, and the steak is all in the hindquarters. The forequarters, where most of the weight is, won't be good for much exceptin' pot roast and hamburger and the likes."

As George talked Harry kept glancing nervously toward the corral, and a little worry began to show in his face. More, I thought, to reassure himself than to advance an argument, he said, "If a steer's got a good layer of fat on him I don't believe a year or two of age will make all that difference in the toughness of his meat."

George looked up from under his hat again, spit, and asked, "Don't Mabel grow radishes in her kitchen garden?"

"Of course she does; all the women folks do."

"Ever notice how tender them first ones in the spring are?"

"Sure have, and tasty."

"Get kind of woody after the first two-three weeks, don't they?"

Harry seemed to get the idea that he was being drawn into a trap, and answered a bit sullenly, "Might be they do. What you drivin' at anyways?"

"Nothin' much," George told him, "exceptin' that a radish and a steer are a lot alike in one way; the faster they grow the tenderer they'll be. The big difference is that it don't cost nothin' to leave a slow-growin' radish in the garden, but a slow-growin' steer in the herd gets outside of just about as much feed in a day as a fast-growin' one.

"Now you take that Hereford herd of Otis Relph's. Only the bull is a purebred, but Otis has been keepin' that kind of sires long enough—tradin' 'em off every two-three years to bring in new blood—keepin' only the best heifer calves, and cullin' out the poorest cows every fall, that now the whole herd is as alike as a row of doves on a fence wire. In country like this valley, where there's good summer pasture and plenty of alfalfa hay for winters, you can't beat them short-legged, wide-backed Herefords like Otis's. Before they're two-year-olds his steers'll average seven hundred pounds apiece; they'll hit a thousand after ninety days on corn, and if they don't top the market when they're shipped they'll come mighty close to it."

"Yep, I suppose they will," Harry said, "and I'd sure like to have cattle like 'em, but I reckon it would cost a heap of money to build up a herd like Otis's or yours, George, and the butter from a mixed herd comes in mighty handy on the store bill."

"I wouldn't misdoubt me you could make the change-over for less'n what you'd save in feed if you done it," George told him. "Bones would allow you a pretty good price on stock as fat as what yours is—even the poorest of 'em—and I reckon you could pick up a dozen of last spring's heifer calves from Otis for around forty dollars a head. If you wanted to take in some different blood, I've got a comin'-two-year-old bull I'd leave you have for an even hundred, and I'd give you a year without interest to pay for him. Of course he ain't purebred, but he's close to it, with a good compact build, and I have a notion he'd sire some awful nice calves out of Otis's heifers.

"You know, it wouldn't surprise me none if your butter was costin' you more than what you're gettin' for it—countin' feed and the smallness of the calves a man gets out of milk cows. Not more'n a week ago I was readin' in the *Country Gentleman* about an Ayrshire dairy herd some place in Ioway. Don't recollect just how many cows there was in it, but there wasn't a one of 'em producin' less'n two pounds of butter a day. I kind of reckon it would cost about as much to get one of them kind of cows out here as what Bones would allow you on four of your milkers, but she'd turn out just as much butter as all four, and you'd save the feed that three of 'em's been gettin' outside of."

Harry sprang to his feet as if someone had pricked him with a pitchfork, reached for George's hand, pulled him up, then told him, "Cull 'em, George! Cull 'em right down close and take the bull. I'll be right proud to have that one of yours, and it won't take me no year to get him paid for neither."

In that single week George culled nearly two hundred and fifty cattle and five hundred hogs, while I booked them, arranged with farmers to haul the hogs in to the Wilson place on Saturday morning, and hired young fellows to drive in the cattle and help with the sorting and loading. George and I did little talking, but in those five days I gained a greater admiration for him than I'd ever had for any man other than my own father. I don't remember his ever calling me Ralph or Bud, but before the week was over he was calling me "Son," and I liked it.

From the time he'd talked to Harry about changing his herd over from mixed breeds to Herefords I'd been thinking about starting a beef herd of my own. When I'd first come to Beaver Township I had no intention of staying a minute beyond the end of wheat harvest, but Effie Simons took me under her wing then, and the country had been good to me every since. At first the high, dry divides with their history of crop failure and poverty, the blazing heat, and the searing wind that blew incessantly from dawn till dusk had seemed ominous to me. But month by month, as I'd made friends, prospered, and learned the richness of the soil in Beaver Valley my dislike had turned to liking. My week with George, my admiration for him, and the enjoyment I'd found in the evenings spent with the Wilsons, convinced me that I would be happy to spend the rest of my life in Beaver Township—and for some reason I couldn't put into words, I had a feeling that my life was going to be longer than the doctors believed.

As George and I rode back toward his place after making our last call, I asked, "Would spring calves winter through all right in a divide pasture that has some fairly good shelter in the gulches?"

"If they was in a herd big enough to give 'em coverage in a blizzard they'd make out all right."

"Would a horse herd do?" I asked.

"Don't hardly reckon it would," he said. "Horses and calves don't mix no better'n horseflies and honeybees. What you got in mind?"

"Well," I said, "I've leased a half-section of good pasture at the top of the high divide, and there's a lot more grazing there than my horses need. I was just wondering how it would work if I put in about a dozen top-grade Hereford heifer calves, and maybe a bull calf from a different strain."

George drew his pony a little closer to Kitten, nodded his head, and told me, "Can't think of a better way for a young fella to set hisself up in business, but was I you I'd wait till spring. Yearlin's wouldn't cost you over ten dollars a head more then than what weanlin's would cost now, and that would be cheap comparin' with the risk you'd run of losin' four or five head in winter blizzards. Besides that, when a bull calf gets to be a yearlin' you can tell a heap more about the way he'll turn out as a herd sire than what you can when he's still a weanlin'. If it was me, I'd just keep both hands in my pockets till the new grass commenced to greenin' up next April." Then he touched spurs to his pony and we made the rest of the homeward trip at a brisk canter.

At sunrise Saturday morning the stock began arriving at the Wilson place, and George "happened over" soon afterward. He stayed right through to help me until the last of the twelve carloads had been put aboard at dusk. There was, of course, no reason for Bob to help, as I was paying him only for the use of his sorting pens, but sometimes he was a hindrance. By an hour after sunrise he'd gathered most of the hog haulers at the scales, offering to bet dollars against dimes that he could guess the weight of any animal in the sorting pens to within 2 per cent, and that no other man in the crowd could come closer than 5 per cent. Right through the day he kept a crowd large enough to be a nuisance to us, and he lost only a few bets on lucky guesses. When the men had gone home he bragged that he'd won every dollar I paid them for hauling hogs.

It was after dark when the train pulled out of Cedar Bluffs and I swung aboard the caboose. The weather on Sunday was cool, so the stock traveled well, and when we reached the Kansas City stockyards early Monday morning I found a strong demand for top grade cattle and hogs, but there was very little demand for culls. George had given the farmers credit for a shade more than sixteen thousand dollars on their mortgages, but the proceeds of the sale—after deducting freight, commission, and my fee—were barely over thirteen thousand. I telegraphed the figure to Bones, spent the rest of the day trying to learn what I could around the stockyards, and caught the night train home, far from proud of the job I'd done.

3

A Different Lesson for Bob

EXCEPT ON Sundays, a freight train—its caboose serving as passenger, mail, and express car—left the main line at Orleans, Nebraska, whenever the night mail train pulled in from St. Joseph, made a run to St. Francis, Kansas, and returned to Orleans about midnight. Arrival time at way stations depended upon the number of cars left or picked up on the run, but the westbound train usually reached Cedar Bluffs in late forenoon and came back at supper time. Saturday was livestock shipping day, and the branch train never failed to make connections at the main line with the "weekender" stock trains for Omaha and Kansas City.

On my return from Kansas City there were few cars to be shunted onto sidings, so we pulled into Cedar Bluffs before ten o'clock. I went directly to the bank, gave Bones the sales tickets, and told him I was sorry to have done no better but that there had been little demand for poor grade cattle and hogs.

"There's never a demand for 'em," he told me, "so there's nothing to be sorry about. Getting that kind of stock out of the herds in this township was worth every dollar it cost me."

Then he looked at me sharply and said, "I didn't expect you back so early, but I'm glad you're here. I've just phoned for Bob Wilson to come up right away. According to what I've been hearing these last few days, he's no more fit to run a business than a five-year-old; stock running loose and scattering feed all over the place while he's sharpening up his eye at the scales so he can skin these farmers by outguessing 'em on cattle weights. Is that right?"

I tried to duck the question, but he looked me squarely in the eyes and demanded, "Is that right?"

"I wouldn't go that far," I said. "He's spent considerable time at the scales when I've been around there, and the feed is badly scattered, but he knows livestock fattening thoroughly. It's my guess that he's always worked under an owner who ran the business, and that he hasn't yet learned to be his own boss."

"Hmmff!" Bones snorted. "I've got no time to watch over him, and it sounds like the longer I let him keep that stock the more money he'll lose for me. I was doubtful of him from the start, so never let him have anything but call loans. He ought to be here any minute now, and I want you to stay."

Bob had evidently scented trouble, for he was barely inside the bank when he began bragging about the weight he was putting on his stock. Bones let him go for a couple of minutes, then broke in, "I'll take your word for that, but I can't afford any more of the slipshod way you're letting things go around there—loose stock running all over the place and scattering feed from Dan to Beersheba while you waste your help's time and your own at the scales. I want you to order cars and ship every head of that stock to market next Saturday."

"Now wait a minute!" Bob shouted. "It's no fault of mine that some of that stock's so puny I have to leave it run loose. Don't forget that you shoved half of it onto me without no chance to say if I wanted it or not, or even to dicker over the price. Some of them cattle ain't been on corn thirty days yet, and it takes that long just to get their insides fat. If I was to ship now they wouldn't bring no more than pasture cattle, and I'd lose all the feed and labor I've put into 'em."

Bones was often hot tempered, but he waited quietly for Bob to finish, then told him, "Part of what you say is true, and I want to be fair with you. If you'll ship that stock Saturday and sign over what's left of the feed, I'll cancel the balance of your notes. That way you can't lose anything. You've had a year's living for your family, and you'll be left with three good horses, harness, a wagon or two, and a couple of milch cows."

Considering the amount of feed Bob had let go to ruin and that hog prices had dropped 40 per cent since he'd bought, the offer was more than fair, but he refused it. "Right at the beginning I told you them steers wouldn't be ready to ship till January," he blustered, "and you said that would be okay. The way I'm putting weight onto 'em now, and the way the fat cattle market's going up, by January I'd have leastways a ten-thousand-dollar profit, and I don't aim to settle for a dime less."

That was too much for Bones. "There's no sense in wasting time with a man who won't talk reason," he shouted. "I'll get a court foreclosure and let the sheriff do the talking." Then he turned to me and said, "Order cars enough to ship that stock Saturday, and I'll pay you at the same rate as before."

Whether or not it was a bluff, it got results. "I didn't aim to be unreasonable," Bob said meekly, "and there's no need of you getting a court order. If you'll leave it up to George Miner, whatever he says will be all right with me."

We found George mending a corral fence, and after listening to the arguments on both sides he said, "The way I see it, neither one of you comes with clean hands. Bob, your claim that you had stock and feed shoved onto you that you didn't want don't hold water. It wouldn't have been shoved onto you if you hadn't been willin' to sign notes for it. A lender has the right to call in his loan, irregardless of due date, if the borrower is heedless or wasteful or mismanages his business, and

I'd say you've been guilty of all three."

Then he told Bones, "Harry, I'd say you've been negligent if you've just found out what's been goin' on over to Bob's place. If you'd called his loans two weeks ago, nobody could of blamed you for it. But now that you've had a tip-off about the bank examiners comin' this way it's unreasonable to foreclose or make him ship half-fat stock. Like he says, the last steers put into that lot won't bring better'n range cattle price if they're shipped now, and the feed put into 'em will be a dead loss. But he knows better'n to believe he'd make anywheres near ten thousand if he was left to feed 'em till January.

"This is what I'd suggest to the both of you: Unless I miss my guess, the hog market's due for an upturn, and the only way to get any good out of that trompled corn is to feed it to hogs. I'd say it would be best for all hands if that feed lot fence was tightened up and the hogs held long enough to turn that beat-up corn into pork. Them steers was too poor a grade to put into a feed lot in the first place, and the sooner they're shipped the better. It seems to me, Harry, like Bob ought to get the same break you had me give folks on the rest of the culls. He'd make a good fair profit sellin' 'em at twelve dollars a hundred—that is, if he'd took reasonable care of his feed and done his own work instead of hirin' a couple of men he didn't need. It'll cost around ten dollars a head to ship them steers, and I doubt me they'll bring twelve dollars a hundred at Kansas City, but I'd say you'd ought to take 'em off his hands at that price, weighed out of his lot on shipping day."

For all Bob's bluster about a ten thousand dollar profit, he agreed readily. Bones seemed less eager, but said he'd take the cattle on Saturday if George would act as weighmaster and I'd handle the shipping. I was glad to agree, but George said, "I'd be willin' to do the weighin', Harry, but I promised Irene to take her to Oberlin Saturday forenoon for her shoppin'." Then he turned to me and asked, "Do you reckon you'd have time enough to sort and load if we didn't start weighin' before one o'clock?"

"One o'clock will be just fine," Bob cut in. "Me and my men'll give him all the help he needs, so there won't be no worry about getting 'em loaded by train time."

I'd left Kitten at the Wilson place when I went to Kansas City, so stopped to get her on my way back from George Miner's. As I saddled I told Bob it seemed to me he'd have done better to take Bones's original offer, but he laughed at the idea. "Shucks," he told me, "that woulda put me out of business, but this way I'll make leastways three or four thousand bucks. Them steers in the lot cost me less'n sixty bucks a head, and I'll get close onto a hundred apiece out of 'em. Sure, there's some feed scattered around, but that don't amount to nothing. I've got plenty left to fatten a thousand cattle, and if a man's got the feed there ain't a banker no place that won't lend him the price of feeder steers and pigs. Soon as ever I get shut of these culls I aim to put in a thousand highgrade Herefords, and by spring I'll clean up a fortune on 'em."

I couldn't tell whether Bob believed what he was saying or it was just more of his big talk, but there was no use in arguing with him. I stopped at the house to thank Marguerite for her kindness, then swung onto Kitten and headed for home. On the way I stopped at the depot and had the agent, "Dad" Haynes, order ten cattle cars for Saturday morning.

There had been a dilapidated three-room house, a fairly large barn, and good pole corrals on the half-section I'd leased. My wheat-hauling crew had repaired and painted the house in spare time, and made me a snug little home with secondhand furniture. At the end of the hauling season we'd stored the wagons and harness in the barn, and turned all the horses except Kitten out to pasture for the winter.

I didn't mind housekeeping, but my diet was a nuisance. The kind of gluten bread that I baked was hard to get down, and the nearest I could come to finding fish and leafy green vegetables was canned salmon and sauerkraut. It was past noon when I got home, so I lighted a fire, put a can of sauerkraut on to heat, and opened a can of salmon. After eating I rode out to see that the horses were all right, then baked two loaves of gluten bread. It was either the worst I ever made, or comparison with Marguerite's made it taste more like sawdust and glue than usual. I opened more sauerkraut and salmon for supper, but when I sat down to the table I had no appetite. I wasn't actually lonesome but had never liked to eat alone, and hadn't realized how much I'd enjoyed mealtime while staying with the Wilsons. I was too restless to read in the evening, so saddled Kitten and rode until I was tired enough to sleep.

I spent all day Friday patching the barn roof—and nibbled at meals of warmed-over sauerkraut, salmon, and soggy gluten bread. Saturday morning I drove down to repair some sagging gates at the Cedar Bluffs shipping pens, and the first thing I noticed was the bawling of cattle in Bob's feed lot. It grew steadily louder, and by ten o'clock I became worried. It was barely a quarter-mile to the buildings on the Wilson place, but I'd seen no one stirring there all morning, so drove over to investigate. No one was at home, and the pump lay dismantled at the foot of the windmill tower. At the feed lot I found all the watering tanks bone-dry, and there was fresh salt in the cracks and corners of all the feed bunks.

I didn't need to be very bright to see through Bob's scheme: He'd get the pump repaired just in time to have those steers so loaded with water at one o'clock that they could hardly waddle onto the scales. As Bones's shipping agent, I felt that I should let him know what was going on, but I didn't like being a tattletale, so decided to ask George Miner for advice. I found him loading baskets of eggs into the back of his Oakland, and as I pulled to a stop he called, "Bob's pump went out of kilter, didn't it?"

"It seems to have," I told him. "There's no one at home, but it's pulled out of the well and dismantled."

George didn't look up, but said, "Them steers have been hollerin' the news since sunup. Bob ought to have thought about that. He could have kept 'em quiet till noontime if he'd waited till after breakfast to salt 'em, and they'd have took on just as big a load of water by one o'clock as they will this way."

"That's what I came over to talk to you about," I said. "I don't like being a squealer, but with Bones paying me to be his shipping agent don't you think I should . . ."

"Don't reckon I'd do it," George said slowly. "This is the kind of a mess where the more you stir it the more it stinks. If I was in your boots I believe I'd keep my trap shut; wouldn't let on to Bob nor nobody else that I had any notion what he was up to. Why don't you ride along to Oberlin with us if you ain't got nothin' better to do this forenoon?"

Then he turned toward the house and called, "Oh, Irene! You about ready? We'd best to get started pretty soon."

Bob must have returned very soon after I left his place. When we passed it on our way to Oberlin he and his hired men were working on the pump and too busy to notice us.

George drove an automobile with as much consideration as he drove a horse, and not much faster. It was noon before we reached Oberlin, and Mrs. Miner spent fully an hour shopping. Then George took us to the best restaurant for dinner, and the service was terribly slow. It was two o'clock before we'd finished eating, and almost three when we got back to Cedar Bluffs. On our way through town George left his wife at Grandma Rebman's, and when we drove into the Wilson yard Bob came hurrying to meet us, calling out irritably, "What's been keepin' you? The weighing-out was to begin at one o'clock, and it's danged near three a'ready."

"Now I'm right sorry about that," George said in an apologetic tone, "but anymore I don't get around as spry as I used to, and sometimes I'm a mite forgetful. Seems like I do recollect askin' Bud if commencin' at one o'clock would allow him enough loading time, and I recall you sayin' that one o'clock would be just fine, but if we agreed on that as a fixed time I sure forgot about it. Oh well, I guess it won't make much odds one way or another. I see you've got the steers all sorted and penned accordin' to sizes, so we'll have plenty of time anyways. It was the sortin' that I was mostly concerned about."

Bob was on a spot where he couldn't holler without prac-
tically admitting his guilt. I knew he was fuming inside, but
he tried to act jovial. "That's all right," he said. "I and the
boys have got everything lined out so's't you won't have to lose
a minute nowheres. I've got the scales all balanced up for you,
and the boys'll put the cattle acrost the platform as fast as you
can set weights on the beam."

The condition of the pens left little doubt as to the amount
of water Bob had managed to get into those steers—or that it
was draining away rapidly. Waterlogged cattle won't eat or
drink again for several hours, so Bob's only hope for any success in his trick was to get his steers weighed as quickly as
possible, but George wouldn't hurry. After he'd spent five or
six minutes sliding the counterpoise back and forth along the
scale beam, Bob called out, "Anything wrong, George?"

"Wouldn't say so," George answered. "Just a mite sluggish
and bound up. Nothin' more than a man might expect if
they're rusted. Stompin' on the corners ought to loosen 'em
up."

For fully half an hour George paid no attention to a few
pieces of lumber, half buried in hay chaff, that lay in the ten-
inch space between the beam housing and the fence at the
front of the scale platform. Then he sang out, "By gosh, I'll
bet that's where the boar got into the cabbage patch. Like as
not there's a rotten plank busted down onto the beam rod." He
bent over and tossed out a ten-foot 2 by 6, along with a half a
dozen shorter pieces of old lumber. "That's it, sure enough,"
he said, wrenched away a sagging plank, and slid the 2 by 6
back to bridge the hole. His face was expressionless, though I
was sure he noticed what I did—the 2 by 6 had been so
placed that, by stepping on it, the gate tender could add his
own weight to that of each batch of cattle put over the scales.

In a last desperate effort to get a few hundred pounds of
water weighed with his cattle, Bob kept his men at a trot as

they drove steers on and off the scales. It was half past three when the first ten were driven on, and four twenty when the last ten were driven off. As George weighed each batch he had Bob and me check the scales, the figure he entered on the tally sheet, and the addition to the previous total. He wrote his name below the last figure brought down, passed the pencil to Bob, and said, "I want both of you to go over my arithmetic and put your name down if you find I'm right, then there'll be no room for arguments later on." As Bob leaned over the tally sheet George looked around at me, and one eyelid drooped for an instant. I had no way of estimating how much water Bob had tried to sell Bones at twelve cents a pound, but his steers would have had to weigh an additional thirteen tons to bring the hundred dollars apiece that he'd bragged they would.

Bob helped with the loading, but didn't go along when George and I took the tally sheets to the bank. Bones made no comment on the weight, but told me to get the cattle auctioned early Monday morning, and to wire him immediately the amount he could draft against the commission agent.

Cattle usually lost 7 to 10 per cent in weight during shipment from western Kansas. But Bob's steers had dried out so thoroughly before George weighed them that the shipping shrinkage was slight, and on Monday morning beef cattle at the Kansas City auctions sold for the highest prices since the war. The steers I brought in did well enough that Bones lost barely fifteen hundred dollars on them after paying freight, selling commission, and my fee. I sent him a telegram as soon as the last carload had been sold, but there was no need of my hurrying back to Cedar Bluffs, so I took a room at the Stockmen's Hotel. It was headquarters for the biggest cattlemen in the West when they came to Kansas City, and there was never an afternoon or evening when they weren't sitting around the lobby discussing livestock and the market prospects.

For the next three days I read every word of livestock news

in the papers, listened to every discussion in the hotel lobby, and talked to every agent, drover, feeder, or stockman with whom I could scrape up an acquantance. When I boarded the train home I was more enthused about the livestock feeding business than I'd ever been about anything in my life.

4

Jointly but Not as Partners

IT WAS nearly noon when the train got to Cedar Bluffs. As I swung down to the platform, two well-dressed strangers climbed aboard, and Dad Haynes told me they were examiners who had been at the bank for the past two days. I went directly there, and from the way Bones was bubbling over with good cheer I knew he'd passed the examination better than he'd expected.

After telling me I'd done a good job in handling the shipment for him, he asked, "Why don't you and Bob go into partnership? He knows how to put fat onto cattle better than any man in Beaver Valley, and with you handling the business end of the partnership you'd make an unbeatable team. The shape I've got the bank's affairs into now, I could guarantee you all the financing you'd have any use for, and you boys would clean up a fortune in the next few years."

I'd have had to be awfully stupid not to see through what Bones had in mind. With the tremendous wastage around Bob's place and the failure of his watering trick, I knew he must be several thousand dollars in debt to the bank. The only hope Bones had of making any recovery was to keep him in the feeding business, but with a partner to offset his lack of business ability. I'd already made up my mind to go into the feeding business, and could have found no better setup for it than Bob's place, but I'd seen too much of his trickery and wastefulness to go into partnership with him. My plan was to rebuild the corrals on the place I was leasing, go into the feeding business there on a small scale, and increase it as I made money from my shipping operations. To avoid telling Bones that I wouldn't go into partnership with Bob under any circumstances, I simply said I'd have to think it over.

That afternoon I started work on the corrals. The first thing Friday morning I took a urine specimen to Dr. DeMay, the McCook doctor who had been treating me for diabetes since I'd come to Kansas. The sugar content was up slightly from the previous week, so he told me to make green vegetables half of my diet until my next visit. I bought fifty pounds of cabbage—the only green vegetable in the stores—and a box of candy for Marguerite and the girls, then dropped in at the Wilson place on my way home. The two milch cows were feeding at one of the haystacks, and a dozen or more shoats were rooting in the corn piles. The hired men appeared to be listlessly repairing one of the pen gates, while Bob sat on the fence directing them.

I stopped to talk to Marguerite a few minutes, and to give Betty Mae a piggy back ride, then went out to the feed lot. I expected Bob to question me about the steers I'd taken to Kansas City—the shipping shrink, what they'd brought at auction, etc.—but he didn't. Instead, he started telling me, in almost the exact words Bones had used, that we ought to go into partnership. He said that with him doing the feeding and me handling the business matters we'd be an unbeatable team, and that we'd both clean up fortunes in less than two years.

"That sounds awfully good," I told him, "but you'll have to count me out. It's better for you to run your own business and me to run mine. Besides, I'm going to have all the work I can handle for the next year. Along with the trading and shipping

I've been thinking of starting my own beef herd in the spring, using some of George Miner's heifers as foundation stock, and I intend to double my wheat-hauling business next fall."

Although Bob still tried to hang on, I wouldn't talk to him any more about our going into partnership, and got away as soon as I could. For the next couple of days I worked from daylight till dark at rebuilding the corrals. The gluten bread I baked was the worst I'd ever made, I got so tired of boiled cabbage and canned salmon that I hated to sit down at the table, and the evenings seemed interminable.

About an hour after sunset on Sunday, Bob came to my place alone, and was no sooner in the house than he began telling me how wealthy we'd become if I'd go into partnership with him. I let him talk for fifteen or twenty minutes, then tried to head him off by telling him I'd always had a dread of debts, and didn't want to get into a business requiring such huge loans as large-scale livestock feeding.

"There won't be no need for you to get into debt more'n ankle deep if you team up with me," he said. "There's a'ready thirty-five thousand bucks' worth of corn and hay piled up on my place, and a hundred and fifty shoats in the lot. All we'd have to sign new notes for would be three hundred feeder steers, and that wouldn't run more than about twenty thousand. By the middle of April we'd have them steers weighing leastways a thousand pounds apiece, and the shoats up to two hundred and fifty. Allowing that the market don't go up another copper that stock will fetch anyways sixty-five thousand bucks. Why daggone it, boy, you team up with me and the both of us'll lay away fifty thousand before another year rolls around."

"I'd sure like to make fifty thousand," I told him, "but I'm not going into partnership with anyone. It's better for you to have your own business and for me to have mine."

"I ain't trying to horn in on your shipping and hauling businesses, Bud," he told me earnestly. "What you make out of them would be all yours, along with half the profits on the feeding, and you'd have as much time as now. I and a couple of men would take care of all the work around the feed lot, and all you'd have to do is look after the banking and such like. You'd double your shipping business inside of a month if you had your headquarters right close to town and the bank and the railroad. Why, man alive, you're plumb loco to be batching way up here on top of the divide. There's plenty of spare room down to my place, and it wouldn't be no trouble at all for Marguerite to cook up that special grub you're supposed to eat."

Bob's offer of Marguerite's cooking and a home with children in it was a great temptation, but I'd have had to be insane to risk partnership with him. In an effort to save his feelings, I said, "I wouldn't be the right partner for you, Bob. What you need is a man who knows the business end of livestock feeding as well as you know how to put fat on the hogs and cattle."

"What I need is the right partner so's that Bones will lend us money to buy feeder steers," he said dejectedly. "He tells me straight out that if we team up he'll leave us have all the money we need to go into the feeding business in a big way, but elseways he won't lend me the price of a haircut. By farming that sixty-seven acres I couldn't make enough to pay interest on the mortgage, leave alone making a living for Marguerite and the kids. Look, Bud . . ."

With all Bob's faults I liked him, and was under obligation for the time he'd spent teaching me what little I knew about livestock trading and weight estimating. Besides, I'd become as fond of Marguerite and the little girls as if they were my own sisters. I didn't let Bob go any further, but told him, "I won't go into partnership with you, Bob, but I'll talk to Bones in the morning, and will do anything I can short of partnership to help you stay in the feeding business."

Monday morning I was waiting when Bones came to open the bank. While the key was still in the lock he began telling me that if I'd go into partnership with Bob, do the buying and selling, and keep my fingers on the purse strings and wastage, we'd make twenty-five thousand dollars apiece within a year. I thanked him for his confidence, but said that a partnership wouldn't work, because neither I nor anyone else could control Bob or make him any different than he was. "You're wrong," he told me. "You could control him easy enough if he knew that he couldn't make a deal or borrow a dime without your say-so, and I'll make that clear to him right from the beginning."

"How deep is he in the hole?" I asked.

"Without knowing how much feed there is out there, I couldn't tell you," he said, "but there's a balance of just under forty thousand on the books. Like you, Bob didn't have a dime when he came here, but he had a family to support. I can't say how much of his balance is for interest and living expenses. But he bought a lot of corn back in September when the price was fifty cents a bushel higher than it is now, and he's probably let a thousand dollars' worth go to waste. I'd be willing to say that ten thousand of his account is water already over the dam, just between Bob and me, and won't have anything to do with the partnership. I'll make up a new note for thirty thousand, then call Bob in, and when you've both signed it you'll be fifty-fifty partners, right down the line."

"I'll risk everything I own in any business I think is a good one," I told him, "but I won't risk a dollar for a man who, because of his own fault, has nothing but debts."

"Don't know as I blame you," Bones said, "but it's a pity for you two not to get together some way. Bob's too irresponsible to handle a business alone, and you don't know stock feeding well enough. But teamed together you couldn't help making a fortune, and to have a prosperous feeding outfit here would be the best thing that could happen to the corn and livestock farmers in this township. As you say, Bob don't have anything to put up as security, so I won't ask you to put up anything either. You team up with him and I'll lend the partnership enough to feed out three hundred steers and half that many hogs, and all the security I'll ask is a mortgage on the feed and livestock. Is that fair enough?"

"Perfectly fair," I said, "but I still won't risk going into partnership with him. Even though you took a mortgage on only the feed and livestock, I'd have the whole debt to pay off if we happened to run into a loss."

"Why do you say *you'd* have the debt to pay?" he asked sharply. "If you fellows happened to run into a little loss—but I don't see how in blazes you could—it would be the debt of the partnership and could be made up out of the profits on the next bunch of livestock you fed."

"Isn't any partner legally responsible for all the debts of a partnership?" I asked.

"Well, legally, I suppose," he said, "but . . ."

"Then there'll be no partnership," I broke in. "I've already told Bob that, but said I'd do anything short of it to help him stay in business. Couldn't he and I buy, feed, and sell livestock together without being in partnership?"

"How do you mean?" he asked.

"Well," I said, "suppose that each of us put up half the money—either our own or borrowed—to buy livestock, hay, corn, and pay all the other expenses, then fattened the stock in a single lot and divided the proceeds evenly when it was . . ."

"Wouldn't work!" Bones snapped. "If all the stock was in one lot and all the feed in one place, how could the lender tell what feed and animals were mortgaged on each loan?"

"That's what I was coming to," I said, "and I think it would keep the arrangement from being a partnership. The feed on hand at any time could be divided by measuring, so there would never be any difficulty in separating the halves. Each man could buy his own half of the feeder stock and hoof brand it before putting it into the feed lot, then separate it by brands at any time. There's just one trouble with that: if one man bought poorer feeder stock than the other and paid half the feed bill, he'd come out with the short end of the stick. To get around that it would seem to me that all the feeders could be bought jointly, put into the lot unbranded, and divided one and one—the way kids choose up sides for a game of one-old-cat—whenever there was any reason for separating the halves."

"Now we're getting somewhere!" Bones said approvingly. "If the chattels can be separated at any time, so that each man can stand alone with his own property and obligations, I don't see how there'd be a partnership even though the stock was fed in one lot with feed from the same stacks and piles. I'm no lawyer, but I'll tell you this: if you and Bob will team up that way I'll make you separate loans—that is if he'll agree to a few things I'd require—and guarantee never to hold you liable for a dime of his debts."

"Would you put that in writing so that no one could ever question it?" I asked.

"I'd write it on the face of your note if you'd like it that way," he told me. "It would then be a part of the loan agreement, and I don't believe there's a court in the world that wouldn't honor it."

"What interest rate would you charge us?" I asked.

"Why the standard rate—ten per cent a year," he said. "But I'll make you twelve-month feed loans and four-month live-stock loans, with the option of repaying any part and cutting off the interest at earlier dates."

"That's okay," I said, "but there are a couple of other things I'd like to get settled before you call Bob. I won't go in any deeper than three hundred steers and half that many hogs. If you put up the entire investment you'd be entitled to considerable control of the business. But I want a free hand in operating my half, and the right to terminate the agreement and separate my stock from Bob's at any time I consider his acts to be negligent, wasteful, or harmful to the business. In exchange, I'll invest two thousand dollars of my own money and put up my horses and wagons as additional security. If we can do business on that basis, and if Bob can do no buying, sell-

ing, or hiring without my approval, I'll agree to feed stock
with him, and to buy half the hay, corn, and hogs on his place
at a value to be set by George Miner."

I think my offer to mortgage my horses and wagons was a
big surprise to Bones. He stuck out his hand to shake, and
said, "As far as I'm concerned, it's a deal, son."

Bob must have been expecting Bones's call, for he got to the
bank within ten minutes. Twenty minutes later he'd consented
to all my conditions and we'd reached an agreement to operate jointly but not as partners in the livestock-feeding business. We also agreed that I would move my trading and shipping operations to his place and have use of the bunkhouse,
sorting pens, and scales in exchange for paying half the land
mortgage interest and real estate taxes. In addition to half the
cost of feeder steers and operating expenses, Bones agreed to
lend Bob six hundred dollars for living expenses during the
four-month feeding period, but demanded that all his notes
become due immediately if our joint venture was terminated.

As soon as all the agreements had been reached I drove over
to ask George Miner if he'd set a value on the hay, corn, and
hogs. He said he'd be willing to do it, but that if he were in
my boots he'd be mighty careful about getting onto thin ice
with as fancy a skater as Bob.

After I'd explained all the terms of our agreement, and that
I could terminate it at any time, he said, "Well that ought to
protect you some, but there's an awful lot of traps layin'
around for greenhorns in the feedin' game. Besides, Bob's
a'ready earned a bad reputation for cheatin', and a man doin'
business alongside of him could awful easy get tarred with the
same stick. I kind of got the notion you aimed to start a little
Hereford herd. Fact is, I picked out a few nice heifers, figurin'
you might want 'em, come spring. There'd be no need to take
'em out of the herd here even then. There's plenty of pasture
and hay land on the place, and Irene and I are gettin' on in
years. What with no boy of our own, I kind of had a notion . . ."

George broke off suddenly, cleared his throat, and said, "Well, what's the odds, anyways? I reckon you've a'ready got your mind made up, or like as not given your word, but I'd be a mite leery about gettin' into the feedin' business in times like these. Hogs are back down to a sensible price, but cattle—specially feeder and fat steers—are awful high, and I'll be jiggered if I can see what's goin' to keep the price up there."

"While I was in Kansas City I listened to all the discussions between the big cattlemen in the Stockmen's Hotel lobby," I told him, "and I talked to more than a dozen agents, feeders, and drovers. There wasn't one of them that didn't think the price of prime steers would be up to at least twenty-five dollars by spring, and some believe it will rise to thirty-five or forty. All the newspapers are saying that America will have to feed starving Europe for ten more years, so there'll be plenty of demand, and the agents tell me that all the export beef is prime grade, so the demand will be for fat steers, don't you think?"

George listened without interruption till I'd finished, then said, "There's lots of smart men down to Kansas City, and they know more about what's goin' on in the world than I do, so I couldn't say they're wrong. But don't forget that there's two Americas—North and South. I was readin' somewheres a few months back that there's more cattle on the pampas down in Argentina than there used to be buffaloes on these prairies when my father was a boy. Of course, they're not corn-fat steers, but I never heard of starvin' folks turning their noses up at good grass-fed beef . . . specially if they happen to be a mite shy on cash the way I understand most of the folks in Europe are since the war. It seems to me like they might go to buyin' their beef in South America if we keep the price of ours too high for 'em."

I was a little disturbed by George's reasoning, and it must have shown on my face, for he went on, "You understand, son, I could be crazier'n a hoot owl about this fat-cattle market bein' too high, so don't let my skittishness worry you. Chances are, those fellows down to Kansas City know somethin' I don't, and even if Europe did go to buying South American beef instead of ours, it wouldn't happen all in a day and without warning. Anyways, you didn't come over here to get a sermon on the livestock market. Are you right sure that Bones and Bob want me to set a value on that stuff?"

I grinned and said, "Well, it's part of the deal, but it wasn't exactly Bob's suggestion."

"That don't surprise me none," George said with just a trace of a smile, "but if you and Bones want me to, I'll go over with you and appraise the stuff."

He brought along an ancient *Farmer's Almanac* containing instructions and tables for determining by measurement the number of tons of hay in a stack, and bushels of ear corn in a pile. After he'd taken careful measurements of each stack and pile and examined samples from them, he spent half an hour figuring, then called Bob and me.

"Well, this is what I make out of it, boys," he told us. "The corn measures to be something over twenty-one thousand bushels, but so much of it's nubbins and the like that I calculate there's no more than sixteen thousand eight hundred bushels of feedable grain. If I owned it I'd be glad to get a dollar and a dime a bushel for it, so that's the price I've put down. The feedable hay measures four hundred and twenty tons—maybe one or two more or less—and a man could buy all he wanted of the same grade, delivered right here on the place, at fifteen dollars a ton. That makes the whole works, hay and corn together, worth twenty-four thousand, seven hundred and . . ."

Bob's face turned grayer and grayer as George talked. Suddenly he broke in angrily, "Now wait a minute, George! Something's all wrong with them figures of yours! There's leastways thirty-five thousand dollars' worth of feed here, and I ain't going to . . ."

George looked up over the tops of his glasses and, without seeming to interrupt, said mildly, "Well now, Bob, I'm not so good at doin' sums in arithmetic, but Dave, the teller up to the bank, he's a crackerjack. Suppose we go on up there and have him do the arithmetic over again. All I know for sure is that I've got the measurements right, and how much yield of corn there'll be to a yard of cobs, and what the stuff's worth a bushel or ton at today's prices. I figure the hogs would net about twenty-seven hundred dollars if you was to ship 'em, so that's what I've valued 'em at."

Bob was so sure Dave would find some big mistake that he was the most cheerful among us on the way to the bank. But his anger flared when Dave came out with the same figure as George's. Again he shouted that the feed was worth thirty-five thousand, and that he wouldn't settle for a dime less. Bones let him blow off steam for a couple of minutes, then he told him, not unkindly, "1 wouldn't like to foreclose on you, Bob, but if you keep on you'll leave me no choice. I believe you boys, working together, can make good profits in the feeding business. If you pitch in and do your best, I'll wager that by this time next year you'll have all your debts paid and be on the road to prosperity."

Holding a grudge, sulking, or staying angry more than a minute or two were not among Bob Wilson's faults. I never knew another man who could forget his troubles so quickly or enthuse more ardently at the prospects of finding a pot of gold at the foot of the next rainbow. To see and hear him when Bones had finished speaking, no one who didn't know the facts would have believed that he was dead broke and more than twelve thousand dollars in the hole. In his own mind he was already far along on the road to prosperity, and his only anxiety was to get started on our venture without another minute's delay. "You don't need to worry none about me pitchin' in," he sang out. "I aim to pay off them men of mine just as quick as the papers get signed up so's I can write checks."

"It wouldn't take Dave more than half an hour to make up the notes and mortgage papers," Bones told him, "and there's no reason why you boys can't sign 'em this afternoon."

"I don't believe it would be good business for me to sign them today," I said.

Bones whirled around toward me and demanded gruffly, "Now what are you backing off about?"

"I'm not backing off from anything," I told him, "but I thought you might want to. Tomorrow will be my twenty-first birthday."

His face turned grayer than Bob's had been. "Why didn't you tell me you were under age when you first came here?" he asked in a voice that wasn't too steady.

"Because you didn't ask me," I answered with a grin.

"Don't you know that notes signed by a minor for anything but food, clothing, and shelter are worthless?" he demanded.

"Yes, sir," I told him. "That's why I thought you might like to wait till tomorrow for the signing."

The note I signed the next morning was for twenty-three thousand dollars and the mortgage covered my horses, wagons and harness, together with "all chattels of whatsoever sort or kind" bought with the proceeds of the loan. Across the face of the note Bones wrote

[*I hereby guarantee not to hold Ralph Moody liable for any debt which he has not personally contracted.*
Harry S. Kennedy, December 16, 1919]

After the signing I moved down to the Wilson place, but all I took with me were the old Maxwell, Kitten and her saddle, what few clothes I had, and the account books from my wheat-hauling business. I'd planned to move enough furniture to fix up a room for myself in the bunkhouse, but Marguerite wouldn't hear of it. She said I was to sleep in the house and be one of the family—and no one was ever happier to join a family than I was to join hers.

5

Old Man Macey's Steers

WITH headquarters adjoining town and the railroad siding, I hoped to double my trading and shipping business. But to do it I needed pasture space so I'd be able to buy any type of cattle and hogs I could get at a good price, then keep them until I had enough of some particular grade to ship a carload. On the Wilson place there was a twenty-acre field north of the creek, and forty acres of rich valley floor to the south, but the fences were only two-strand barbed wire. The day I moved there I made a deal with Bob that I'd pay three quarters of the taxes and mortgage interest on the place, and half the cost of fencing it with hog-tight woven wire. In exchange I was to have year-around use of the north field, and use of the south field until May. We would then plant it to corn, sharing the work and dividing the crop equally.

Loose hogs were still rooting in the corn piles, and the hired men still loafing around the place. I suggested to Bob that he set the men to repairing the feed lot fence, and said I'd pay half their wages until the end of the month if they'd fence the two fields and a stackyard around the hay and corn piles. "There's no sense keeping 'em another day," he said, "and I

51

aim to pay 'em off tonight. You and me can do the whole dag-gone job without a lick of help. It won't take us scarcely no time to string up the fence, and we can do it in odd hours while we're buying feeder steers."

"I don't want to start buying feeders until the fencing is done," I told him, "so I'll be able to pick up shipping stock at the same time. Men are cheaper than interest, so hadn't we better keep them a few days? One could go to Oberlin for hog wire in the morning, while the other repaired the feed-lot fence and dug post holes for the stackyard."

"Look, Bud," he said, "you don't need to worry none about me not pitchin' right in on the work. You go get the wire in the morning, and I'll fix the feed-lot fence and dig the stack-yard post holes while you're gone. With posts a'ready set around the rest of the place it won't take the two of us next to no time to staple up the hog wire. I'm going to Oberlin for groceries tonight anyways, so I'll pay the boys off and take 'em along. It ain't right to pay men off without you ride 'em back to town."

Right after supper Bob drove away with the men, it was way past midnight when he came back, and at four o'clock in the morning I left to get the wire. Bob had the biggest and showiest team of horses in Beaver Township. They were bright bays weighing a ton apiece, but were slow afoot, and it was well after eight o'clock when I pulled into the Oberlin lumberyard. "How come you wasn't at the celebration last night?" the yardman called.

"What celebration?" I called back.

"The one Bob Wilson throwed over to Scott's pool hall," he told me. "Bob, he sure must have made a heap of dough on them cattle he shipped a couple of weeks back. Wouldn't let nobody else spend a dime, and he bought Scotty plumb out of sody-pop and near-beer and ceegars."

I didn't want to hear any more, so asked, "Have you got a dozen rolls of four-foot heavy-duty hog wire on hand?"

"You betcha!" he answered. "Bob, he give me the order last

night. Tells me you're putting in a thousand top-grade white-
face steers and five hundred shoats, and got to fence the whole
place hog-tight and bull-strong to hold 'em. Bob, he's sure a
big-time operator, and you're a lucky kid to get teamed up
with him."

The more I heard the less lucky I felt, especially when I
found that the bill had already been made out to Wilson and
Moody. I didn't bother to explain that there was no such firm,
but paid for half the wire and had the other half charged to
Bob.

When I got back to the Wilson place Bob wasn't there, only
one post hole had been dug, and there was a drove of shoats
rooting in the corn piles. For a moment my temper flared hot
enough to make my mouth dry. I started turning the team, to
drive up to the bank and tell Bones the whole deal was off.
Then Betty Mae came running toward me from the house,
singing out gaily, "Hi, Balp! Gi'me horsie wide."

With that happy little face beaming up at me I couldn't
stay angry, and I couldn't go off and leave her. "You wait right
there, so you won't get stepped on," I told her, stopped the
team, and jumped down to pick her up. With her squealing,
clinging to my back like a monkey, and hugging me around
the neck with both chubby little arms, I took her for a piggyback ride to the back door, put her inside, and told her, "You
stay right there till I come in for dinner. If one of those horses
stepped on you he'd mash you flatter than the grasshopper
that sat on a railroad track."

I'd unhitched the horses and was leading them toward the
barn when I heard the chattering valves of the Buick behind
me. The moment the motor stopped Bob shouted. "I sure got
us off to a flyin' start this morning!"

I didn't look around, but he followed after me, calling out,
"Daggoned if I ain't just stole us nine of the prettiest white-
faced steers you ever seen. Every one of 'em will scale mighty
close to seven hundred and thirty-five pounds, and they're
worth leastways a dime a pound, but I bought 'em at sixty

bucks around."

To keep any sound of anger out of my voice I waited until I'd put the horses in their stalls, then turned toward Bob and asked, "Where did you get the steers, and how did you pay for them?"

"Didn't have to pay for 'em," he told me jubilantly. "I got 'em off'n old man Macey, and his stuff is mortgaged clean up to the ears. All we got to do is tell Bones and sign up a note for the five hundred and forty bucks."

"Did you tell Mr. Macey that top grade feeders were worth only eight dollars a hundred?" I asked.

"Shucks, no!" he laughed. "The old geezer reads the drover's news like it was mail from home, so you can't catch him up much on the pound price, but he don't know nothing about cattle weights. He hung out for an average of eight hundred pounds at first, but I kept on telling him they wouldn't scale an ounce over five hundred, so we finally come together on sixty bucks a head."

"Bob," I said, "there are a few things we'd better get settled before we go any further." Then, after telling him where I drew the lines between haggling and cheating, I said, "You've already earned the reputation in this township of trying to cheat on every deal you get into. Unless that reputation is cured right at the start, any man doing business alongside of you will be tarred with the same stick, and I'm not going to get tarred. From now on you'll make no deal that I'm in any way connected with unless I'm right there and agree to it. We'll do our buying and selling together until you try some more tricky stuff, but the first time I find you trying to cheat me or anybody else in this business I'll pull out of it."

Bob stood with his head down until I'd finished. Then he looked up with the expression of a little boy whose mother has told him he's been naughty, and said, "Daggone it, Bud, I didn't aim to cheat the old man—all I done was to tell him his cattle weighed less'n what they did. But I savvy what you mean about them lines, and I'll stay inside of 'em if that's what you want."

"As long as you do we're in this together," I told him. "Now let's go see what Marguerite's got cooking for dinner."

During dinner Bob acted as if he hadn't a care in the world, but after we'd eaten he pitched into the post-hole digging as if he expected to find a gold piece at the bottom of each one. I let him dig alone for a couple of hours while I mended the feed-lot fence to make it pig-tight. Then we worked together, setting stout posts to enclose a one-acre stackyard. We'd stretched woven wire drum-tight around them, and were hanging the gate when Mr. Macey climbed out of his ancient top buggy at the roadside and drove nine steers into the dooryard.

I needed no one to tell me that those steers were out of stock originally from the Miner herd. They were as alike as if they'd been cast in the same mold: broad through the shoulders and hips, straight backed, stubby legged, and deep in the brisket and buttocks, giving their bodies the appearance of being square. For a minute I was at a loss for any way of paying the old gentleman what they were worth without admitting that Bob had tried to cheat him. Then an idea struck me, and I called out, "Bob tells me he made a deal for those fellows at a dime a pound. Drive 'em right back here to the scales, and we'll weigh them."

The old man looked at me as if he thought I'd gone out of my head, and said in a confused sort of way, "Well now . . ." Then stopped and began again, "Well now . . ."

Before he had a chance to say that the deal had been for sixty dollars apiece, Bob broke in loudly, "Daggoned if them critters don't look a quarter again bigger now I get a close-up look at 'em than what they did out there in the pasture, Mr. Macey. Fetch 'em right on back to the scales so there won't be no guesswork about the weight."

What the scales showed was the unerring accuracy of Bob Wilson's eye. He had told me the steers would average close to 735 pounds apiece, and the nine scaled 6,598 pounds—just seventeen off the mark. As the beam hung teetering I turned to the white-bearded old gentleman and asked, "Are these cattle mortgaged to the bank?"

"Yes," he said, "so the check goes to Harry."

On the list Bones had furnished me, showing what I could pay directly to his borrowers for mortgaged stock, the figure opposite Mr. Macey's name was 25 per cent. As he turned away I pulled out my check book and told him, "Wait a minute. The cattle are yours. The bank only holds a mortgage on them, and we have an agreement with Harry to pay you a quarter of the price in cash."

He watched with trembling hands while I made him a check for $165, then turned it over and wrote on the back: "I hereby sell to Robert Wilson and Ralph Moody nine Hereford steers for the sum of $659.80, 75 per cent to be paid for my account to the First State Bank of Cedar Bluffs."

When I passed it to him his hand shook so violently that he could hardly hold it, and his voice was unsteady as he tried to thank me. But he hurried back to his buggy almost at a trot, and drove rapidly away toward town.

Bob was obviously as happy as I to see the old man's joy. But I was sure that he felt no remorse at having come so close to cheating him out of more than a hundred dollars. Remorse seemed to have no part in his makeup—nor greed, either. I didn't believe his trickery was actually an attempt to rob anyone, but an effort to convince himself that instead of being a failure at business he was smarter than the man with whom he was dealing.

We'd been back at work no more than half an hour when Marguerite called from the kitchen doorway that Bones wanted to see me at the bank right away. When I got there I found him furious at Bob. "That man has no more sense of honesty or responsibility than a grasshopper," he stormed. "I had an idea that your teaming up with him in stock feeding would be good business for all hands concerned, but there's no sense in either of us trying to deal with a man that can't be trusted as far as you could throw him. Do you know that he was over to Oberlin last night, bragging his head off, and that he spent over fifty dollars treating all the bums in town at the pool hall?"

Without waiting for an answer he stormed on, "Grandpaw Macey was just in here, so broke up he couldn't hold still. He tells me Bob swore up and down that his steers didn't weigh over five hundred pounds apiece, and that he'd have stolen them for sixty dollars a head if you hadn't stepped in. Folks hereabouts know he can guess cattle weights right down to a T, and he uses it to steal from 'em. Given a chance, he'll cheat you or me or anybody else out of our eye teeth. I hate to foreclose on a man with a wife and family like his, but he leaves me no choice."

"I wish you'd give him one more chance," I said. Then I told him about the talk I'd had with Bob that noon, and said, "What he needs now is for you to give him a rough-shod raking over the coals."

Bones sat listening glumly while I talked, and when I'd finished he said, "If you want to risk it, I'll go along for the time being, but I'll foreclose on him the day I hear of his pulling one more of these shenanigans." Then he cranked the phone and asked Effie to have Bob come to the bank right away.

6

Our First Buying Trip

To AVOID meeting Bob on his way to the bank, and because I thought it would be good business to have line calls made, I crossed the street to the telephone office. The moment I opened the door Effie demanded, "What's all this mishmash I been hearin' about you goin' into partnerships with Bob Wilson?"

"It's sure-enough mishmash if you've heard anything like that," I said. "We're going to feed livestock together, but we won't be partners."

"Hmmmff!" she sniffed. "Kind of like a woman movin' in with a man she wouldn't darst to marry, ain't it? What in this wide world are you gettin' tangled up with Bob Wilson for?"

"Because he knows more about fattening livestock than any other man in this part of the country," I told her.

"Hmmmff!" she sniffed again. "And Jesse James knew more about robbin' banks than any other man in this part of the country."

"What's that got to do with it?" I said. "Bob's no robber."

"Didn't say he was, did I?" she flung back. "But he'll skin the hide off'n your eyeballs with you lookin' right at him. Part-

58

nership or no partnership, you get mixed up with Bob Wilson and I'd bet every hair on my head you'll come out owin' all the bills."

"Don't you worry about that, honeybunch," I told her; "Bones has guaranteed that I'll never be stuck for a dime of Bob's debts."

"Don't you honeybunch me!" she flared. "And don't you take Bones Kennedy's glib guarantees too literal neither. When he's got a roastin' ear in too hot of a fire he ain't above gettin' somebody else to haul it out for him, and you wouldn't be the first one that's got his fingers burnt."

"It was no glib guarantee he gave me," I said; "he put it in writing on the face of my note and signed it."

Effie cooled down considerably. "Well," she said, "that's somethin' else again. If Bones put it in writin' and set his name to it, you can bank on it, but what in this wide world do you want to get mixed up in the feedin' business for? Ain't you makin' all the money you've got any need for in the haulin' and shippin' businesses?"

"I've been doing all right," I said, "but there won't be any more hauling till next August, and there isn't shipping business enough in Beaver Township to keep me busy in the meantime. Besides, everybody in the Kansas City stockyards says there'll be big profits in feeding cattle as long as the United States has to feed Europe, and the newspapers say that'll be for another ten years."

"Fiddlesticks!" Effie exploded. "I don't reckon they know a tinker more about it than what you and I do. Thought you told me you aimed to buy some of George Miner's yearlin' heifers, come spring, and start a beef herd of your own."

"I do," I told her, "but that's nearly five months away, and it'll take only four months at most to fatten one batch of livestock. Unless all the stockmen in Kansas City are dead wrong, I ought to make enough out of feeding a hundred and fifty steers to pay for half that number of top-grade yearling heifers, and that would start an awfully nice herd."

"Did ever you hear about the dog that lost his meat 'cause he thought he seen a dog in the river with a bigger piece?" she asked.

"I guess every school kid has heard that one," I said, "but you don't need to worry about me; I'm not giving up either my shipping nor wheat-hauling business to go into livestock feeding."

"Well, anyways, it does worry me," she said in an almost sorrowful tone. "What does George Miner say about it?

"He's just about as enthusiastic as you are," I said, "but he thinks the hog market is going up, and he doesn't believe there's any danger of a sudden drop in fat cattle prices, so there can't be much to worry about. Bones and I had him set the price that I paid for half of Bob's feed and feeder pigs."

"Well," she said, "if you've paid it the milk's a'ready spilt, so there's no sense in us arguin' about it. You goin' to move down to Bob's place?"

"I'm not going to move my furniture down there—not yet, anyway—but I'm going to live with the Wilsons."

"Stayed there nights while you was workin' with George on the cullin', didn't you?"

"Yes," I said. "Having the children around in the evenings was almost like being back home again."

"Kind of lonesome up there on top of the divide now the haulin' season's over, ain't it?"

"I hadn't noticed it much till this last week," I said.

"Reckon a man batchin' all alone get's mighty fed up on his own cookin' too, specially if it's stuff that ain't scarcely fit to eat anyways, like that bread you was tellin' me about."

"Bob's wife can bake it so it tastes almost good," I said. "She's an awfully good cook."

"Far as I can find out she's an awful good girl, poor child, and hard-workin' too. It's a shame she couldn't of married somebody else besides a sharper like Bob Wilson. Oh well, she'll make you a good home down there."

"I know it," I said.

"Had a lot to do with you goin' into the deal with Bob, didn't it?"

"A little, maybe."

"Thought so, and I don't know as I blame you for it, but don't you leave him skin you out of the start you got in the haulin' business, and don't leave him skin them poor tenant farmers on top of the high divide, Bud. Even if we have had four or five pretty good crop years in a row, some of them folks are still mighty hard up."

"I've told him already that I'll pull my stock out of the feed lot and quit him the first time I learn of his trying to cheat anybody," I said.

"Wouldn't want anybody to get cheated, but . . ."

Effie broke the sentence off short, then said in a businesslike tone, "Well, if you're aimin' to buy feeder stock I reckon you'll want me to put out line calls. What'll I tell the folks?"

"Tell them I've moved my trading headquarters down to the Wilson place," I said, "and that Bob and I are going to feed cattle and hogs together, but that I'll carry on my trading and shipping business alone. We already have enough pigs, but starting Monday morning we're going to buy three hundred top grade white-faced feeder steers. Right now we're fencing the place hog-tight, so I'll be able to buy any kind of shipping stock at any time and hold it till I can make up uniform car-loads. You could say that we'd be glad to hear from anybody with cattle or hogs to sell, regardless of grade, type, and whether or not they're mortgaged to the bank."

"Want me to say you'll stand personal behind any deal Bob makes or anything he says in dickerin' for a deal? If you do you're a fool, and if you don't the folks in this township are goin' to be mighty skittish about offerin' stock."

"Then I'm a fool," I said.

Effie squeezed her lips together so hard that a white ring showed around them, then blew out a gusty breath and told me, "Well, there's no cure for foolishness. I'll put out line calls for you, but I've got a feelin' that I might as leave be givin' you a ticket to the poorhouse. Wouldn't do it if the folks in this township didn't need a dependable stock feeder so cussed bad. Now get out of here so's't I can simmer down before I make them line calls."

There was nothing more I could say, so I kissed a forefinger, touched it to the tip of her nose, and got out of there.

Bob was at the bank for more than an hour. When he came home he tried his best to act as if he'd had a nice sociable visit with Bones, but he did none of his usual bragging. Next morning he set to work in good shape when we began fencing along the McCook-Oberlin road. But Effie had stirred up considerable interest with her line calls, farmers by the dozen came by to say they had stock for sale, and Bob stopped to visit with every one of them. Some were top-of-the-divide tenants, so poor that only their wives and children were unmortgaged, but even with them Bob acted as if he were ashamed to be caught working, and he could no more help bragging than breathing. Before the day was over he was pushing most of the fence building off onto me by lengthening his visits with the callers. Still, I had to admire his acting ability, for he gave no appearance of trying to kill time, and his bragging always had a fresh, convincing quality.

We finished fencing on Saturday, and by that time nearly every farmer in Beaver Township had either phoned or come by to say he had livestock of some kind for sale. By investing in the feeding business I'd drawn my trading funds down to less than fifteen hundred dollars, so before the bank closed I went up for a talk with Bones. After he'd given me an up-to-date list of the cash percentages we could pay on mortgaged stock, I told him, "A good many on this list have some shipping stock to sell. I believe I could pick up two or three carloads while we're out buying feeder steers, but to do it I'd need a temporary loan until the stock is sold."

"There's no need of making the loan now," he told me. "Go ahead and buy as much stuff as you want to, then I'll make the loan for whatever amount you've overdrawn your trading account. I'd like to see a good bit of that mortgaged stock shipped out of here before winter sets in."

It hadn't occurred to me that it was the last Saturday before Christmas until I got home from the bank and found Marguerite and the girls dressed in their going-to-town clothes. We all went to McCook that evening, I made my weekly visit to Dr. DeMay, and the sugar content of my specimen was down enough that he let me go back on my regular diet. After we had supper I took care of the girls while Bob and Marguerite did their Christmas shopping. I don't believe we missed a toy, notions, or candy counter in the department store, and I had fully as much fun as they. I mailed trinkets to my brothers and sisters at home, and sent my mother a check. Then before we left town I bought Effie the biggest box of candy I could find.

I spent all day Sunday cleaning the trampled hay and corn from around the stacks and piles in the stackyard. Then at daylight Monday morning Bob and I saddled up and set out for the south end of the township on our first buying trip. On the way we laid our plans for making deals. Top grade feeder steers were bringing eleven dollars and a half a hundredweight at Kansas City, and shipping costs from Beaver Township were a dollar fifty, so we decided to buy only the best and to pay about a dime a pound. But livestock was almost never bought from farmers by weight, because no farmer was happy with a sale unless he'd dickered the buyer up a few dollars above his original offer. To provide for it we made our original offers three to five dollars below the actual value of each animal, then let the seller dicker us upward.

By noon word had spread that we were in the neighborhood, and we seldom rode into a yard that we didn't find the farmer waiting for us with the stock he wanted to sell corralled for inspection. If a man had steers for sale that were of the size and quality we wanted we always bargained for them first. Then Bob stood aside while I dealt alone for the shipping stock. I'd expected to do a fairly good business, but was un-

prepared for the deluge of stock offered me on our first day
out. Some of it was because farmers wanted to get rid of surplus stock before severe weather set in. But, particularly
among the tenants, I think it was mainly because the wives
wanted some Christmas spending money. Whatever the reason, I was offered well over a hundred cattle and hogs that
day, and bought every one on which I thought I could make a
reasonable shipping profit.

As the animals were bought, whether for feeding or shipping, we marked their faces with a line of identification dye,
and told the farmer to deliver them on the Saturday after
Christmas. Since Bob would never bother to fill out stubs, I
wrote all the checks: against my trading account if for shipping stock, and against my feeding account if for steers
bought jointly. I made the checks for whatever percentage of
the purchase was allowed by Bones's list. On the back of each
one I wrote out, as I'd done on Mr. Macey's check, a bill of
sale describing the stock, and a statement of the balance to be
paid to the bank for the seller's account. Then, for our own
records, I entered the same information on the check stub.

The divide farmers were wheat growers, so their cattle were
mostly milch stock, and they raised few more hogs than were
needed for the family meat supply. Bob and I found only sixty
feeder steers of the size and quality we wanted, though I
bought more than three carloads of shipping stock, largely dry
cows and veal calves. But in Beaver Valley, where corn and
alfalfa were the chief crops, many of the hog herds were large
and most of the cattle were beef stock.

Our first call in the valley was on Alfred Ashton, one of the
most prosperous farmers in the township. He led the way to
the corrals and showed us sixteen white-faced steers of exactly
the type we wanted. As we climbed the fence he looked me
squarely in the eyes and said, "According to what Grandpaw
Macey's been telling around the valley, there's no need of you
and me wasting time at haggling, so name your best bid right
off the bat."

"If you put it that way," I said, "I'll have to say seventy dollars a head, all the way around."

"It's a deal," he said. "That's right where I had 'em pegged. Want to make me an offer on about forty shipping hogs?"

The hogs were of excellent quality and weighed about 275 pounds apiece. Top grade bacon hogs were bringing only thirteen fifty at Kansas City, down ten dollars since September, and I expected them to go lower. None too anxious to buy, I told Ashton, "I'm sorry, but the best I could offer is thirty dollars a head."

"I'll take it," he said without a moment's hesitation.

When we moved on, one farmer after another asked for our best offer on his steers, and accepted it without a quibble. Then, at prices fully two and a half dollars a hundredweight below the Kansas City market, he sold me all his hogs except his brood stock. By mid-forenoon I became frightened. With the most successful farmers in the township selling off their hogs I was afraid to buy any more, but refusing might cause hard feeling that would hurt my future business. There was only one man whose advice I dared take, so I told Bob to wait for me at the next four-corners, then set out for George Miner's as fast as old Kitten could cover the ground.

I found George sitting in a sunny corner of the wagon shed, picking the Christmas turkey. He kept right on picking while I told him what was worrying me, then without looking up he asked, "Ever herd sheep?"

"No, sir," I told him, "I was never around sheep."

"Well," he said, "let an old ewe start to blattin' and head off some place—no matter if it's off the top of a bluff or out into a blizzard—and the whole flock will follow after her unless there's somebody close by to head 'em back. I was minded of sheep last night when Irene and I went to a little Christmas shindig over to Dave Goodenberger's. Folks got to talkin' about you and Bob buyin' feeder steers, and about old Grandpaw Macey, and you buyin' up stuff to ship, and the likes. Al Ashton said he'd a'ready waited too long for the hog market to turn back up again, and reckoned he'd wasted every bushel of corn he'd fed in the last month. Said he aimed to sell every hog on his place, exceptin' only his brood stock, if you made him a reasonable offer. Well sir, before you could say scat-my-cat every hog farmer in this valley was singin' the same tune."

George went back to picking feathers as if there were nothing more to be said, so I asked, "Are you going to sell?"

"Why, someday, I reckon," he said, "but I ain't in any hurry about it. It appears to me like it's fat cattle and feeder steers that's too high, not hogs."

"Then you'd advise me to keep right on buying?" I asked.

"Wouldn't advise you one way or the other," he answered. "A man ought to make up his own mind . . . specially in the livestock tradin' business." Then he peeked up at me through his bushy eyebrows and asked, "Hadn't you best to be goin' along if you and Bob aim to get them steers bought before Christmas?"

After our talk I stopped worrying, and the deluge continued. With no haggling to be done, Bob and I moved rapidly from farm to farm. At almost every one we bought a number of excellent feeder steers, and I seldom failed to pick up a dozen or two hogs, along with a few shipping cattle. By dusk on Christmas Eve, we had bought what we believed to be the three hundred best feeder steers in Beaver Township, and I was fairly swamped with shipping stock. Altogether, I'd bought more than five carloads of hogs, and four of mixed cattle and calves, together with five hundred bushels of corn and twenty tons of hay.

Christmas was the best I'd ever spent away from home. As soon as the girls had opened their presents and we'd had breakfast I saddled Kitten, took the box of candy up to Effie, and rode on to my place to spend the forenoon with my horses. Marguerite's dinner was glorious, and I ate as though I'd never heard of a diet. In the afternoon we popped corn and played games with the children, then gathered around the player piano in the evening, singing carols and hymns till bedtime.

7

Blizzards and Backaches

THE morning after Christmas I got out the books I'd used for my wheat-hauling business and headed up pages for two new sets of accounts—one for the livestock-feeding business, and the other for my trading and shipping records. It was well past noon before I finished, and it took Bones more than two hours to handle the paper work at the bank. He would almost gloat over my having bought an old cow from some poor top-of-the-divide tenant farmer. As he wrote a voucher for transferring the thirty-dollar mortgage balance to my account he'd tell me, "If that cow is less than twenty years old, I'll bet I've held a mortgage on her from the day she was born. Never did think I'd live to collect it."

But when the mortgage transfer amounted to only six hundred dollars on a thousand dollars' worth of stock bought from a prosperous valley farmer, he'd say, "Now that's the kind of business I like to see: a man getting everything but his brood stock sold and off his place as soon as it's ready for market. Don't forget that every head of livestock shipped out of a township brings in fresh money that makes prosperity for you and me and everybody else."

When we'd finished the paper work I signed a new note for twenty-three thousand dollars, making my total indebtedness to the bank forty-six thousand dollars. As I swung onto Kitten and started back to the Wilson place I was a bit proud of being a big enough businessman within two weeks after my twenty-first birthday that a banker would lend me any such an amount.

Saturday morning Bob and I were out at the crack of dawn, getting everything ready for receiving the stock we'd bought. We were none too early, for soon after sunrise a farmer drove into the dooryard with a load of hogs. Before I could check them off the list and show the man where to unload, two more had arrived. Within half an hour the yard was filled with wagons, and along the roadway as far as Cedar Bluffs men and boys herded little bunches of cattle, waiting to get in and deliver them.

In some ways Bob Wilson was the most amazing man I ever knew. No matter how large the amount, he never bothered to fill out check stubs, and invariably forgot the amount within two minutes. But he could ride for no more than ten minutes through a herd of fifty cattle, never see them again, and tell each one's markings and weight a month later. He fidgeted impatiently while I checked in the first few loads of hogs, then told me, "There's no sense wasting time with all that messin' around. I know every feeder steer by sight, and if you can't remember what-all you bought these fellas can tell you." Fortunately, he soon gathered a crowd around the scales, and forgot everything else in the excitement of betting dollars against dimes that he could guess the weight of any "cow critter" to within less than 2 per cent.

I'd planned to ship all my trading stock that evening, but the westbound train left me only three cars, so I had to hold most of it over. There were still half a dozen men at the scales with Bob when, in late afternoon, I drove what stock I could ship to the railroad siding. It was dusk before I finished loading, and full dark before the cars were shunted into the eastbound train. With the lot full of new steers, there was no possibility of my accompanying the shipment, so I telegraphed my agent what was in transit, then swung wearily into the saddle. When I rode into the dooryard the corn wagon stood right where I'd left it that morning, and Bob was coming from the scales, whistling merrily and swinging a lantern. "You sure ought to been around the scales this afternoon," he sang out gaily. "I skun them gazabos out of close onto ten bucks. How'd the loading go?"

I had trouble to keep from shouting when I called back, "Haven't you fed those cattle yet?"

Bob didn't seem to notice my peevishness, but told me, "Well, daggone it, I aimed to, but anymore the days are so short it gets dark on a man before he can say Jack Robinson."

He stood for a minute or two, watching me strip the saddle off Kitten. Then, probably because I didn't say anything, he want on, "Well, shucks, it won't make no difference no ways. The moon ought to be up by the time we've eat supper, and we can feed 'em just as good by moonlight as daylight."

By the time we'd eaten, the sky was completely clouded over and the night so black that a man couldn't see his hand six inches from his eyes. The temperature had dropped at least 10 degrees, the wind had veered into the north, and it was salted with particles of snow that cut like glass slivers. There was no need of corn-feeding the steers, but with a storm coming on they must have at least a ton and a half of hay, and my hogs in the pasture a ton or more of corn.

Wearing double suits of overalls and jumpers, earlapper caps, and heavy gloves, Bob and I set out for the stackyard, carrying a lantern and a couple of pitchforks. As I hung the lantern where it wouldn't be blown out Bob started up a ladder, shouting that he'd pitch down from the top of the stack. By chance, I'd hung the lantern in such a position that I was left in deep shadow, but the light shown upward onto Bob as though he were an actor on a stage. He'd tossed down no more than a hundred pounds when I saw him plunge his fork tines deep into the matted hay, slip a knee under the center of the handle, and throw his full weight onto the extreme end. There was a sound like a rifle shot as the handle broke, and Bob imitated a howl of pain so well that anyone might have thought he'd been hit by the bullet. He clamped both hands over his spine and wailed, "Daggoned if it don't feel like I busted my back with that lifting. Don't know if I can make it down from here by myself or not."

I didn't try to control my anger, but shouted, "If you don't get another fork in a hurry, I'll bust the handle of this one the same way you did yours, and come up there after you."

With any other man I ever knew that would have started a fight or brought him to terms, but not Bob Wilson. He hobbled down the ladder as if he were in agony, leaned against the stack, and groaned, "Just leave me have a couple of minutes to rub some of the ache out, and maybe I can try it again."

"I saw you break that handle intentionally," I told him, "and I don't believe you've got any more backache than I have. If I could prove it I'd take my half of the stock out of this feed lot before daylight."

Even that didn't bring him around. "You don't reckon I'd try to fool you at a time like this, do you?" he asked between groans. "Just leave me hold the lantern for you a spell, and I'll be all right soon as ever this pain eases up."

With all Bob's ingenuity he couldn't find a way to pitch hay without as well as admitting that his back injury was a fake, and I made him pay for it. When the temperature is only a few degrees above zero and there is icy sleet in the wind, pitching hay and shoveling corn are a lot more comfortable jobs than standing and holding a lantern, and I kept Bob holding that lantern for more than two hours. When at last we headed for the house he was so nearly frozen that his face had turned blue, but he was still sticking to his story.

When I woke at dawn Sunday morning a full-fledged blizzard was raging out of the northwest. I had no concern for the steers, as the feed lot was well protected by the buildings and the thick growth of trees along the creek. But I was badly worried about my shipping stock, for the creek flowed through a deep, narrow gorge along the eastern side of the pasture, so the trees afforded no protection from a northwest storm. I dressed in my warmest clothes, built a fire in the kitchen stove, then shouldered the door open and went out.

The wind was so thick with powder-fine snow that I could see only three or four feet, but I groped my way to the barn and saddled Kitten. Trusting to her mustang instinct, infinitely more reliable in a blizzard than a man's reasoning power, I led her to the pasture gate, opened it, mounted, and let her have her head. As if the little mare knew my intention by telepathy, she struck off downwind at a jogging trot. After a few minutes she veered sharply to the left, my right leg brushed against fence wire, and a cow's head loomed out of the whiteness at my left. I didn't need sight to know that the cows and calves had drifted with the storm and were wedged tightly into the southeast fence corner.

Stepping from the saddle I pushed my way among them, expecting to find several dead and trampled calves. There was only one down, and it was still alive, simply given out from cold and weakness. Kitten stood quietly while I lifted the limp, gangling calf across her withers. The moment I swung back into the saddle she began crowding the dazed and bewildered cattle out of the fence corner, nipping their rumps and driving them into the battering force of the storm. Probably by scent, she kept track of every cow and calf in the little band, headed off those that continually tried to turn back, and drove them to the gate as unerringly as if she could see through the blinding storm.

After putting the exhausted calf into the barn and the rest of the cattle in the sheltered horse corral, I turned Kitten back to the pasture. But that time I had to depend upon my own reasoning, for mustangs have little instinct concerning hogs. I rode downwind to the corner where she'd found the

cattle, back along the fence to the creek gorge, and let her
pick her way down the steep bank. The ravine was about
thirty feet deep, and below the rake of the wind the visibility
lengthened to ten yards or more. The creek was frozen solidly,
three feet of snow had sifted down onto the ice, and the bottom of the gorge looked like the Valley of Ten Thousand
Smokes. The hogs had burrowed into the snow, and the smoke
was steam from their breathing, rising through blowholes.
They were as warm as if wrapped in blankets, and with plenty
of fat over their ribs they wouldn't need feeding for several
days.

When I went to the house for breakfast I found Bob lying
on the parlor sofa, groaning pitiably as Marguerite put a bottle of hot water against his back. It was evident that he had
her as fully convinced of his injury as I was unconvinced, but
I couldn't tell her it was all a fake, and he was smart enough
to know it. "Daggone it, I hate to leave you do the whole job
of feeding on a morning the likes of this," he told me. "Them
steers will need a load of corn along with their hay, but the
way my back feels I don't reckon I could handle a fork or a
shovel to save my neck."

After breakfast the visibility improved a little, but the wind
was still bitter cold, and icy snow crystals scoured my face
like sandpaper. Alone, the feeding took me until after ten
o'clock, then I saddled Kitten and rode through the gorge to
be sure the hogs were still all right. When I came back I
heard Bob's voice from the feed lot, calling to the steers. From
just outside his range of vision I watched him for several minutes; calling to the steers, looking them over, and breaking
ears of corn on the edge of a feed bunk. He seemed as happy
as a boy with a new toy, and showed no signs of backache.

I started toward him angrily, intending to tell him that he'd
either do his half of the work without any more faking or I'd
quit him the minute the blizzard was over. But as I neared the
feed bunk one of the steers picked up a three-inch piece of
corn ear and began wallowing it around in his mouth. Instead

of groaning about his backache as I expected, Bob looked up and told me, "You got to learn 'em to shell the corn off'n short pieces of cob first. Elseways they'll lose fifteen or twenty pounds before ever they get onto the trick of takin' a whole cob into their mouths and shelling it."

I realized instantly that his knowledge of livestock feeding was more than enough to offset whatever work he might shirk onto me, so I held my tongue. Together we broke corn until Marguerite yoo-hooed to let us know dinner was ready, and I enjoyed it in spite of the cold and cutting snow.

The blizzard continued through Tuesday, but when the sun rose bright and clear Wednesday morning my hogs came out of hibernation, looking as fat after three days without feed as they'd been when I bought them. I shipped every head of my trading stock the following Saturday, and the profit on it was more than I had dared to hope for.

With the big shipment out of the way, Bob and I fell into a routine that we seldom varied. He always had a backache if there was anything to be done that he considered work, but he'd spend five or six hours a day opening and closing heavy gates, rounding up steers in the feed lot, and weighing them one by one. Within ten days from the time we'd put the three hundred steers into the lot he could tell exactly how much each one had gained or lost. If a steer wasn't gaining he took it out of the lot, put it with other non-gainers in a separate corral, and brought them all up to full feed with a minimum loss of weight.

The only actual labor required for the feeding operation was two hours of hay-pitching and corn-shoveling morning and evening. I was willing enough to do it as my share to match Bob's know-how, but it presented a couple of difficulties. One, that cattle won't eat well in darkness, and the trick in fattening is to get them to eat all they can digest, so I had to start the afternoon feeding at least two hours before dark. The other, that Beaver Township was stripped of cattle and hogs that farmers wanted to sell, so I had to widen my buying territory or give up the shipping business until spring.

Monday through Friday for the rest of the winter I was on the road by seven o'clock, worked in the adjoining townships until two, then hurried home to do the evening feeding. I seldom called on more than four or five farmers in a day, and usually had to dicker half an hour before buying an animal at a price that would allow me a reasonable profit. Haggling with livestock dealers was the only entertainment some farmers had during the winter, and they liked to make it last as long as possible.

On Saturdays I started feeding at four o'clock and was out with Kitten by daybreak, rounding up the stock I'd bought during the week and getting it on the road for home. Hogs were the only stock I required sellers to deliver, but most of them helped with the cattle driving, usually bringing along an animal or two for trading. I always planned to get home before noon, and our place soon became the cattle and hog trading center for the whole surrounding countryside. Some trades were made directly between the farmers, but more often with me, and I always tried to make a dollar on each deal. Bob never failed to gather a crowd at the scales on trading days, or to make a pocketful of change by betting dollars to dimes on guessing cattle weight.

February 1920 was bitter cold, cattle prices dropped sharply, and though I never missed a day from my territory there was little profit to be made. The first half of March the weather behaved as if it had been designed especially to punish stockmen. At dawn on the eighth the thermometer stood at twenty-two below zero. Six inches of snow covered the pasture, with a crust hard enough to support my heaviest trading cattle, and the wind was strong enough to blow the lighter ones off their feet. By noon on the ninth, summer seemed to be just around the corner. When I came home at three o'clock a balmy Chinook wind was blowing out of the southwest, and Bob had taken the family to Oberlin—partly to get fresh meat, but more to give Marguerite and the children a little outing. The cattle sunning themselves contentedly in the pasture stood in ankle-deep slush, and the feed-lot steers waded equally deep in sloppy muck and manure.

I pulled off my jumper before starting to load the corn wagon, and didn't notice that the wind had shifted into the north until my sweat-soaked shirt slapped against my back, as cold as if it had been dipped in the creek. Before I'd finished loading, the wind had veered into the northeast, there was a raw edge to it, and though it wasn't actually raining, there was enough moisture in the air to wet my face. As I filled the feed bunks in the lot the steers stood motionless, tails to the driving wind and heads hung low—a sure sign of a coming storm. The pasture cattle behaved the same way when I fed them, and few came to eat. By the time I'd finished feeding and had unharnessed the horses, the temperature had dropped to fifteen above zero and the moisture in the wind had turned to fine sleet.

So the house would be warm when the family got home, I lighted fires in the kitchen and parlor stoves, then went out to do the milking. I'd just finished stripping the brindle when the Buick clattered into the dooryard, so I went to lend a hand with the children. After I'd carried Betty Mae and Arvis to the house Bob told me, "You'd best to saddle up while I unload the groceries and Marguerite gets us a bite of supper. If we don't keep them cattle on the move till this slush crusts over hard enough to keep 'em from busting through, there'll be so danged many frozen feet around here that you couldn't count 'em."

I've spent some rough nights in my life, but I think that one was the roughest. The temperature never dropped below fifteen or rose above twenty, but all night long the wind veered from north to northeast and back again, striking in almost horizontal blasts of cutting sleet. If left alone ten minutes, the cattle turned tail to it, humped their backs, and stood waiting to freeze, so we couldn't work in relays. Bob had to be constantly with the steers in the feed lot, and I with the cattle in the pasture, keeping them on the move to stir the circulation in their legs and prevent their feet from freezing in the slush and mud that extended above their hoofs.

I'd saddled Bob's sorrel, but rode Kitten bareback so that the warmth of her body would keep my legs from stiffening too badly. Even then they ached with a dull grinding pain, and although the feed lot was somewhat protected by the trees along the creek, Bob, riding on a saddle, must have suffered much more than I. All through the night no hour passed that Marguerite didn't come to the pasture fence with scalding-hot coffee, swinging a lantern to signal me in. Then as I rode back I'd see its glow moving on toward the feed lot.

As often happens in a storm of that kind, the wind let up at dawn. The sky cleared soon after daybreak, the temperature dropped to zero, and a crust strong enough to support an elephant formed over the feed lot mud and pasture slush. Bob and I reeled like drunkards as we put our tired horses in the barn and headed for the house, too weary and numb to speak. When we stumbled into the kitchen we found two tubs of steaming water sitting in the middle of the floor, with rough towels and dry clothes hung over a chair in front of the oven door.

During the next few days the temperature moderated to the mid-forties, while Bob and I worked constantly with the cattle. Each day we put every one of them across the scales, checking its weight, the gloss of its coat, and for any sign of leg swelling or tenderfootedness.

By the end of the week we were satisfied that we'd come through without a single frozen foot. But as the weather warmed I had from fifteen to twenty phone calls a day, all from farmers anxious to sell me crippled cattle. I had to explain that I couldn't buy them because they'd be unable to stay on their feet for so long a haul to market, and advise the man to butcher any cripples immediately, so as to save the meat before gangrene set in. Bob and I estimated that more than a hundred cattle in my trading area went into corned beef barrels that week, and that an even larger number were shot, skinned, and their carcasses left for the coyotes.

On March 15 we had wind close enough to hurricane force that it scattered half the haystacks in the township. Then, as if winter had exhausted itself in a final burst of violence, spring came to stay, the frost drew out of the ground, mud dried to loam, and the first sprouts of new grass appeared. By mid-April our steers came into the bright bloom of corn-fat cattle that have reached their prime.

8

The Hog Cycle

AFTER seventeen consecutive weeks of decline, the prime steer market held steady during the third week of April, and Bob was sure it would bounce back to its December peak any day. I had no such illusions and—with a little help from George Miner—convinced Bob that it would be wasteful to hold our stock another week. Our hogs were already becoming overweight, and after cattle reach their prime any added weight is lardy fat that reduces their value.

I decided to ship six carloads of trading stock I'd accumulated at the same time we shipped the feed-lot stock, so ordered eighteen cars for the twenty-fourth of April, and applied for returning stockmen's passes for Bob and me. That Saturday I had my biggest trading day of the spring, and more than twenty men stayed to help load the stock and see the train away. As always when I accompanied stock to Kansas City, I wore blue denim jeans and jumper, taking along only a change of underwear. But Bob wore his Sunday suit and carried a suitcase.

Riding two nights and a day in the caboose of a cattle train and trying to sleep on a bare wooden bench is no fun under any circumstances. But it is infinitely worse in wet clothes, and mine were sopping almost the entire trip. It began raining an hour after the train pulled away from Cedar Bluffs, and there was no letup. Bob, in his best clothes, was no help, and with so many cars I had to run forward a quarter-mile at every stop, to make sure we had no cattle down and injured. It was still pouring when we reached Kansas City, and in spite of the discomfort I was pleased, for on long hauls livestock shrinks less in rainy weather than in fair.

Our train was one of the first to pull into the stockyards Monday morning, and our stock came through in exceptionally good condition. The yards were six inches deep in muck, so Bob didn't help with the unloading, but I'd brought along a pocketful of half-dollars for the roustabouts, and was able to get our stock penned in good positions. I had all the hogs penned close together, with my trading cattle nearby, but the steers—being prime—had to be penned fully a quarter-mile away. Regardless of the muck and rain, Bob wanted to stand as owner beside the auctioneer when our steers were sold, and I was glad to be free so I could look after the rest of the stock.

The hog market was good that morning, up half a dollar from Saturday, and although our feed-lot hogs were somewhat overweight they did well, netting almost five thousand dollars. My trading stock did well, too, averaging a little better than sixty dollars profit per car.

It was eight o'clock when my last cattle were sold, and when I went to our agent's office Bob had been gone more than an hour. "He ran into some friends," the agent told me, "and they went celebrating as soon as the last carload was auctioned. Bob said you'd look after the paper end of the deal."

There was nothing but paper work to be done regarding the feed-lot stock. As was customary with mortgaged stock, ours had been shipped subject to attachment for the amount of our loans. And since the loans were greater than the value of the stock, the entire net proceeds had to be paid directly to the First State Bank of Cedar Bluffs. Even so, I couldn't blame Bob too much for doing a bit of celebrating. In spite of the poor-quality feed and the drop in fat-cattle prices, our steers had brought very close to thirty-three thousand dollars net.

As soon as the agent and I had completed the paper work and I'd sent Bones a telegram, I picked up my bundle from the train caboose and went to the Stockmen's Hotel. Not because I expected Bob to have been there, but to make conversation as I signed the register, I asked, "Seen Bob Wilson this morning?"

"I sure have," the clerk told me. "Him and his friends come in half an hour ago, celebrating Bob's good luck. He tells me he brought in ten carloads of prime steers this morning, topped the market with 'em, and cleaned up a profit of better'n thirty thousand bucks. A train whistle spooked some of his cattle while he was unloading, and they run him down in the slop. He was plastered with muck from head to heels, and on his way uptown to buy some new clothes."

I thought I smelled a mouse, so asked, "Did he just stop in to leave his suitcase and cash a check?"

"Yeah," he said, "the poor guy couldn't wait around for the banks to open up—not in the shape his clothes was in—but three hundred bucks was all I had on hand."

There was no sense in telling the clerk that Bob hadn't a dime in the bank and that the check was worthless. But with a roll in his pocket I knew he'd be off on a wild spending spree, and there'd be less sense in trying to find him.

I spent the rest of that day and all the next around the hotel lobby, waiting for Bob to show up and listening to the stockmen and agents. Those who had been the most optimistic in December were wailing that any man who stayed in the feeding business was bound to go broke. My own agent still thought the prospects were good, and a stockman with agricultural school training argued that a feeder could break exactly even at the current prices. His argument interested me particularly, for Bob and I still had nearly enough corn and hay on hand to feed three hundred steers for four months.

Bob came back to the hotel just in time for us to catch the Denver night express. As I expected, he was barely able to keep on his feet, couldn't remember where he'd been, and didn't have a penny in his pockets. He was wearing a new brown suit and hat—the worse for rain and mud—but was carrying three or four packages that were dry and in good shape. "There's presents in 'em for Marguerite and the girls," he told me groggily, "shirtwaist with lace on the collar, and the likes of that." He slept every minute until we transferred to the branch line, and then became as restless as a hound with fleas. The moment we pulled into Cedar Bluffs he hurried away toward home with the parcels, but forgot his suitcase.

I left it with Dad Haynes and went to the telephone office with the box of candy I'd brought for Effie. She looked as sad as if she were at a funeral, and her eyes failed to light up as usual when she saw the candy box. "You shouldn't have went and spent money on candy for me," she said, "not after the kind of lickin' you must of took on them steers you fed. I was scared for you right from the start-off. How bad did you get hurt?"

"Not enough to amount to anything," I told her. "My loss on the whole deal was barely more than five hundred dollars, and that's nothing when you consider that the price of fat cattle dropped thirty per cent while we had our steers on feed."

"Nothin'!" she scoffed. "You might call five hundred dollars nothin', but I sure don't. Up till the war commenced that's more'n what I got for mindin' this switchboard a whole year. And look at the four months of hard work you lost to boot."

"I'd like to lose four months the same way every winter for the next fifty years," I told her. "Since Christmas I've made enough on my trading and shipping business to pay my share of the living expenses, buy hog-wire fencing for the place, pay interest on my trading-account loans, and save eighteen hundred dollars. Besides that, I've learned enough about livestock feeding to be worth every penny it cost me."

Before I'd finished, Effie had lost her mournful appearance and was eyeing the candy box hungrily. "Well then," she said, "I ain't goin' to feel so bad over you fetchin' me candy—exceptin' only that you're goin' to fat me up like a Poland China sow if you don't quit it. You don't aim to go back into the feedin' business, do you, Bud?"

"I don't know yet," I said. "Most stockmen at Kansas City are afraid of cattle feeding now, but our corn and hay will go to ruin if it isn't used before winter. I'm not going to do anything until I talk with George Miner."

"Now you're beginnin' to show a smidgen of common sense," she told me as she eagerly untied the candy-box ribbon, "and you'd better go see Bones before he jumps clean out of his hide. He's called up three times a'ready, tellin' me to send you right over to the bank as soon as ever I laid eyes on you."

When I crossed the street to the bank, Bones came hurrying to meet me as if I were the Governor instead of a kid in dirty blue denims, congratulating me on how well we'd done with the steers in the face of a demoralized fat-cattle market. He led me back to his desk, pulled up a chair, and began urging that Bob and I put five hundred steers into the feed lot right away.

I told him about the conversations I'd heard at Kansas City, and said I wasn't going to make up my mind until I'd talked with George Miner. Snatching up the phone receiver, he whirled the crank and asked Effie to get George on the line. I thought it might be a good time to get in a whack for Bob, so as we waited I said, "Oh, by the way, Bob had to write a check for some cash while we were down to the city. The rain and muck at the yards ruined his suit, and while he was getting another one he bought some clothes for his wife and the children."

I was careful not to mention the amount of the check, and

Bones didn't ask. He just waved a hand and said, "That's okay. Tell him to drop in and sign a note for it the next time he's . . . Hello! Hello, George! This is Harry. Bud Moody is here with me, just back from the city, and we've been talking about him and Bob putting in another bunch of feeder cattle. We'd like to get your ideas on it if you could spare time to drop by. Fine! Much obliged, George."

George came right away, but he wouldn't do any talking until I'd repeated all that I heard in Kansas City. "Well," he said at last, "down there where the tradin' goes on every day they'd ought to know what the fat-cattle market's goin' to do if anybody does, but I misdoubt me that anybody does. Instead of bein' the worth of stuff, market price is only a measure of how bad one man wants somethin' and another man wants to get rid of it. You take the way prices have been runnin' lately: bacon hogs fetchin' a dollar a hundred more'n prime steers. That's hind-end-foremost. Ever since I can recollect—exceptin' when the market was on a spree, you understand—fat steers have fetched around a dollar more than top grade hogs. Sooner or later it'll straighten itself out again, but your guess on when it'll come about is as good as anybody else's."

"But aren't hogs as apt to drop two dollars as fat steers are to go up?" I asked.

"I don't reckon so," he said. "Most stockmen never take note of it, but the hog market generally always runs in nine-month cycles, and it's only four months since the upswing commenced—right after Christmas."

"What do you mean by cycles?" I asked.

"Well," he said, "I suppose you know that it's close to four months from the time a sow's bred till she has her litter. If she's a good brood sow and the pigs are put on corn as soon as they're weaned, they'll be bacon-hog size and ready for market by the time they're five months old. That's what I call a hog cycle, and if a man pays careful heed to it he ought to be able to figure out—by and large, of course—about how the hog market will behave for a spell ahead."

"I understand the cycle," I said, "but not how it would help a man figure what the market is going to do."

"Then you don't know farmers as good as a livestock dealer ought to know 'em," he told me. "When the price of hogs goes down, ten farmers out of a dozen stop breedin' their sows, figurin' there's no profit in raisin' pigs. Nine months later hogs get scarcer'n hen's teeth, so the price goes to shootin' up, and every one of them farmers goes to breedin' his sows again. By the time another nine months rolls around bacon hogs are plentiful as flies around a slaughterhouse, and there's just about the same demand for 'em, so the bottom drops out of the market. Of course, that nine months can stretch out to ten, or even eleven, dependin' on the price of corn. If it's high, most farmers hold back a mite on the feed, so it takes the hogs a few weeks longer to grow to market size."

"How long is the cycle for beef cattle?" I asked.

"If you put it that way, I'd have to say there wasn't one," he told me. "You see it's upwards of three years from the breedin' of a cow till her calf is ready for the beef market. That's so long that raisers don't pay much mind to a couple of dollars up or down in the market. Mostly, their breedin' depends on how much pasture they've got, how the grass is doin', and how many head of stock it will support. Of course, there's what you might call a cycle in the price of prime fat cattle, because it takes only three or four months to put the fat on 'em. Most generally you'll find that feeders are like hog farmers. When the market's bad there won't many of 'em put a new bunch of steers onto feed, so in about four months there's a shortage of prime beef. Then the price goes to risin', every feeder goes to fillin' his lot, and in another four months the seesaw goes down again."

It seemed to me that George was trying to give us his opinion in a roundabout way, so I said, "It's more than four months since the fat-cattle market began falling, and feeder steers are way down too, so there can't have been many put into feed lots lately. Don't you think this might be the right time for Bob and me to put another bunch into the lot?"

The slightest trace of a grin broadened George's lips, and he told me, "Well, son, like I told you about hogs last December, I ain't sellin' any cattle right now, but I ain't advisin' you to buy none either. A man ought to make up his own mind and not go too much on what somebody else thinks. How does Bob feel about puttin' in another bunch now?"

"You know Bob," I said. "He'd have put in a thousand head last December if he could have borrowed enough to buy them."

George got up, stretched, and said, "Yep, old Bob, he kind of likes to jump in with both feet, don't he? Sometimes a man wins big by doin' that, but it's awful easy to get mired if he happens to light on a soft spot. Reckon I'd better be gettin' on home or Irene might suspicion that I've run off with the new schoolma'am."

After listening to George, Bones seemed no more anxious than I to risk lighting on a soft spot, but agreed to lend Bob and me whatever we needed to put in another three hundred steers and half that number of pigs—on the same terms and conditions as our first loan.

For the next three days Bob and I were on the go from dawn till dark, and lucky there were fourteen hours of daylight at that time of year. Late Friday afternoon we finished our rounds, having bought a hundred and fifty pigs and nearly five hundred steers. By six o'clock Saturday morning stock began pouring in from every point of the compass. George came over to help me check it in, and Bob did the sorting. All the pigs and the three hundred best steers were put into the feed lot; the remainder divided into six carloads for shipping. During the afternoon George and I loaded the cars while Bob, with a couple of boys to help him, put all the new feed-lot steers across the scales, and no feeder could have wished for finer stock.

9

Mustang Auction

SUNDAY morning I was up long before daylight, had my feeding done an hour after sunrise, and by seven o'clock Kitten and I were climbing the divide. The rain of the previous week had left the soil in our south field as mellow as meal and, as my grandfather used to say, "a-hankerin' for the plow." It was time for corn planting, but I couldn't use Bob's two-ton team for both feeding and plowing, so had decided to bring down four of my heaviest mustangs for the planting job.

I can't remember many days when I've had more fun than on that Sunday. My mustangs had come through the winter in fine condition: were as round and sleek as otters and wilder than falcons. No matter how carefully a mustang is broken, or how tractable he may become during the working season, his instinct is to fight restraint after a winter's freedom. All forenoon I worked with the four I'd use for corn planting: harnessing them to a wagonload of dirt, then letting them fight it till they'd blown off their excess steam and would answer the reins willingly.

I spent the whole afternoon playing: roping other broncs, saddling them, and riding them in a pole corral. Every one bucked furiously, but they showed no viciousness, and though I was tossed several times, I was unhurt—except for a few bruises and having the wind knocked out of me two or three times. I would like to have stayed and played with the horses till dark, but I knew Bob would find some excuse for not feeding the stock. With the sun still two hours above the horizon, I gave each mustang that I wasn't going to use for plowing a slap on the rump, dodged its flying heels, and watched it race away to the pasture and a few more weeks of freedom.

In western Kansas the topsoil is deep, and because of the scant rainfall the plant-feeding chemicals haven't been leached out of it; so few farmers dress their land. But I learned farming from my New England father, and couldn't bear to plant corn on undressed land when there was a foot-thick blanket of manure in the feed lot. Bob and most of the neighbors told me I was wasting my time when I started hauling manure, but George nodded his head and said, "If I was in your boots I wouldn't pay 'em no mind. Sure, a calf will live and grow on skimmed milk, but he'll grow a sight faster if he gets the cream."

I spent the whole first week of May hauling manure and spreading it over the forty-acre south field, then another two weeks plowing and planting, often with Betty Mae riding on my knee. The corn planting kept me too busy to work my territory, but there was always a trading session on Saturdays, and the six carloads of surplus steers we'd shipped made a profit of three hundred dollars.

That spring of 1920 was glorious for me, and Sundays were the best days of all, for I spent them at my place on the divide, getting ready for the wheat-hauling season that would begin in late July. To have the whole day free, I arranged to mail my specimens to Dr. DeMay and told Bob I wouldn't be home to do the Sunday evening feeding.

I spent the forenoons reassembling my wagons, resetting the tires, making repairs, touching up the paint, and putting harness into first class condition. Then I devoted the afternoons to

rounding the horses into shape: trimming their hoofs, hitching
each pair to a heavily loaded wagon, driving them enough to
sweat off their winter softness, breaking down their resentment of control by firm but gentle handling, and finally re-
training each four-horse team until it responded as a unit to
every command or touch of the reins.

I'd finished the corn planting and been working my trading
territory a week or two when a lightweight truck passed me on
the road. It was the first truck I'd ever seen on a country road,
but five more passed me by the end of the week, all driven at
breakneck speed by young fellows I'd never seen before. I
should have had sense enough to know why they were there,
but it never occurred to me until a farmer told me they were
contracting to haul wheat at little more than half the price-per-
mile I'd charged the previous summer. Even though I owned
my horses and wagons clear of debt, I couldn't afford to meet
any such rate.

The coming Sunday would be Fourth of July, and harvest
would start that week. At an auction just before harvest,
horses and wagons would bring more than at any other time,
and although I'd never owned anything I hated so badly to
part with, common sense demanded that I sell quickly. The
bigger the auction crowd the higher the bidding, so I headed
straight for the telephone office. I told Effie my reason for having an auction and that it would be held at my place on
Fourth of July afternoon, with the biggest barbecue ever seen
in Beaver Township and fifty dollars' worth of fireworks in the
evening. Then I asked if she'd put out line calls and have the
operators in all the nearby towns do the same.

Next I went to see Bones, told him what I was going to do,
and asked if he'd get as many bankers as he could to come.
Bankers were nearly as important to me as bidders, because I
intended trying to sell my rigs as units: the four mustangs that
had been trained as a team, their harness, and a pair of tan-
demed wagons. Few farmers, especially just before harvest,
could write a check for as much as I hoped one of those rigs

would bring unless his banker was on hand to approve a mortgage loan. From the bank I went to Oberlin, hunted up the best auctioneer in the county, arranged for him to handle my sale, and told him I'd pay an extra 1 per cent commission on rigs sold as a complete unit. At the Oberlin Cash Store I had an order sent off for skyrockets, Roman candles, and other fireworks.

That evening I told Bob about the auction, and that he'd have to do the evening feeding for the rest of the week, but that I'd load the hayrack and corn wagon for him each morning. I spent most of Tuesday and Wednesday collecting the hogs I'd bought during the past weeks. It not only gave me a chance to drive my teams, but let the farmers in four townships see how sleek and well-trained they were.

All four mustangs in the team I'd driven myself during the 1919 hauling season were old Kitten's offspring: the smallest, toughest, wildest, and most unmanageable of all my horses. The former owner had nearly ruined them with cruelty, but they were highly intelligent and had become tractable under careful handling. By the end of the season they'd obey the reins with such machinelike precision that, in showing them off to Effie, I'd put them through a figure 8 in front of the telephone office while hauling 120 bushels of wheat on a pair of wagons hitched in tandem. I decided to train them in the stunt at a run, not only as entertainment for the auction crowd, but to show prospective buyers how strong, dependable, and controllable my little mustangs were. Along with collecting hogs and hauling supplies for the barbecue, I schooled the team morning, noon, and evening all week. By Friday they'd pull a pair of loaded wagons at a full gallop along the level quarter-mile stretch of road leading to the buildings on my place, swing through a figure 8 in the dooryard without slacking speed, and slide to a stop exactly in front of the corral gate.

A steady rain set in before daylight on Saturday, and lasted most of the day. It made schooling the horses impossible, but was so valuable to our corn crop that I was glad to have it. I spent all day and late into the evening getting ready for the auction, then stayed at the place all night. An hour before dawn on Fourth of July, I drove down to the Wilson place to feed the stock, and took my furniture along. It was all second-hand and nothing fancy, but I'd become sort of attached to it and didn't want it auctioned off, so stored it in Bob's empty bunkhouse.

Bob and Marguerite went back with me as soon as I'd done the feeding, and we took along a man from Cedar Bluffs to do the barbecuing. While they started getting the food ready I hitched up all seven rigs, put the teams through a final work-out, then lined them up for display in the big corral. By noon there were jalopies of every kind and description, some fine automobiles, buggies, buckboards, carriages, and wagons lined up on both sides of the driveway and a quarter-mile down the county road. The dooryard was swarming with people, and Bob was acting as traffic cop to keep it free of vehicles.

It was customary not to serve the free lunch until after the auctioning, but it seemed to me that men with full bellies would bid more freely. When everyone had eaten and drunk all he could hold, the auctioneer climbed up on the corral gate and made a flowery speech about my four-horse tandem-wagon rigs being "famous throughout Decatur County and the whole region round-about." After orating for more than ten minutes about my mustangs being the best trained, fastest, toughest, and strongest horses—pound for pound—in the world, he shouted that it would be a downright crime to break up any one of the teams, so he was going to auction each com-plete rig as a single unit. "I'm not asking you to take my word about these little horses," he bellowed. "Before they're put up for sale we will give you a fantastic demonstration of their strength, speed, sure-footedness, and ease of handling."

As Bob and the auctioneer harangued the crowd, clearing the driveway and dooryard, I climbed to the high wagon seat behind my figure 8 team and gathered the reins in my hands.

When the gate swung open I drove out into the empty yard, then stopped the team and called out, "I need a four-ton load here. How about fifty of you heaviest men and boys coming along for a ride?"

Four tons was far more than I wanted, but I was sure the boys would outrun the heavier men—and they did. Within ten seconds both wagons were packed tight, but the whole load weighed less than three tons. The driveway was straight and flat, hard-packed from the recent rain and heavy traffic of the forenoon. I let the team pick up a brisk trot as we neared the county road, swung them in a wide turn, still at a trot, and cautioned my riders to hold tight.

As I'd done in practice, I snugged the reins the moment the leaders were facing back toward the buildings, then sang out, "Yi-ya! Ha! Ha! Ha!" The four little mustangs—no one of them weighing over eight hundred pounds—sprang into their collars as if each Ha! had been a whip lash. In a dozen strides they'd picked their speed up to a full gallop, and by the time we reached the dooryard they were fairly flying. With the crowd yelling insanely, we swung so close to the corral that the skidding rear wheels of the trailer wagon missed the fence no more than an inch or two. By that time the leaders were halfway across the yard, streaking toward the house, then swinging back toward the barn to complete the bottom circle of the 8; across the yard again, and into the reverse circle at the top of the figure. As we'd always done in practice, I hit the brakes hard at the top of the circle, and the rig slid to a stop squarely in front of the corral gate.

Almost instantly there was a man at each bridle, and the crowd gathered tightly around us, wild with excitement. The auctioneer was too smart to let the opportunity slip away. He started the auctioning as soon as the crowd had quieted enough for bids to be heard, and within three minutes had sold the rig for nearly seven hundred and fifty dollars. No other rig brought so much, but they all sold above seven hundred. Even my six old tote horses brought sixty dollars apiece. Spare harness and other odds and ends sold for another couple of hundred, bringing the total for everything except Kitten and my saddle to slightly more than fifty-seven hundred dollars. I wasn't at all displeased with the amount, but far from happy otherwise. As men climbed to the high seats and drove my teams away I felt almost as guilty as if I'd sold my own brothers and sisters.

After the auction there was nothing I wanted less than a big celebration, so I asked Bob to host the rest of the affair, then saddled old Kitten and rode away. It seemed unbelievable that only a year had passed since I'd come there, dead broke, and as part of a rag-tag harvest crew. I'd planned to stay only to earn railroad fare to Denver, but the place had become my home, and I found myself riding away from it with an ache in my throat.

For an hour or more I let Kitten have her head as I thought back over the year and how good it had been to me. I'd made far more than I'd ever dreamed of making in a single year, and if the stock Bob and I had in the feed lot did as well as we expected, I'd make as much again before the summer was over.

For the next month I worked my territory every possible hour and shipped two car loads of stock a week. In early August there was a cloudburst near McCook, and an inch of rain fell at Cedar Bluffs. It was fine for our corn, but I had to cultivate right away to keep the moisture from evaporating in the scorching heat. By the time I'd finished there was no doubt that Bob and I would make a huge profit on the stock we were feeding, for the price of fat cattle had risen steadily since early June. Because we were nearly out of feed, I suggested shipping on August 14, but Bob insisted that the steers needed another two weeks to reach prime, and George agreed with him.

I'd never seen George so optimistic about livestock prospects. Prime steers were bringing seventeen dollars a hundred, bacon hogs sixteen, and corn had leveled off at a dollar sixty. He had a theory that the whole market was in balance when hogs were ten times the price of corn, and prime steers a dollar higher. "A man might as leave predict which way a flea will jump as to forecast the livestock market," he told us, "but I'll say this: the way the price of corn and hogs and prime steers have pulled into line is the healthiest sign I've seen since the war."

Bob cut in to predict that prime steers would be bringing twenty-five dollars a hundred before Christmas, but George told him, "I'd stake anything I own that you'll see another war before you again see fat cattle as high as twenty dollars, leave alone twenty-five. But I look for 'em to stay right around seventeen or eighteen while corn brings a dollar sixty."

With George confident that the market was in a healthy condition, Bob and I wanted to put another bunch of stock on feed as soon as possible after shipping. Next morning we went to see Bones about the financing, and found him not only willing but eager. He urged that we put in double our present amount of stock, enough high-quality feed to fatten it, and do all our buying immediately to avoid higher prices. When I pointed out that it would require an eighty-thousand-dollar investment he said he knew it and had ample funds to provide the financing.

Bob would have jumped right in, but I could see no reason for paying interest until we actually needed the money, and since George felt as he did about the market I doubted that prices would rise to any great extent, so I told Bones, "I'd like to put in another batch after we've sold this one, but I think five hundred steers and half as many pigs should be the limit, and I don't want to buy feed more than a month before it's needed."

I didn't work my territory during the last two weeks of August, but spent all my spare time grinding feed to put our steers in top-notch condition. When we loaded them onto the cars they were as near perfect as any feed-lot cattle I'd seen, and our hogs were equally good. Unfortunately the last weekend of August was the hottest of the summer, so our shipping shrinkage was almost twice as high as on our first shipment, but we still came out wonderfully well. Three carloads of our steers and two cars of our hogs topped the market, with the others close behind. Bob stood proudly beside the auctioneer as owner of the steers, and I stood as owner of the hogs. But the net receipts, of course, had to be paid directly to the bank at Cedar Bluffs.

The day we got home and settled with Bones was one of the proudest of my life. After paying every dime I owed, I sent my mother a check that left my bank balance an even nineteen thousand, five hundred dollars. Bob's share brought his debt down to barely more than eight thousand, and there seemed little doubt that he could pay it off by the end of the year.

By the following Friday evening we'd bought our full quota of steers and pigs for our next operation, and feed enough to last us a month. The stock was delivered on the fourth of September, and that afternoon Bob and I signed notes for our new loans. Bones insisted that he have a mortgage on all our stock and the feed we'd bought, but didn't ask either of us for a mortgage on our corn crop.

With seven hundred and fifty head of stock in the feed lot and my trading business to take care of, I was busy from dawn till dark and had no reason to go to Cedar Bluffs in more than two weeks. Then, on the twenty-first of September, Bones phoned and told Marguerite that he'd like to see me at the bank right away. When I went in he asked me to come back to his desk, looked around as if to make sure that Dave Sawyer, the cashier, wasn't listening, and said in a low whisper, "You'll have to keep this strictly to yourself, but I've got to . . ."

Then he seemed to catch himself and change his mind. He cleared his throat and started all over again, "No, son, I can't tell you what I was about to, but I'll say this much: it would be best for you and Bob to take out loans enough now to cover whatever feed you'll need till the end of the year. I'll make the due date January fourth, like your other notes, so you'll be in a good safe position if anything should happen."

I signed a note bringing my loan up to twenty thousand dollars, and said I'd have Bob drop in to sign his, but I did it only because there was something about Bones's behavior that left me no doubt of his absolute sincerity. He walked to the door when I went, laid a hand on my shoulder, and told me, "Son, it's been good to do . . ." Then he turned and, without another word, walked slowly back to his desk. I left the bank as puzzled as ever in my life, but I never told anyone what Bones had said to me, though I had Bob go in and sign a new note.

On the last Monday in September the whole township was abuzz, for there was a terse announcement in the *McCook Gazette*, "Harry S. Kennedy of Cedar Bluffs reports that he has sold 90 shares of stock of the First State Bank of Cedar Bluffs at $400 per share. Atwood men to take over the bank."

The next morning Bones phoned for Bob and me to come up and meet the new bankers. When he introduced me he said some nice things about my having arrived there as a harvest hand and become one of the most successful livestock traders and feeders in western Kansas. The new men seemed friendly enough, but I couldn't help the feeling that they were looking me over in the same way Bob and I looked over a steer when considering whether or not to accept him. When we left, one of them walked to the door with us and said pompously, "Bank examiners are due here in a few days, and like as not there'll be some scuttlebutt whispered about, but don't pay it any mind. We're putting in enough new capital to make this little bank as strong as The Bank of England."

The rise in feed and livestock prices that Bones had predicted was short-lived and followed by a sharp decline. By the end of October corn had dropped below a dollar a bushel, prime steers were down two dollars a hundred, and bacon hogs more than three. But I could see nothing for Bob and me to worry about; there was plenty of time for livestock prices to recover before our stock would be ready to ship at the end of December, and the lower corn went the less our feed would cost.

10

A Skunk under the Woodpile

THE FIRST HALF of November was wonderful for Bob
and me. Our corn crop shucked out better than eighty bushels
to the acre, the price of prime steers bounced up a full dollar,
and hogs not only stopped their plunge but turned upward
twenty-five cents. Besides that, our stock was gaining weight
faster than any we'd fed, and there seemed no possible doubt
that we'd make an enormous profit when we shipped at the
end of the year. The only disturbing market factor was that
the price of wheat took a sharp tumble at the middle of the
month, though corn held fairly steady.

Sunday evening I went for a visit with George Miner, to
find out what he thought had caused the sudden drop in the
wheat market. He was more concerned than I'd ever seen him,
and told me, "If I don't miss my guess, there's a skunk under
the woodpile, and I've been smellin' him ever since the first of
the month. The big grain speculators in Chicago must know
about somethin' goin' on in the world that the politicians
down to Washington are holdin' back from the farmers, and
that's what is drivin' the price of wheat down. It's been
slippin' off steady for six months now, but the crop was

smaller this year than last. That's pretty good proof that the demand has gone all to pot, and the only reason I can think of is that Europe has raised a good enough crop to feed its own people. If that's so, you're goin' to see some mighty tough times ahead for American farmers, what with the way the government's kept us increasin' production since the war end. If my guess is worth a tinker, farmers won't be the only ones to get hurt neither. Maybe we've been wastin' our tears over Bones for havin' to sell that bank stock."

George walked to the gate when I left, and told me, "I didn't aim to make it sound like the whole shootin' match was goin' to the bow-wows, and I hope my runnin' off at the mouth didn't upset you none. What with corn fallin' only a nickel, and fat cattle gainin' back most of their loss, and hogs on the way up again, it don't look to me like you and Bob have too much to worry about. It's only six weeks till you'll be shippin', and it ain't likely that we'll run into any trouble to speak of before the end of the year. But if I was in your boots I'd be a mite leery, come January, about puttin' another big bunch of cattle and hogs on feed. Good night, son, and don't lose no sleep over what I've said to you. Irene give me mince pie for supper, and it could be I'm lookin' at the dark side of things on account of it layin' heavy in my stomach."

When Bob and I were in Kansas City in August, the *Kansas City Star* had just completed a radio sending station so powerful that it could be heard clearly for five hundred miles. Every noon one of the newspaper men at the stockyards broadcast the market report for the day, telling how much stock of each type had arrived and the high and low price each grade had brought at the morning auctions. I bought an instruction book on building radio receivers and the materials for a crystal set, but was so busy after we got home that I didn't get it finished and working well until corn-shucking time. Half the farmers in Beaver Township wanted a radio as soon as they'd heard mine, so I agreed to build one for anybody who would shuck a hundred bushels of corn for us and send to Sears Roebuck for materials. The materials arrived the Monday after I'd had my visit with George, so I fixed up a bench in the bunkhouse and spent every moment I could spare from feeding and trading on radio building. As I worked I picked up nearly everything coming over the air, and the more I heard the more it seemed to me that George was right. The price of wheat slipped off another dime, corn dropped to sixty cents, and hogs nose-dived three dollars, though fat steers held steady.

By the end of the week I was so worried I could hardly sleep, but Bob was gay and carefree as a robin in May, for he'd believe anything that was to his advantage and nothing to his disadvantage. When I tried to explain the nine-month hog cycle, the fact that the upward phase had ended in September didn't bother him at all. He laughed uproariously and told me, "Shucks, the only trouble is that them hogs don't know they've fell off'n their cycle yet. Soon as they find it out they'll get up and start to running like the devil was after 'em. And when they do you'll see the market jump right back to twenty dollars or better. Did ever you try to stop a scairt hog when he got to running?"

After that I never tried to discuss the market with Bob, but all that kept me from going for another visit with George was that I didn't want to act like a scared kid. The day before Thanksgiving hogs took another sharp drop. When the broadcast ended I was willing to admit being scared. I saddled Kitten and had ridden to the Miners' front gate before I noticed the McCook taxi standing in the dooryard. George had all his cattle corralled, and there were two well-dressed strangers with him, looking them over. I didn't think anyone had seen me, so turned Kitten back for home, my mouth dry with nervousness and worry.

As soon as I'd unsaddled I set to work on a radio requiring enough concentration to leave no room for worry. I had no idea how long I'd been working on it when the bunkhouse door opened and George came in. "Reckoned I'd drop by and see how you go about makin' one of them contraptions," he told me as he ooched his behind up onto the bench beside the coil I was winding.

For maybe ten minutes I tried to tell him about sound waves and frequencies, and things like that, but we both knew that we were only making talk. At last he chuckled and told me, "I'll be jiggered if I ain't gettin' to be as superstitious as Effie. Reckon I'd light out and run myself to death if a black cat was to cross the road in front of me."

Trying to act offhand, I kept my eyes on the coil and asked, "What are you getting superstitious about?"

"Well," he told me, "like Effie'd say, the moon ain't in exactly the right phase for settin' a hen, and it's seemed to me like the stink from under the woodpile was gettin' a mite ranker here of late. So when a couple of buyers from Ioway happened past this afternoon, lookin' for Hereford breedin' stock, I let 'em have a few carloads to be shipped Saturday."

I still didn't look up, but asked, "What did you do, run advertisements in the Iowa newspapers?"

"Oh, a couple of 'em," he said. "You know, I ain't as young as what I used to be, and Irene's been at me of late to take things easier. Without us havin' a boy of our own, and with good help hard to come by, I reckoned I might as leave cut the herd down to a few good heifers."

"Do you think it's getting dangerous enough that Bob and I ought to ship our stock this weekend?" I asked.

"Wouldn't say so," he said thoughtfully. "Before I come in I stopped by the scales and lost a couple of dimes to Bob. Your steers look mighty good for bein' less than ninety days on corn, but Bob says they need another month to top 'em out real good, and I'd agree with him. If you was to ship now you'd do well to get thirteen dollars a hundred at the auctions, and you'd take an awful lickin' on your hogs. They need another month's growth to bring 'em up to bacon size, and it's plumb crazy for hogs to be sellin' like they are now, at six-fifty below fat cattle. One or both of 'em's got to move till the gap's no more'n two dollars, and I can't believe fat cattle will take any such a drop till things get a lot worse than what they are now."

For the rest of the month the news coming over the air wasn't disturbing enough to keep me awake nights. Then, on December first, the fat cattle market went to pieces like a homesteader's shack in a cyclone. By the fourth the price of prime steers had dropped from $16.75 to $12.85. But instead of coming up to help close the gap, bacon hogs dropped to $9.75, though wheat remained steady and corn actually went up a nickel.

Bob quit listening to the livestock reports when the fat cattle market disintegrated, went to McCook or Oberlin every day, and often failed to get home until after midnight. He stopped weighing steers, seldom went near the feed lot, and when I tried to talk to him about shipping he told me, "Shucks, them cattle and hogs don't belong to me no more. If the big shots up to the bank want 'em, they can come and get 'em."

Two of the bankers came on December sixteenth—my twenty-second birthday—when prime steers at Kansas City had dropped to $10.50 and bacon hogs to $9.10. What brought them was Bob's having overdrawn his bank account by more than a hundred dollars. He wasn't at home, and when I told the bankers that I didn't know where he was, one of them became as pompous as a turkey gobbler in April. He strutted to the feed lot, looked over the gate, and told me roughly, "Order cars and ship this stuff before the price goes any lower! We've taken all the loss we aim to on it."

Ever since the noon broadcast I'd considered shipping on Saturday, but I've never liked being roughly ordered around, so decided not to do it. I waited for the man to finish, then said, "The notes and mortgages on this stock aren't due until January fourth, and I don't believe you hold them, do you? Didn't Mr. Kennedy discount them to a Kansas City cattle loan company?"

His face turned almost purple and he bellowed, "That don't

make any difference. We're guarantors on the loans, and we're not going to risk any further loss. Ship this stock Saturday!"

"I can't talk for Mr. Wilson," I told him, "but if you want my half shipped this Saturday I'd suggest you get a court order."

The man wasn't too careful of his language when he told me how sure I might be that he'd get a court order, and he drove out of the dooryard so fast that the spinning wheels burned rubber off his tires.

That evening Bob came home while I was feeding, so I called him out to the lot and told him about his overdraft and the bankers' demand that we ship our stock on the coming Saturday. "Them guys don't scare me none," he blustered. "Any time they want this stock they can send the sheriff after it. They can't take no more away from me than what they've got a mortgage on."

"Oh, yes, they can," I told him. "With those bad checks they can easily get an attachment on your half of the corn crop, and you know there's a bad-check law in this state. It might be you they'll send the sheriff after."

He blustered a bit more, but for the first time there was a sound of worry in his voice, and he went to the house muttering to himself. All through supper he was irritable as a dog with canker in its ears, went to bed while I was milking, and drove away toward McCook soon after I went out to feed the stock next morning. I was working on a radio in mid-forenoon when I heard Bob's contagious laugh and the sound of unfamiliar men's voices. I stepped to the bunkhouse window as Bob and two strangers came out of the stockyard, climbed into a new Buick touring car, and drove away. About an hour later Bob came back in the old Buick, pulled to a stop in front of the bunkhouse, and sang out jovially, "Let the daggoned bankers try stealin' that corn now and see how far they get."

I opened the door and asked, "What did you do, trade your half of it for that 1921 Buick?"

He lowered his voice and said, "I ain't that big of a fool. I put enough cash in the bank to make them checks good, but that's all they're going to get their fingers on. Sure, I made a deal for a new Buick, but I only paid a hundred bucks down. That way the dealer'll keep the ownership papers, and these smart guys up to the bank can't steal it away from me. Don't say nothing to Marguerite about it. I aim to save it for a Christmas surprise—or maybe New Year's. It'll take a week to get the model I dealt for out here from Omaha."

With money in his pocket, a new Buick on order, and the new bankers outwitted, Bob was fairly prancing. At every chance he flashed a roll of bills that would have choked a bull, and Marguerite must have believed he'd struck it rich. They made four shopping trips to McCook, each time coming home with armloads of packages.

The Thursday before Christmas, Bones phoned and asked me to come to his house. When I got there he led me into the parlor and told me, "I hope you understand that I don't have the say about what goes on at the bank any more—that is, no more say than one vote gives me, and that's precious little."

"I understand," I said. "Are they after my hide?"

"I wouldn't exactly say that," he told me, "but you got their dander up when you told them to get a court order. You know, of course, that mortgaged stock can't be moved across a state line without authorization from the mortgage holder. Well, they've taken up you boys' notes from the loan company, aiming to force you into shipping your stock in the bank's name by refusing authorization for it to cross a state line otherwise. If you ship that way, the entire proceeds will have to be paid to the bank, and I have a notion that they plan to impound every dollar of it, claiming that you and Bob are in partnership. They know different, but you'd have to sue to get your money, so the burden of proof would be on you."

"Is there any way to avoid it?" I asked.

"That's what I called you up here for," he told me. "If you were refused shipping authorization on your half of the stock—subject to mortgage, of course—you'd have a legal damage claim. It would include any loss sustained because of market decline, feed, and care of the stock from the time of refusal until ultimate sale. The bank's only defense would be to prove partnership, and the burden of proof would be on them. They know it, and I don't believe you'll have much trouble in getting an authorization when they find out that you know it."

"Is there any legal reason to keep Bob and me from dividing our stock now?" I asked.

"Of course not," he said. "You can divide it any time. That's part of the agreement under which the loans were made."

"And could Bob turn his half over to the bank before the mortgage is due, whether or not the new men agree to it?"

"If he stopped feeding the stock they'd have to take it. What else could they do to save their situation?"

After thanking Bones I drove around the back way and pulled up in front of the bank as though I'd just come from home. When I went in the man who had ordered me to ship the stock was at Bones's old desk, and there were only he and the cashier in the bank. I stepped to the rail and said pleasantly, "Good morning. I plan to ship my stock on Christmas Day, so dropped in for an authorization, subject to the amount of my mortgage."

"There'll be no need of an authorization," he told me without looking up. "Ship the stock in the bank's name!"

"Maybe Mr. Kennedy forgot to tell you," I said, "but the bank doesn't hold title to the stock, only a mortgage on it."

He looked up, stared at me, and said roughly, "That makes no difference. The mortgage is for more than the stuff's worth. Now get out of here, kid, and do as I told you! I'm busy."

I bent over enough to rest an elbow on the rail, and said as though we were having a pleasant conversation, "That's true of Mr. Wilson's stock, but he won't be asking for an authorization. He'll be turning his stock over to the bank on his mortgage, probably this afternoon. If you'd like, I'd be willing to ship it for you at fifty dollars a carload. Whoever decided not

to give me an authorization probably didn't realize how fast
the market is falling, or that my note isn't due until January
fourth, or that I'd have a damage claim against the bank
for . . ."

I stopped in the middle of the sentence and started toward
the door, but before I got my hand on the knob a panicky
voice called out, "Hold on a minute, Moody, will you?"

When I looked back the man was coming toward the railing
with a forced smile on his face. "It does sound like the man
that made the decision didn't have all the facts before him,"
he said. "You see, Harry Kennedy hasn't been well of late—
that's why we had to take over the management here—and
we're finding that there's a lot of things he forgot to tell us,
the way a sick man will. Let me have about an hour to get
hold of my associates and I believe we can find some way to
give you and Wilson shipping authorization. You'd both ship
if you had the authorizations, wouldn't you?"

"That's right," I told him as I stood in the open doorway,
"but don't bother about them unless your associates are perfectly willing. Now that I've come to think of it, I can see that
I'd make more money the other way. Anyhow, I'll drop back
in an hour." Then I stepped outside and closed the door.

I drove around the back way again, stopped to tell Bones of
the conversation, then went on to Oberlin to do my Christmas
shopping. I wasn't feeling as affluent as Bob, so made five dollars cover candy for Marguerite and Effie and a toy for each of
the girls. It was exactly an hour from the time I left the Cedar
Bluffs bank until I was back, and my reception was somewhat
warmer than before. The man at Bones's desk came to the railing with an envelope in his hand, and saying heartily, "It was
just as I suspected. Poor old Harry forgot to give us all the
facts, but now that we've got the straight of it we're more than
glad to accommodate you. I've got the authorization all made
out here. Look it over and see if it fills the bill."

It was typed on the bank's letterhead and released our stock
for shipment and sale, subject to a claim for one half the net

proceeds plus $20,667—the amount of my note and accrued interest for four months. Below the bank's name the man had scrawled his own name illegibly, with V P after it in large, clear letters. From that day on, he was always spoken of around Cedar Bluffs as V P.

I read the release carefully, put it in my pocket, and said, "That's okay. We'll ship Saturday, and hope to get the stock into the earliest auctions Monday morning. Do you want our agent to mail you a check, or would you rather I'd telegraph you the amount, so you can draft on him by wire?"

V P walked to the door with me, saying, "Send me a telegram, will you, Bud? Since we took over the management, this bank is as safe as a church, you understand, but—Harry overlending like he did—we've been a bit tight for ready cash." He opened the door for me, and as I climbed into the dilapidated old Maxwell, he called out cheerily, "Drop in whenever we can do anything for you. Always glad to accommodate our friends."

After going by to show Bones the authorization, I stopped at the depot and ordered seventeen cattle cars and three double-decked hog cars. The rest of the afternoon and all day Friday I spent getting ready for the big shipment, but Bob paid no attention to the stock, and gave me no help. While he and Marguerite were trimming the tree that evening, I went up to the telephone office, partly to take Effie her box of candy, but mainly because I knew she'd find me the help I needed. To move as much stock as we had from the feed lot to the shipping pens, sort, and load it, would be impossible for one man, or even two, and with conditions as they were I didn't feel that I could afford to hire help. Effie had known for more than a week that I'd lose almost everything I had on the stock in the feed lot, and had shed many a tear over it. After we'd visited for maybe fifteen minutes, I mentioned that Bob and I were going to ship our stock next day.

"On Christmas?" she asked incredulously. "I never heard the likes! What you doin' that for?"

"Because it falls on Saturday," I said, "and I'm afraid to wait another week with the market falling the way it is."

"Hmmfff," she sniffed, "I'd think it would be hard to get help on Christmas Day. Who-all did you get?"

I grinned and told her, "I haven't got anybody yet, but George Miner always lends a hand, and I'm going to try to put a burr under Bob. As my grandfather used to say, 'I'm feelin' porely of late'—or maybe it's just plain stingy—but there won't be much left out of this shipment for paying help."

That time Effie didn't sniff, but snorted. "My lands! Why on earth didn't you let on about it sooner. Here it is ha'-past-eight a'ready, and if it was any night but Christmas Eve half the folks in this township would be abed. Now sit still and keep your trap shut while I get out a line call. There's any Lord's quantity of folks in Beaver Valley that would be glad to lend you a hand if they knew about your shippin'."

As she spoke her thumb was pushing the key in the 4-4-4 ring that signaled a line call. She made the call sound as though our shipment would be the greatest historic event of the century, and that taking part in it would be an honor. "There! That ought to do the trick," she said when she'd pulled the line plugs. "Now you go on home and get some sleep. You look plumb beat out." She took the headphones off and walked to the door with me, then gathered me into her arms as if I were still a little boy, gave me a kiss full on the mouth, and told me, "God bless you, boy, and a merry Christmas to you. Don't get any notions in your head that the folks in this valley don't know what you're goin' through."

"Well, the last couple of minutes of it has been mighty sweet," I told her, kissed her again, and went out to the old Maxwell, feeling happier than I had for many a day.

There was little celebrating in Beaver Township on Christmas Day, 1920. Wheat that had cost two dollars a bushel to raise, harvest, and thresh, was bringing a dollar forty-five at the elevator, shelled corn was bringing sixty cents, and no one had the slightest idea how much lower livestock prices might plunge. Many farmers knew only that everything they'd gained during the war years had suddenly been swept away by a force they could neither fight nor understand, that their mortgages were greater than the value of their assets, and that they had new bankers whom they neither knew nor trusted. Only Bob seemed untouched, for he still had a good-sized roll of gold-backed twenties to flash.

The westbound train left our cars early Christmas forenoon, so I hauled a load of corn to the siding and spread a few bushels in each car as bait to make the loading easier, but Bob never left the house all morning. Marguerite had, of course, heard Effie's line call the night before, and she must have listened in on some of the morning gossip on the line. When I came back from the siding she came out to tell me dinner was ready, and she seemed to be on the verge of tears. "How are things, Balp?" she asked nervously.

"I've seen 'em better," I told her, "but they're no worse for us than for most of the farmers. Unless the market goes all to pieces between now and Monday there'll be a few shekels left over from this shipment. Don't you worry about anything until I tell you it's time to worry. Has Bob said whether or not he's going to Kansas City with the shipment?"

"Mmm-hmm, I packed his suitcase," she said tonelessly, then burst out, "Oh, Balp, I wish . . ." That was the nearest I ever heard her come to complaining, but she suddenly bit the sentence off and turned back to the house. I waited a few minutes to give her time to get hold of herself, and when I went in to wash for dinner she was humming. Throughout the meal she tried to act as if she were happy, but it was obviously a hard task.

After dinner I had barely time to stow a razor and clean underwear in my war bag before a couple of dozen neighbors came to help sort and load the stock. With so many helpers and the cars well baited, the loading was easy, leaving me plenty of time for completing the bills of lading before the arrival of the eastbound train. As it pulled away with our cars

Bob, dressed in his Sunday best, showed up and swung aboard the caboose. As always, I wore blue jeans and jumper, but there was little need of working clothes on that trip. Our stock was in as fine condition as any we'd shipped and the weather was crisp and clear, so there was little for me to do but inspect the cars at each stop to be sure we had no fallen or injured animals.

Considering the demoralized market, our stock did well in the auctions. After all deductions, my share was about three thousand dollars more than the mortgage and interest claim against it. While I was settling with the agent, Bob told us he was going to see a Junction City friend who would lend him money for another feeding operation, and he hadn't returned at train time.

It was well past noon on Tuesday when I got home. I stopped only long enough to tell Marguerite that Bob had gone to see a Junction City friend, then drove to Oberlin, for I'd decided to move my bank account to the Farmers National rather than risk having it impounded at Cedar Bluffs.

I've met few men whom I liked and trusted right from the beginning as I did Charley Frickey, president of the Farmers National Bank. We visited for more than half an hour, and though he knew about my wheat hauling, livestock dealing, and feeding businesses, he seemed more interested in how I'd happened to come to Decatur County, what I'd done before coming there, and the family at home. He said the First National would make no livestock-feeding loans until the economy settled down again, but that he'd make me short-term loans in reasonable amounts for my trading and shipping business. When I left he walked to the door with me and said, "Drop in whenever you come to town; I'll be very much interested in how you're getting along."

11

Foreclosures

THE DAY AFTER we returned from Kansas City I was working on a radio when Marguerite came out to the bunkhouse and told me that V P had phoned and asked if I'd come to the bank right away. When I went in he didn't mention my having withdrawn my account, but thanked me for sending the telegram, gave me my canceled note, and told me, "We don't aim to foreclose on anybody or anything unless we're forced to, but poor old Harry let this bank get into such awful shape with past-due and poorly-secured loans that we'll have to take proceedings in a few cases. What I'd like to do is work out a deal with you for handling and shipping any livestock we find it necessary to foreclose on."

Although V P accused me of being a robber, we finally made an agreement, put it in writing, and both signed it. I was to be paid fifty dollars a carload for shipping and accompanying to market all stock delivered to the Cedar Bluffs loading pens on shipping days. If cattle had to be brought in from the farms, I was to receive an additional dollar a head, plus fifty cents for each day they had to be cared for and fed before shipment. The rate for hogs was half those amounts. I was to take my pay in livestock, valued at what it would bring as butchering stock at Kansas City, less a dollar fifty per hundredweight.

I hadn't seen George Miner since shipping, so went over for a visit right after supper. It was bright moonlight when I came home, and there was a new Buick touring car in the dooryard. I knew that Bob must have come home by way of McCook and picked up the auto he'd ordered when he sold the corn. I stopped a minute to look the Buick over, and had started toward the kitchen door when I heard Marguerite say in an almost hysterical tone, "You'll do no such a thing, Bob Wilson! Tomorrow morning . . ."

I turned back to the bunkhouse, lighted a lamp, and went to work on a radio set. By the time I'd finished the job the house was dark and silent, so I went in quietly, and to bed.

In winter I'd always built the fire before going to do the milking so the kitchen would be warm when Marguerite came out to cook breakfast. But when I woke next morning I could see the reflection of a light in the kitchen, and as I dressed I heard the rattle of stove lids. When I went to the doorway Marguerite was standing at the stove as though in a trance, staring down at a basket of cobs she held in her hands. She looked tired enough to fall, utterly discouraged, and her swollen face and eyes showed plainly that she'd been crying. I stepped forward, took the basket, and said, "Let me build the fire for you. Why didn't you call me?"

She looked around with a vacant expression and said, "I suppose you know Bob's home. He's out milking."

In the year I'd lived there Bob had never before been up earlier than I, or done the milking if I were at home. Between the shock of it and trying to avoid admitting that I'd overheard her scolding him, I had no better sense than to say, "I thought so when I saw the new Buick in the yard last night."

"Well, that's all he brought," she said, "and we're not going to keep it. I don't know where he's been or what he's been doing, but he didn't go to Junction City and he hasn't got a nickel to his name. There's going to be another baby next fall, and I don't know . . . Hasn't Bob made anything out of all the stock you've fed together?"

"Neither of us has made a nickel on it," I told her, "but I've still got enough to carry on the shipping business, and Bob could make a good living from it if he'd settle down and go to work." Then I went out to tell him what I thought of him.

Lantern light shone full on Bob's bloated face, and for the first time since I'd known him it showed deep worry, if not stark fear. "I've been an awful fool," he said in a dull voice. "I don't know if I spent or lost it, but all I got for the corn is gone . . . and Marguerite's expecting again in the fall. I come home through McCook and picked up the Buick, but I didn't know then that Marguerite was expecting. After breakfast I'm going to take it back. If they won't give me no refund, will you leave me have a hundred or two till I get back onto my feet again?"

"I won't lend you a penny," I told him. "If you honestly want to make a living for your family you can work for me in the shipping business and help farm this place, but every dollar you get out of it you'll earn with your own two hands. The first time you shirk or groan about that phony lame back I'll quit you."

"You don't need to skin the hide off'n me; Marguerite done that last night," he said. "All I'm asking is a chance."

I doubted that his repentance would outlast his hangover, so told him, "One is all I'll ever give you; it's all up to you."

Right after breakfast Bob took the new Buick back to the dealer in McCook, and managed to get a fifty-dollar refund. I followed in the Maxwell to bring him home, and on the way we passed a field with a dozen fine young hogs in it. "Daggone it," he said, "if I'd a-thought of it, I'd sure have butchered one of them good bacon hogs of ourn before we shipped."

"Then it's a good thing you didn't think of it," I told him. "V P would have you thrown in the hoosegow if he found out that you'd butchered a mortgaged hog, but I'll make a deal with you: If you'll give Marguerite the fifty bucks when we get home, I'll buy one of those hogs in the pasture for you to butcher."

As soon as we got home I went with a wagon for the hog, while Bob heated water for scalding and got ready to do the butchering. Neither he nor Marguerite ever told me he'd given her the money, but it showed on their faces when I got home. The afternoon was crisply cold, and we did the slaughtering behind the barn, out of the children's sight. By twilight we had the halves hung high in a tree where coyotes couldn't reach them during the night. Marguerite fried fresh liver for supper, and though it was taboo on my diet I ate my full share. That evening was the best we'd had since Thanksgiving. I brought in the powerful radio I'd been working on, and was able to tune in the New Year's Eve broadcast from a big Chicago station.

New Year's Day was a busy and happy one. Bob was up as early as I, built the kitchen fire, and fed the horses and cows while I did the milking. The temperature had dropped to zero during the night, so after breakfast we brought the pork into the kitchen. Bob cut the chops, then trimmed the hams and bacon slabs, and packed them in salt to cure for smoking. My job was to bone the shoulders and neck, and grind fifty pounds of meat for sausage. Marguerite seasoned the meat as I ground it, fried thick patties slowly in deep fat, packed them in stone crocks, and poured in hot fat to seal out the air and preserve the sausage. By bedtime we had more than a two-month's supply of meat packed away in the cave cellar.

With only two cows and four horses to take care of, there wasn't much work to be done around the place, but Bob was up at the crack of dawn on Sunday, and kept himself busy all day, doing half a dozen odd jobs that he'd been putting off ever since I'd lived there. I spent most of the day loafing, telling the girls stories, finding them programs they liked on the radio, and writing letters to my folks back home.

Bob's notes fell due on Monday, so he went to the bank to

sign over his half of the remaining feed. He was gone about half an hour, and when he came back he told me, "That guy acts like he's mad at everybody. The only way I could keep him from foreclosing on the whole shebang was to sign over both cows along with the feed. He wants to see you right away."

When I went in V P came to the railing with a sheaf of papers in his hand, held it out to me, and said in a disagreeable tone. "The sheriff's serving papers on these foreclosures now. I want the stock shipped out of here Saturday, every head of it. If anybody gives you any trouble, let me know right away."

The foreclosures were against eleven of the finest young farmers on the lower benches at either side of Beaver Valley, and listed on each of the orders V P gave me there were anywhere from a dozen to fifty cattle and hogs of various classifications. From calling on those farmers I was well enough acquainted with their stock to know that they were being stripped right down to their last milch cow and brood sow. I also knew that the only reason their horses and farming equipment weren't being taken was that no market could be found for them. After looking the papers over, I asked, "Is this stock going to be delivered to the railroad shipping pens on Saturday?"

"No," V P snapped irritably, "you'll have to go get it."

I knew in reason that the foreclosed stock would net the bank far less than the new management expected, and that I'd leave myself open to claims of dishonesty unless I had proof as to the stock I received and shipped, so I told him, "Then there will have to be a bank representative to check the stock into and out of my hands, sign receipts, and set the value on stock I hold out to cover my charges."

"Be reasonable," he told me. "You know I can't chase all over this township to check in a few head of livestock."

"That's not necessary," I told him. "It can be any man who knows livestock, is trusted by the farmers being foreclosed on, and who has no mortgage obligation to this bank."

There were only three or four men who could qualify, and after a few seconds he asked, "How about Miner?"

"He'd be okay with the farmers and me," I said.

V P had Effie get George on the phone, talked to him a minute or two, and told me, "He'll do it and be ready to start out in the morning. I want all that stock shipped Saturday, and there ought to be more to go along with it."

I told him I'd do my best, went out, and crossed the street to the telephone office. The bank had a private line so that no one (except Effie) could eavesdrop on conversations, but it worked both ways. No one on the bank phone could listen in on line calls or the gossip continually flowing back and forth over the party wires—and I planned to start a little gossip. No farmer could help having some resentment toward me—even though he knew I had nothing to do with the foreclosure—if I came to his place and took his stock away; but he'd have none if he delivered the stock himself and was well paid for doing it, particularly if he'd just had his bank balance seized.

"I've got a job to do that I don't like," I told Effie. "Will you get Bill Hornbuckle on the line for me?"

She raised her eyebrows questioningly, then plugged a jack into the valley line receptacle and rang the Hornbuckle's combination. A moment later she said, "Hello, Dotty. Is Bill right handy? Bud Moody wants to talk to him." She covered the mouthpiece with her palm and whispered, "Be careful what you say if you don't want it to get around. I a'ready heard five or six receivers lifted on that line."

I picked up the receiver on the wall phone, waited for Bill to come on the line, and told him, "I've just been given a shipping job that I don't like worth a . . ."

"I know it," he said in a discouraged voice. "The sheriff served the papers this morning. The sooner you come get the stuff the more feed I'll have left for my horses."

"That's why I called you, Bill," I said. "The bank has given me more of these jobs than I can handle by myself, and is allowing me a dollar a head for cattle and fifty cents for hogs to bring the stock in. I'd sure like it if I could get you to bring yours in at those prices. The list I've got calls for nineteen cattle and twenty-two hogs."

"That's right," he said, "including my brood boar and bull, and Dotty's two milk cows. Sure, Bud, I'll bring 'em in, and much obliged for giving me a chance to earn a dollar."

Effie had, of course, listened to both ends of the conversation. I'd no sooner hung up the receiver than she jerked the line plug and demanded angrily, "How many other folks did that young whippersnapper foreclose on?"

For answer I fanned out the papers V P had given me, and said, "There'll be more, but I don't know how many. I'd sure appreciate having any of them bring their stock in at the rates the bank will be paying me—the ones I told Bill."

"Is everybody getting cleaned out like Bill, right down to his last milk cow?" she asked.

"That's right," I said, "and every herd bull and boar."

"It's a dirty shame," she snapped. "A farmer's milk cows are part of his family, and I'd about as leave take away one of his kids as one of his . . ." She half choked, then spluttered, "Get on out of here before I set myself to bawlin'! Anymore, I'm gettin' to be a sentimental old fool."

Sentimental or not, Effie had given me an idea that would be of inestimable value to Beaver Township—and to me. The more ambitious and better farmer a young man was, the less security Bones had required on loans. It was they who had overexpanded and improved their stock the most during the war years, so they were first to be foreclosed on by the new bankers. Each of them had one or more excellent milch cows, and their herd bulls and boars were among the best in the township. But as butcher stock bulls and boars, regardless of their breeding qualities, would bring little more than two cents a pound above shipping costs, and my agreement with the bank was for payment of my charges in livestock at its butchering value.

"I'm to take livestock for my pay," I told Effie, "and aim to take the cheapest—milch cows, bulls, and boars—but it would break me to feed them through the winter. If any of the folks being foreclosed on would keep a cow or two for me till spring I'd sure appreciate it. And an/body who wants a good herd bull or boar can come and pick one out, then pay me back pound-for-pound in bacon hogs when I start shipping for myself again."

Effie bounced out of her chair, smothered me in a bear hug, and told me, "Now get on out of here! I've got work to do."

By supper time every man on whom I had an order had phoned to say he'd bring his stock in, and would be glad to keep a cow or two for me until spring. That evening George and I made plans for checking in the stock, next morning he came over at sunrise, and soon after that the discouraged farmers began to arrive with their cattle and hogs. As each animal was received I painted an identification number on its shoulder, Bob weighed and penned it, while George entered its description and estimated value on a receipt with carbon copies for the bank and me. When each man went home he took along one or two of his best milch cows, a receipt for his stock, and a check for delivering it.

In mid-afternoon George and I took the receipt copies to the bank and V P gave me another sheaf of orders, most of them on the more prosperous tenant farmers on the divides. Before bedtime every one of them had phoned to say he'd bring in his stock, and to ask if he might keep a milch cow or two for me until spring. By Thursday all the foreclosed stock had been delivered, and we had eleven carloads of it in the feed lot and sorting pens. Thirty-seven excellent milch cows had been lent to their former owners, and nineteen equally good bulls and boars had been traded for one fat steer and nearly ten tons of bacon hogs for future delivery. In addition, I'd taken the feed and two cows that Bob had signed over to the bank, fifteen calves, and ten pigs too small to ship.

George had placed a value barely under two thousand dollars on the stock and feed I'd taken, and my fees amounted to a shade less than seventeen hundred, so I gave V P a check for the difference before leaving for Kansas City. I'd also paid the farmers nearly four hundred for bringing in their stock, but instead of their holding resentment I had a township full of friends. No man to whom I'd lent a cow, or traded a bull or boar, failed to come and help us load the shipment.

12

Bankruptcy

JUST BEFORE I left for Kansas City with the stock, Marguerite discovered that Bob hadn't paid anything on the grocery bill for months, and she was worried sick about it. When I got back I found him as restless as a hound with fleas and no hunting to do. Unbelievably, he seemed to have fallen into the habit of working again, and to like it. "Why don't we butcher that steer I got for the Hereford bull?" I said. "One steer would be a nuisance around the place, and with conditions as they are he wouldn't bring much on the hoof. But I'll bet we could trade beef for butter and eggs to turn in on the grocery bill, and chickens to make up for the ones I've eaten from Marguerite's flock."

Bob was all for it, so right after dinner we tackled the job of converting a steer into a beef. For me it was a new and nauseating experience, but Bob was very evidently an old hand at it. He wasn't a good workman with most tools, but had the knack of handling a skinning knife so deftly that he could strip the hide off a carcass as cleanly as if it were a glove. My contribution was little more than disposing of the offal and sawing down the center of the backbone to separate the halves. By dusk we had them hung from a cottonwood limb ten feet above the ground, safe from coyotes and where the meat would chill thoroughly during the night.

After a good supper of fresh liver, I went up to Joe's store for wrapping paper, and took Effie a box of candy I'd brought her from the city. I mentioned that we'd butchered a steer, and said, "We don't plan to sell the beef, but if any of the folks want some we'll trade a pound of steak for a dozen eggs, two for a pound of butter, or three for a good roasting chicken." She seemed as happy about it as she'd been about the milch cows, shooed me out of her office, and had made line calls before I got home.

Right after breakfast next morning, Bob and I stacked my furniture and radio materials tightly into one end of the bunkhouse. Then we planed the bench top smooth and clean, swept and scrubbed the floor, hung up meat hooks, and made ourselves a little butcher's shop. We'd taken one side of beef down from the tree, cut it into fore and hind quarters, and were carrying them to the shop when our first customer drove into the dooryard. The heads of several chickens were sticking up through holes in a gunny sack on the floor of the buckboard, and there was a basket of eggs on the seat beside her. From then till the meat was gone there were seldom less than six or eight jalopies, carriages, or wagons in the dooryard, and a cluster of men and women waited at the bunkhouse door.

I didn't know any more than a jackrabbit about meat cutting, but Bob was pretty good at it. He could cut steaks and roasts as fast as I could weigh the meat and take in whatever the people had brought to trade for it. Some of them had come ten miles or more; I don't believe anyone took less than five pounds of meat, and some took as much as twenty-five. No one was a bit fussy, and when all the steak was gone they were glad to take stew meat and shortribs at the same rate of exchange. Every scrap of meat was gone by eleven o'clock, the bunkhouse floor was packed solidly with baskets, buckets, and boxes of butter and eggs, and the heads of more than a hundred bewildered chickens stuck through holes in a row of gunny sacks outside. All we could do was to tell the folks who had come too late that we'd butcher beef again within a few days.

We'd put the chickens in the hen yard and were packing boxes of butter and eggs when Marguerite called that I was wanted at the bank right away. I went in, washed, put on a clean shirt, and had just come out when George Miner drove into the yard. He asked if I'd been called to the bank, and when I said I had he told me, "Come ride with me. I have a notion that we're goin' to be busier'n horseflies in harvest time for a spell."

"What's up, now?" I asked as we started out the driveway.

"Well," he said, "I'd guess they've a'ready got all the foreclosures they can, and are still over the barrel for cash. V P's been phonin' up everybody with a livestock-secured note fallin' due in the next month or two, tellin' 'em that if they'll pay off now he'll let 'em turn in cattle and hogs at Kansas City stockyard prices. That's where you and I come in. The stock's to be delivered here, and I'm to do the gradin'."

"When did V P tell you about it?" I asked.

"To come right down to it, he ain't told me yet. I reckon that's what he's called us in for. But you know how women are. Irene, she happened to have the receiver down when some of the talk was goin' over the wire."

"Do you think many of them will bring stock in?" I asked.

"Most of 'em, I'd guess, and pretty quick, too," he said. "They're scairt that prices will keep right on goin' down, and they're even more scairt that the bank'll foreclose on 'em if they leave their notes run till the due date."

V P was even more ill-tempered, nervous, and jumpy than usual, and told us nothing that we didn't already know. When he demanded roughly that every head of stock brought in be shipped the following Saturday, I said, "I'll do the best I can, and at the same feeding and shipping rates as before. But if I'm to be paid in livestock it will have to be at two dollars a hundred under the prices you're allowing the farmers. My shipping costs are a dollar and a half, and I won't risk this falling market without a fifty-cent margin." He was ugly and disagreeable about it, but George told him it was only reasonable, and he finally agreed to it.

V P's behavior annoyed George, and when we came out of the bank he told me, "Like Bones says, these new men are scairt and desperate, and there's no tellin' where they'll stop. This kind of monkey business will do the bank more harm than good, and the senseless foreclosures they put through will blight this township worse than the grasshoppers did in the eighties. It would have been better if they'd taken everything away from the poor devils—horses, machinery, and everything else."

"I can't see how," I said. "A farmer can't make a living without horses and machinery."

"That's right, and that's the reason it would have been better," he told me. "The boys that bought places on the benches along the valley paid upwards of a hundred dollars an acre for that land at the start of the war. I doubt me there's one in ten with a mortgage balance under seventy dollars an acre, but that land wouldn't bring fifty now, because the price of land in Kansas follows the price of grain. The way it is, those boys will work their hearts out, tryin' to keep up their mortgage payments and interest, and go deeper and deeper into the hole.

"If the bank had taken their horses and machinery, there'd be only one thing those boys could do: declare bankruptcy. Then they'd be able to make a fresh start and hope to raise their youngsters with full bellies, and give 'em an education so they'd know enough not to make the mistakes their daddies made. I'm dead against any man runnin' out from under his debts because he's too lazy to work his way out. But when a man has worked his best and saved every dollar he can, then gets caught in a bind like the one we're in now, the best thing for him to do is go through the wringer. That's what the bankruptcy laws were made for."

"How about the man who hasn't tried his best, and never saved a dollar in his life, but seems to be trying to make up for it this past week or two?" I asked.

"Well now," he said, "that's a horse of a little different color. Lazy and squanderin' as Bob has been, it don't seem right to leave him off scot-free, and if he was a single man I'd be against it. But his wife and children shouldn't have to suffer for his sins all the rest of their lives. Then again, how would he have come out if the farm economy in this country hadn't been left to go all to blazes while you boys had that last bunch of cattle and hogs on feed?"

"If the market at the end of the year had been anywhere near the September level he could have paid off every cent he owed and had at least ten thousand dollars left over," I said.

"Then if I was in his boots I'd go to see Jake Noble—he's the best lawyer over to Oberlin—and have him file me a petition in bankruptcy. According to my understanding there's not much to it, just that a man has to swear that he owns so much and owes so much, and who he owes it to. Then if I recollect right, it has to be advertised. Anyways, when the court declares him bankrupt all the debts he's listed in his petition are wiped out forever. Do you have any idea what Bob owes and owns?"

"I'd make a bet that he owes almost everybody who ever gave him credit," I said, "and that he himself has no idea how much or who he owes. Until this past week I don't believe he ever worried about a debt in his life. But all that I actually know of his owing is about twenty-two thousand to the bank here, and a few hundred to John Bivans on his grocery bill. He owns nothing but the place and his furniture, the old Buick, three horses, harness and saddle, and maybe a hundred dollars' worth of odds and ends—all mortgaged to this bank."

"Well," George said, "the furniture and the place ought to be left out. I don't believe a judge would let the bank foreclose on a family man's furniture, and the mortgage on the place is held by a widow woman over to Oberlin. It's way more than what the place is worth now. When you come right down to it, that big team of Bob's is all he's got that's worth a tinker, but it's the best one anywheres around, and you'll need a good team if you aim to farm that place next summer. If I was in your boots I'd go have a talk with Bones. He takes care of all the widow's business, and if Bob was to sign title to the place back to her, I have a notion you could lease it for less than what the mortgage interest amounts to now."

I went to Bones's house right after noon, and before I'd been there two minutes it became apparent that George had already told him about the talk we'd had. Bones agreed that the best thing for Bob to do was to file a petition in bankruptcy, but said that he should first sign title to the place back to the mortgage holder, and all his other assets except the furniture over to the bank. He told me that if the title were signed over the widow would lease me the place for a year, and he finally agreed to a rental of nine hundred dollars, but insisted that it be paid in advance. I disliked cutting into my trading funds so deeply, but we had to have the place, and Bones wouldn't rent it otherwise for less than a hundred dollars a month.

"You're making no mistake," he told me. "That's a fine place and you ought to buy it as soon as the economy in this country and land values in this valley become stablized again. If you buy it before your lease is up I'll see to it that you get credit for your nine hundred as a down payment. I suppose Bob has told you that I'm holding the deed. You bring him up at three o'clock this afternoon and I'll have the mortgage holder here. Then we can do the whole thing at one lick."

Before going home I stopped in at the bank and told V P, "If you'd like him to, I think Bob would sign everything he has except his furniture over to the bank, and I'd agree to take it in on my shipping bill at five hundred dollars. Or if the bill doesn't run that much I'll pay the difference in cash." He fairly jumped at the offer, and had me wait while the cashier typed out the agreement for Bob and me to sign.

It seemed to me that it would be best if Marguerite could be kept from knowing the situation Bob was in. So as soon as I got home I asked him to come out to the stackyard where we wouldn't be overheard, then repeated in detail all three conversations I'd had. "If you want to do it," I told him, "I'll lease the place and buy the rest of your stuff back from the bank. Then, after you've been through the wringer and can make a fresh start I'll return the stuff as your share of the profit on handling and shipping stock for the bank. There's just one more thing: before you have a petition filed—if you decide to do it—I think you should go in to see Bivans and tell him you're going to pay his bill in full, regardless of the bankruptcy. What do you think about the whole thing?"

Bob knew nothing about bankruptcy, and at first he was as afraid of going into it as a child would be of going into a pitch-black cave. But when I'd explained it to him he told me, "I'll do anything you and George say is right, and I'll sign anything you tell me to if it'll leave me have a clean start. I'd sure like to get the stuff around here back free and clear, and I'll work the best I can for it."

At three o'clock Bob and I left the signed agreement at the bank and went on to the Kennedy house. The widow and George Miner were there, and Bones had the deed, a quitclaim, and a lease in my name laid out on the table. The lease was less than half a page long, simply giving the legal description of the place, stating that it was leased to me for the calendar year 1921 in consideration of nine hundred dollars, the receipt of which was acknowledged, and that the full amount would be applied against the purchase price in the event of my buying the place within the lease term. The signing required no more than fifteen or twenty minutes, and by three-thirty Bob was on his way to lawyer Noble's office—the old Buick loaded to the door tops with butter and eggs for John Bivans.

During the rest of January, Bob and I butchered five fat

young cows, four hogs, at least two hundred chickens, and shipped more than six hundred animals for the bank. To do it we had to be up before five o'clock every morning and were seldom in bed before eleven at night. Marguerite was fully as busy as Bob and I, taking care of the house and children, cooking meals, and waiting on customers who came to trade butter, eggs, and chickens for beef and pork. During the evenings she packed cases of eggs and boxes of butter to be turned in on the grocery bill, while I picked chickens to be sold to a shipper at McCook, and Bob cut meat for the next day's trade.

All month the cattle market continued steadily downward, and corn dropped another dime, but hogs held fairly steady. As the market declined V P became more irritable, disagreeable, and difficult to deal with, but he had cause for it. As near as George and I could estimate, the bank had lost five thousand dollars on stock that he had taken in at Kansas City prices.

In spite of the falling market and the huge loss on our last feeding venture, January thirty-first was as happy a day at the Wilson place as December thirty-first had been sad and worrysome. Our earnings from feeding and shipping stock for the bank had been enough to redeem Bob's assets, pay for the cattle and hogs we'd butchered, and leave us fully four hundred dollars' worth of trading, butchering, and shipping stock. Bob had been adjudged bankrupt, and the load of butter and eggs taken to Bivans that day cleaned up the grocery bill. When Bob got home I gave him a bill of sale for everything he'd signed over to the bank, and told him that he had a half interest in all the other stock on the place—excepting only Kitten.

13

The Sign in the Window

My JOY was short-lived. The next day I received notice that suit had been filed against me by the First State Bank of Cedar Bluffs in the amount of $22,186, principal and interest owed to the plaintiff by the partnership of Wilson and Moody.

I took the notice straight to Bones and found him furious about the filing of the suit. "They know they haven't a leg to stand on," he stormed. "I told them before ever they bought the bank stock that there was no partnership between you and Bob. The trouble with them is that they're new at the banking business, they're scared, and the examiners will be here any day now. What these fellows are up to, now that Bob has taken bankruptcy, is trying to make a dead loss look to the examiners like a recoverable asset. There isn't one chance in ten of the case ever coming to trial, but you'll have to get a lawyer to make answer and defend you anyways. I suppose you'll go to Jake Noble, won't you, the same as Bob did?"

"That's right," I said.

"You tell him what I've said," he told me, "and that he can count on me for the testimony to win the case if it's ever brought to trial."

I went directly to Mr. Noble's office, gave him the notice, and told him exactly what Bones had said. "I don't believe you have much to worry about," he told me. "Not with Harry Kennedy backing you up. I'd be inclined to agree with him that this suit is nothing more than window trimming for the examiners. I'll get in touch with Harry and file a reply, and if the case is called I'll appear and get a continuance. I might have to get two or three of them before the suit is finally dropped, and I'll let you know if there's anything further to be done. In the meantime, don't let it worry you."

A few days later the examiners arrived and a card was put in the bank window, announcing that it was temporarily closed by the State Banking Commission. When Effie tried to pump Bones for information he told her, "The card speaks for itself. There's nothing further I can tell you or anyone else."

With the bank closed there would, of course, be no more shipping to be done for it, and Beaver Township had been so stripped of cattle and hogs that there would be little or no trading business for several months. Then too, since the grocery bill had been paid off, Bivans was less happy to be deluged with butter and eggs. The day the sign was put in the bank window I had a long talk with George Miner. That evening Bob and I made our plans for the rest of the year, based on George's theory of a nine-month cycle in the hog market.

Hog prices had risen steadily during the first nine months of 1920, then plunged downward for six weeks, and were still slipping off, though at a much slower pace. George believed the trend would continue until the cycle ran out in June, and that hog prices would then rise rather sharply, but to nowhere near the 1920 peak. Bob and I decided to trade the stock we had on hand for weanling pigs, corn-feed them through the spring and early summer, and market them as bacon hogs in July. We wouldn't operate as partners, but each would own his half of the hogs and furnish half the feed, then we'd split the profit. I told him that if he kept working as he had been, he could have all the profits from butchering, and half the net income from trading and shipping.

We had no difficulty in trading our stock for a hundred and twenty-two pigs, and Bob did excellently on the butchering. We had Effie put out line calls that we couldn't take butter, eggs, and chickens any longer, but would exchange four pounds of beef or three of pork for each bushel of ear-corn brought in. By the end of February Bob had nearly a thousand bushels of corn cribbed up in the stackyard, and owed me only a hundred and fifty dollars for stock we'd slaughtered. In the meantime I'd collected and shipped the hogs I had coming to me for bulls and boars, and they'd brought nearly twelve hundred dollars.

From our March shipping profits Bob and I bought enough more pigs to bring our herd up to an even two hundred. I ran out of feed and it seemed a shame to use corn from our last year's crop when I knew that a good many farmers would like some of it for seed. At George Miner's suggestion, I had Effie put out a line call, saying that I'd trade one bushel of seed corn for two of feed corn. The trading brought in thirty-five hundred bushels of ear-corn that was plenty good for hog feed, and I still had enough seed left for our own field.

With Beaver township fairly stripped of livestock I was obliged to extend my trading territory farther to the west each week. When the distances became too great for traveling back and forth every day I stayed out in the territory all week, then shipped from the nearest railroad town on Saturdays. Bob stayed at home to take care of the butchering business, feed the hogs, and get ready for the spring planting. Although he'd ridiculed my fertilizing the corn field the previous spring, he began hauling manure without any suggestion from me. By the end of April he'd spread a thick layer of it over the entire south field, plowed it under, and planted the seed.

The weather turned unseasonably warm on the first of May, Bob had to quit butchering for lack of refrigeration, and for a few days I felt as though I had spring fever. My head and joints ached, my mouth became so dry I could hardly swallow, and I didn't want anything to eat but canned tomatoes and cold milk. Then pimples broke out on my arms, legs, and the back of my neck. By the end of the week there were thirty-one of them, swollen the size of egg yolks, bright red, and as painful to the touch as if hot coals were being pressed into me. I had trouble in collecting and shipping the stock I'd bought, and Sunday morning I went to see Dr. DeMay. He had no idea what had caused the eruptions, but said they were carbuncles, poulticed them, and told me I'd have to come back every day until they'd all been brought to heads, lanced, and the cores removed.

To be where I could easily get to Dr. DeMay's office every morning, I went back to working my old valley route in Beaver Township. There had been considerable change on the route since the end of the year. Most of the young farmers whose cattle and hogs had been foreclosed upon had been obliged to go into bankruptcy. A few had made loans from friends or relatives and were still hanging on; renting the land they had lost, trying to farm with too few horses, and to start new herds with a couple of brood sows and a few heifer calves. The rest had quit; some moving away, and others going to work for the more prosperous of the valley farmers.

Every man who quit had brought back the milch cow or two he'd had on loan, and each time Effie had put in a plea for some newly arrived sharecropper whose only cow had gone dry. Since the beginning of March several "croppers" had moved into the township from Arkansas or Missouri to farm the land lost by boys who had quit. They'd come by railroad, bringing their families and what little furniture, farm equipment, and livestock they had in a single emigrant car—simply a boxcar with a hole for a stovepipe to stick out through.

There were few cattle for sale in Beaver Valley, but the week my carbuncles were being lanced I bought two carloads of hogs. Saturday noon I hauled some corn to the Cedar Bluffs siding for baiting the cars, but the westbound train was late. It was a beautiful day, and Dad Hanes was sitting on the edge of the platform, whittling a stick and spitting tobacco juice out across the track. I hitched the team and went to sit beside him. He didn't look up, but asked, "How's the boils doin'?"

"Better," I said, got out my jackknife, and started whittling a horse's head from a scrap of soft wood I'd picked up.

There was no reason to ask Dad when the train would get in, because he didn't know any more about it than I did, so we just sat and whittled. A hundred yards down the siding, just beyond the grain elevator, there was an emigrant car that had come in from Arkansas the day before. We'd been whittling for about ten minutes when I heard an angry-sounding voice shout, "Shut up and stay in there!"

I glanced up to see the tousled heads of three or four children in the car doorway, and a big stoop-shouldered man starting along the track toward us. He came on steadily until he was directly in front of Dad, then folded his arms across his chest and announced belligerently, "I'm movin' onto the Bill Hornbuckle place. What kind of neighbors will I find there?"

For the first time, Dad looked up from his whittling, turned his head to spit, and asked in his quiet twang, "What kind of neighbors did you have where you come from?"

The mention of his Arkansas neighbors seemed to drive the man into a frenzy. In as violent an outburst of swearing as I ever heard, he told us they were the worst bunch of thieves and scoundrels in the world. When the tirade ended, Dad looked up again, spit accurately at a rail, and said mildly, "You'll find 'em just the same here," then went on whittling as if he were alone. For a moment the man bristled as though he might attack, then dropped his arms and lumbered back down the track.

With my carbuncles healed, the corn planted, our hogs growing like mushrooms, and the shipping business making us a good living, Saturday nights became our blowout time. When I'd get home from the territory Marguerite and the girls would be dressed in their Sunday best, Bob would have the chores done, and Betty Mae would come running to meet me, calling, "Huwwy up, Balp! We're going to see Bibbins."

To her, going to Oberlin was a trip to see John Bivans—looked forward to by both of them with equal joy. She'd hardly allow me time to take a bath and change into clean shirt and jeans, then we'd be off for town—Marguerite and the baby in front with Bob: Arvis, Betty Mae, a basket of eggs, and me in the back. We didn't spare expenses but had the dollar dinner at the best restaurant, then went to the early movie. Before the show was half over we usually lost Betty Mae, but it didn't worry us. She'd have sneaked out to the store, and we'd find Bivans waiting on trade with her riding pickaback on his shoulders, munching cookies and jabbering like a little monkey. If we weren't his favorite customers he made us feel that we were, and he was certainly our favorite storekeeper.

Actually, our Saturday night blowouts were far from wild or extravagant, but they were enjoyable, and although we were working hard for every dollar we made, I'd seldom in my life been more contented. I'm sure Bob and Marguerite felt the same.

Since the bank closing Bones had aged terribly, avoided any question about its affairs, and kept to his house most of the time. The "temporarily closed" sign was still in the bank window, though everyone knew that the examination must have long since been completed. None of us had seen or heard from the new bankers since closing day, and not even George Miner had any idea what might be going on.

Mr. Noble phoned on the third Sunday in May, asking me to come to his house that afternoon, and to bring any books or records I'd kept on the livestock feeding business. When I got there he showed me into the parlor and told me, "The affairs of the Cedar Bluffs Bank have been taken over by the State Banking Commission and a receiver appointed. He's a fine and reasonable man, but he's obliged to prosecute any suits that have been instituted, and the bank's suit against you is scheduled for trial before a justice of the peace on June tenth."

For nearly an hour he questioned me about my dealings with Bob and the way we'd done our buying, feeding, and selling. He'd evidently spent several hours with Bones, for he had eight or ten pages of notes about our loans and the various agreements we'd made, including the provision for separating Bob's stock from mine at any time by one-and-one choice.

My biggest worry was that I'd neglected to have Bones write on my last two notes, as he'd done on the first one, that he guaranteed not to hold me liable for any debt I hadn't personally contracted. "It's the intent of the parties that governs in such matters," Mr. Noble told me, "and Harry Kennedy states definitely that all your loans were made with that understanding on his part. With him standing squarely behind you—and he is—I don't foresee much danger of an adverse decision."

He walked to the door with me, and as I was leaving he said, "You might ask Bob and George Miner to drop in at my office the next time they come to town. There's no need for either of them to make a special trip, but there are a few questions I'd like to ask them. Don't let this thing worry you, and go right on about your business in the usual way. I shouldn't have to bother you again for a couple of weeks."

Bob and George went to see him Monday, but for the next couple of weeks I was so busy that I had no time for worrying about the trial. I was working territory in the northwestern corner of Kansas, and business was good. The ranches were large, and I was sometimes able to buy eight or ten cattle from a single rancher. Our feed-lot hogs, nearing the two-hundred-pound mark, were stowing away fifty bushels of corn a day, and Bob ran out. As soon as we were sure our May profit was going to be a big one he bought twelve hundred bushels at forty cents, but had to haul it six miles.

On the last Sunday in May Mr. Noble phoned, asking me to

come to his house again. When I got there he had only a few more questions to ask, and as I was leaving he said, "That just about wraps it up until June tenth. Barring the uncertainties of law, I can foresee nothing that should prevent us from defending against the action handily."

14

Flood

THURSDAY forenoon, June 2, I was working in the Republican Valley southwest of St Francis. There I heard of a cloudburst at Atwood, thirty-odd miles up Beaver Valley from Cedar Bluffs. Cloudbursts weren't uncommon in spring, so I paid little attention to the report and spent a couple of hours dickering over a few cattle. When I moved on, the next rancher told me that a second tremendous cloudburst had followed the first and that Atwood was flooded, with water at the highest point ever known. Beaver Creek was certain to overflow at Cedar Bluffs in any such flood and Marguerite, the children, and the stock might be in serious danger unless there was plenty of advance warning, so I put in a phone call right away.

Effie said that word had been telephoned through within minutes after the first cloudburst struck, that she'd put out line calls up and down the valley, and that everyone was safe. Bob, she said, had left for a load of corn just before the word came through, but made it back in time to get the family, horses, and cows out. "Bill Justice and a couple of boys from town here fetched out the furniture," she told me, "and they're down there with Bob now, trying to get the hogs out. You'd

134

best to get here just as fast as you can. Don't try to come straight east on the Phillipsburg road; the Atwood bridge is out, and you can't come by way of McCook because our bridge here is out. You'll have to go south to Goodland and come on to Oberlin by way of Colby and Selden."

Effie hadn't told me that the probability of getting our hogs out was far from good, but I didn't need to be told. The bridge on the McCook-Oberlin road—no more than fifty yards from the house—was four feet higher than our feed lot. If the bridge had been washed out there was little doubt that the feed lot had gone with it. The only hope was that Bob had managed to get the hogs to high ground before the bridge went.

The old Maxwell nearly rattled itself to pieces, but covered the 140-mile circuitous route from St. Francis to Cedar Bluffs in three hours. There was no need of my having rushed, though, and nothing I could do when I got there. From the corner where the road pitched downward to the town from the top of the bluff, Beaver Creek looked like the Missouri River.

Swirling brown water, spotted with floating buildings and all manner of debris, covered the entire valley floor. At the far side, the buildings of the Miner place stood at the water's edge, the corrals already awash. On the near side, the eighteen or twenty houses of Cedar Bluffs huddled like frightened sheep at the foot of the high divide, saved from the flood only by the railroad grade that skirted the south edge of the valley. All I could see of our place was the tops of trees marking the course of the creek, the peak of the submerged house, and the bunkhouse—afloat and apparently caught in the big cottonwoods behind the barn. What puzzled me was a yellowish cast to the water in an irregular circle covering most of our corn field.

Guy and Effie Simons's house was farthest back in the village, safely above any danger from the flood. There I found Marguerite and the children, frightened and worried, but unharmed. Bob, with the rest of the men, was filling gunny sacks with dirt and piling them along the railroad track to form a higher dike. He was mudsoaked, bedraggled, and nearer discouraged than I'd ever seen him.

"Daggone it," he told me, "we done the best we could, but never saved one measly hog. A wall of water three foot high hit us before ever we got 'em out of the lot. It washed 'em away like rolling logs, and we'd a-gone with 'em if we hadn't been on horseback. I've seen lots of floods, but never the likes of this one. The water come up so fast it was knee-high to a mounted man before we could get out of the dooryard, and when the bridge went out it stove the feed lot fence all to kindlin'. The worst of it is that there wasn't any need of us losing a single daggoned hog. If I'd been there when the line call come through, instead of off . . ."

"Forget it!" I told him. "A man has nothing to grieve over if he's done the best he could, and we're a long way from licked. There's still time to replant the corn if this water drains off in a few days, and before another winter we'll be right on top of the heap again. But if we don't get this dike built up in a hurry the town's going to be flooded. The water has risen six inches since I got here."

Until the crest passed, just before sunset, every man and boy in town, and many who came down from the divide to help us, had to work furiously to build the railroad grade high enough to keep water out of the town. It was possible only because the creek channel turned away from the railroad just above Cedar Bluffs, crossed the valley to surround our buildings and feed lot in a U-shaped loop, then returned to the railroad line east of town. Strangely, the flow of water past our dike was sluggish and moving up the valley instead of down.

Old Kitten, being straight mustang, could swim like an otter, and I could do fairly well myself. Partly to find what was causing the backwash, but more to discover the reason for the yellowish appearance of the water covering our corn field, I decided to swim Kitten out there. Instead of bridling her, I braided a two-foot strip of rawhide into her mane, stripped to my B.V.D.'s, wound the rawhide around one hand, and plunged her off the built-up railroad grade at the shipping pens. The moment we hit the water I slid off her back and turned her head in the direction of the barely visible house peak, straight across what had been our corn field that morning.

The water was deep enough that Kitten swam over the fence without touching it, and by the time we were a hundred feet out from the track the reason for the yellowish color became joyfully apparent. The surface of the water was blanketed with floating ears of corn, moving in a clockwise direction as if they were laid out on a thirty-acre, slowly-revolving table. I eased Kitten into the edge of the mass and soon learned the reason for it. Trash and broken planks from the bridge and feed lot fence had lodged in the limbs of the big cottonwoods at the elbow-bend of the creek. It formed a bulwark against which the current hurled itself in a roaring, foam-crested torrent and was deflected southward across what had been the stackyard. Friction of the current as it followed the U-shaped channel was forcing water inside the U to turn in a slow-moving whirlpool.

To insure good drainage, I'd set the corn cribs on a knoll in the stackyard, standing about four feet higher than the surrounding land. That had kept the cribs from being swept away by the first wall of water, the whirlpool had been set in motion, and the corn had simply floated when the water level reached the tops of the fifteen-foot-high cribs.

There had been well over three thousand bushels in the cribs, and from the size of the floating mass I didn't believe that we'd lost 10 percent of it—yet. If we'd been well-equipped fishermen we might have been able to surround the corn with a purse net and tow it ashore. But with neither nets nor boats there was nothing we could do but hope that by some miracle our corn would be left behind when the flood had passed.

In spite of all the change in Bob since the end of the year, he had never lost the illusion that he'd some day find a rainbow with a pot of gold at both ends. When I told him that little if any of our corn had yet been swept away, he began talking about putting in another two hundred pigs as soon as the flood went down. But Marguerite must have had a terrible fright between the time of Effie's line call and his getting home to take her and the children out. Though the water level had dropped a foot and all danger was over before dark, she couldn't look out across the valley without trembling uncontrollably. She wouldn't let the baby out of her arms, or Arvis and Betty Mae out of her sight. At any mention of going back to the place she became almost terror stricken. In hope that talking to her mother would quiet her nerves, Effie put through a call to Junction City that evening, but it didn't help much.

Nearly every bed in Cedar Bluffs was filled with women and children evacuated from homes on the floor of Beaver Valley, and the men spent the night wherever they had taken their livestock. Bob and I slept under his load of furniture, just outside Simon's corral, but we were up at the first gray of dawn. The water level had fallen about six feet during the night, but when the sun came up it showed no yellow cast to the brown water that still circled slowly above our corn field.

The current above the channel was still swift but no longer a raging torrent. As near as we could make out from the railroad embankment, the water was even with the eaves of the house, and the bunkhouse appeared to have settled onto the barn roof. Not far outside the southeast corner of our corn field the creek had cut a new channel, ripping out the railroad along the foot of the bluffs for which the town was named. The water covering the corn field was draining off slowly in the direction of the washout, though the slope of the land was slightly the other way.

With our corn having disappeared Bob could find no rainbow, to say nothing of a pot of gold. He tried to keep up an appearance of confidence for Marguerite's benefit, but couldn't do a good enough job to deceive her. All day Friday he and I rode along the south margin of the flood below town, hoping to find some of our hogs that had managed to swim until they'd reached high ground, but we found only their bloating carcasses. The warning had come early enough that our neighbors had been able to save their horses, cattle, and most of their hogs. Almost no poultry had been saved from places on the valley floor, and drowned turkeys, hens, and roosters hung from the box elder trees all along the creek channel.

We and most of the men along the south side of the valley spent all day Saturday plowing trenches just above the mud line, dragging in carcasses, and burying them before the stench became unbearable. Although the valley telephone lines were down and all communication cut off, we knew that conditions on the north side must be equally bad, for we could see men with teams and stone boats dragging carcasses up from the margin of the flood.

When we went back to the village that evening, Effie took me aside and asked, "Has Bob got anything left that he can call his own besides that load of furniture?"

"Certainly," I told her. "He doesn't owe a nickel, his big team is worth four hundred dollars even with conditions as they are, and there's the Buick, his saddle mare, and a couple of milch cows. I suppose you know that he'd just paid nearly five hundred dollars for corn and was hauling the last load of it home when the flood struck. But he still ought to have about a hundred dollars left, and I owe him seventy from last week's shipment."

"Well," she said, "I don't reckon it's any news to you, but Marguerite's expectin' in September. When a woman's that way she's liable to get lots of notions into her head that she wouldn't get otherways, and that's what's happened to Marguerite. She's as scared of taking them little children back to live in that house again as the devil is of holy water, and ever since she talked to her mother she's been so homesick she can't hardly stand it. It'll be leastways a month before that house can be dried out and cleaned up enough to live in, and she'll go stark-starin' crazy if she has to sit here that long with nothin' to do but worry. What I been thinking was that if Bob could afford the train fare he'd ought to send that girl home to visit her folks till the house is ready and signs of the flood kind of wore off from the valley. Like as not, by that time she'll be over her fright enough that she'll be glad to come back. Why don't you kind of drop a hint to Bob?"

I didn't drop a hint, but told Bob straight-out what Effie had said, and that I thought she was right. He did too, and I never saw a woman happier than Marguerite was when he told her. There wasn't much getting ready to be done, and Sunday noon she and the girls took the train from Oberlin.

By Monday the water had drained off enough that the creek was back in its gorge, leaving the floor of Beaver Valley a half-mile-wide morass of soft mud, spotted with mounds of wreckage and debris. From what remained of the railroad grade, Bob and I could see that the house and barn—protected from the main current by the big cottonwoods and the built-up bridge approach on the Oberlin-McCook road—appeared not to be badly damaged. The bunkhouse sat squarely atop the low-pitched roof of the barn, but all the smaller buildings were completely gone, along with the haystacks, corn cribs, and most of the feed-lot fence. Miraculously, the woven wire fence around the corn field looked to be very slightly damaged, though banked high with debris and mud.

Late Tuesday afternoon I thought the mud might have dried out enough to hold up my weight. Wanting to find out how much damage had actually been done to the house, I took off my boots and socks, rolled up my jeans, and set out from the shipping pens. The bank of the railroad grade was fairly firm, but at the first step onto cultivated ground I sank to my knee, and on the way down my bare toes raked across something that felt like an ear of corn. I reached into the muck with my hand and found the ear buried under five or six inches of silt that had been brought down by the flood.

There was no sense in trying to reach the house. But since I was already as dirty as if I'd fallen into a hog wallow I took a few more steps, and at each one my foot struck an ear of corn. I spent an hour wading around the field, and discovered the story of our corn as well as if I'd been able to watch every ear. The reason for its disappearing the first night was that the cobs became waterlogged and the kernels coated with mud, causing the ears to sink a few inches below the surface. Their position left no doubt that they had continued circling, and had settled gradually with the silt as the water, slowed by the debris caught in the fence, drained slowly away. The number of ears I found made me believe that nearly all of our corn was still right there on the place. Although buried under a few inches of mud, I thought it could be salvaged by turning hogs into the field as soon as it had dried out enough to bear their weight.

After scrubbing myself under the fire hydrant at the grain elevator, I took Bob to the edge of the field and showed him the bushel or so of corn I'd dug out of the mud. I explained why I believed that three thousand bushels might still be on the place, and told him how I thought it could be salvaged. He agreed that most of the corn might be there, but said it would rot before hogs ever rooted deep enough to find it. We were trying to figure out some other way of salvaging when Harry Witham shouted from the elevator, "Telephone!" As we hurried back along the track he sang out, "It's for you, Bob. Effie say it's Marguerite calling from Junction City."

Harry and I stayed outside, but after Bob had talked a minute or two he rapped on the window and motioned for me to come in. From the look on his face I knew he'd found a rainbow—one with a pot of gold at each end. "The tenant on the Webking place died last night," he told me when I went in, "and that's the best half-section of corn land anywheres around Junction. Marguerite's folks have been to see Miz

Webking, and she'll leave me have the place for the rest of the year if I can come right away. The corn's all planted, and she'll give me a third of the crop for farming and shucking it."

"Take it," I told him. "It will be too late to plant corn here when the land dries, and you could never make as much on cattle shipping as on a deal like that. Besides, I don't think this house will be fit for Marguerite to live in again. The only thing I'm not sure about is whether or not Mr. Noble will need you here for the trial."

It took three or four more phone calls, but before the evening was over everything had been arranged. Bob had a lease on the Junction City place for the remainder of the year, with a promise of renewal if he'd done a good job. We'd ordered an emigrant car into Oberlin for shipment of his horses, cows, and furniture. It would be shipped on June ninth, and he would follow in the Buick after testifying on the tenth.

15

Three Little Pigs

THE Banking Commission had two lawyers when my case came to trial on June 10. One was an Oberlin man, and the other a tricky Topeka attorney who did all the cross-examining. The first witness called was the cashier who came to the Cedar Bluffs bank when the new management took over. The Oberlin lawyer had him identify some of the bank's books and records, and testify from them for half an hour. Among other things he testified that I had written nearly all the checks when Bob and I bought stock or feed, but that the amounts had often been charged equally to Bob's loan account and mine. He also testified that proceeds of our sales had been credited to us in exactly equal amounts.

As his final witnesses, the lawyer called several farmers from whom we'd bought stock. I don't believe any of them realized what the trial was about, and they all seemed embarrassed, but each one testified that he understood he was selling to a partnership and had heard Bob call me partner.

When the prosecution rested its case Mr. Noble told me there hadn't been a shred of damaging evidence produced. He said that Bones's testimony would nullify any implications by the cashier, and that it was customary in the West for one man to call another partner as a common term of address.

So that Bob could get away as early as possible, Mr. Noble called him as our first witness. He testified only a few minutes—just long enough to state under oath that he and I had never been partners, but that each had owned half the livestock and feed, which could have been separated at any time. Bob admitted that he'd called me partner, but said he'd called hundreds of other men by the same name. The Topeka lawyer didn't even bother to cross-examine him, and we had only a chance to nod good-bye before he left for Junction City. The rest of the forenoon was taken up by neighbors and farmers from whom we'd bought, testifying that Bones, Bob, or I had told them we were not in partnership though we fed stock together.

Bones was our first witness in the afternoon, and a good one, talking more as though he were telling a story than testifying at a trial. He recited, almost word for word, the conversations he and I had in early December, 1919—my refusing to go into partnership with Bob but agreeing to feed stock with him if some way could be found for doing it as individuals. He explained the method we'd worked out, and testified that he'd told me, "If the chattels can be separated at any time, so that each man can stand alone with his property and obligations, I don't see how there'd be a partnership. If you and Bob will team up that way I'll make you separate loans and guarantee not to hold one of you responsible for a dollar of the other's debts."

Mr. Noble presented my original note to the justice of the peace for identification, then passed it to Bones and said, "I hand you a promissory note dated December 16, 1919, upon the face of which is endorsed, 'I hereby guarantee not to hold Ralph Moody liable for any debt which he has not personally contracted. Harry S. Kennedy.' Please state whether or not the signature is yours, and if the endorsement had been made at the time the note was signed by the defendant."

Bones looked up at the justice and said, "The signature is mine, and the endorsement was on the note at the time it was signed by the defendant."

"On subsequent loans to the defendant, was the same or a similar guarantee endorsed upon the notes?" Mr. Noble asked.

"Not to my recollection," Bones testified, "but the same guarantee was nevertheless a part of the loan agreement."

For the next half hour Mr. Noble had Bones testify as to dates and amounts from the bank's books. I think it was mainly to establish that Bob was in debt more than twelve thousand dollars in excess of his assets at the time we started feeding stock together.

On cross-examination the Topeka lawyer had Bones repeat three different times that Bob's debt to the bank after our second shipment was only eight thousand dollars. He asked the justice for the note that had been placed in evidence, then paced slowly back and forth, appearing to study it intently. After a minute or two he stopped in front of Bones, passed him the note, and asked if the signature under the guarantee was his. When Bones answered that it was, the lawyer told him, "Please state the name of the payee on the instrument you are holding."

Bones looked up, scowled a bit in irritation, and replied, "The First State Bank of Cedar Bluffs, Kansas."

"Then the endorsement is your personal guarantee, not that of the lender. Is that correct, Mr. Kennedy?" the lawyer said as he reached for the note.

Bones flared, "When that loan was made I was virtually the sole owner of . . ."

"Answer yes or no," the lawyer broke in suavely.

Bones looked as though he were on the verge of exploding when he grated out, "Yes."

"That is all," the attorney said with an inflection of finality.

George Miner followed Bones, and Mr. Noble had him testify as to the value at which he had appraised Bob's feed and hogs at the time I bought half of them—evidently to again establish that Bob had then been deep in debt. In closing, he had George tell of meetings between Bones, Bob, and me at which he had been present, of agreements we'd made in his hearing, and that we had all told him no partnership existed.

The Topeka lawyer didn't cross-examine George more than five minutes. He asked a few questions about dates of meetings, where they were held, what had been said, and who had said it. When George had answered all the questions the lawyer began pacing slowly, and said, "Now if I remember correctly, there were three separate feeding operations; the first commencing in December, 1919, the second in April, 1920, and the third in September, 1920. Is that correct, Mr. Miner?"

"That's right," George answered.

Still pacing, the attorney asked, "Now these meetings that you attended, they were all held prior to the first feeding venture or during its very early stages, were they not?"

George thought a moment, and again answered, "That's right."

The lawyer stopped directly opposite him, stuck both hands into his pockets, and asked slowly, "Since September first of last year has anyone told you, Mr. Miner, that no partnership existed between the defendant and Robert Wilson?"

George said hesitantly, "Well, I don't recollect anybody tellin' me in just so many words, but . . ."

"That is all," the attorney broke in, then walked away.

I was my last witness—and my worst one.

Mr. Noble put my account books for the trading, shipping, and feeding business into evidence. Then he had me testify from them more than an hour, showing that each business had been operated independently, and that in the feeding business Bob's assets, liabilities, profits, and losses had been recorded entirely separate from mine. To prove that the bank officials were thoroughly aware that no partnership existed, Mr. Noble entered in evidence all the agreements and bills of sale in connection with shipping bank livestock—every one of them made out in my name alone. Before completing my testimony, he had me identify each document, then turned me over to the Topeka attorney for cross-examination. It lasted about two minutes.

After pacing back and forth a few times, he stopped in front of me and said, "Now you have testified repeatedly that you and Mr. Wilson each owned a distinct half of the livestock in question and a distinct half of the feed, though I understand that the livestock was generally kept in a single enclosure. How many times were the halves physically separated?"

"We had agreed on a method by which they could have been separated at any time," I said, "but . . ."

"Answer the question I asked you!" he said coldly.

"None," I answered. "There was never any reason for it."

He shoved both hands into his pockets, faced me a minute without speaking, then asked, "How many cattle have been lost by death since you and Wilson began feeding stock together?"

"None," I answered.

"How many hogs?"

"No hogs," I replied, "but we lost three small pigs from the last lot of stock we fed."

"Were they yours or Wilson's?" he asked.

I knew what he was up to instantly, but there was only one answer I could make: "They belonged to us jointly, since no division had been made at that time."

He strode back to the counsel table, saying, "That is all." It was, too.

The justice ruled that Bob and I had been "de facto" partners in our third livestock feeding venture, but not in the first two or in the trading and shipping businesses, and that I owed the bank $13,136 plus interest from January 4, 1921.

Bones was irate at the ruling though he stood to gain by it. He was still a stockholder in the defunct bank, and so large a recovery would substantially reduce his loss. Mr. Frickey had attended the trial, and was among the first to come up after the judgment was rendered. He said he was surprised and shocked by it, and suggested that Mr. Noble, Bones, and I come to his office where we could discuss the matter in private. We were no sooner in the office than Bones insisted that an appeal must be filed immediately, but Mr. Noble didn't agree with him. He said an appeal would be a drawn out and expensive matter, and in the light of some of the evidence, particularly that regarding the three pigs, he doubted that a reversal could be obtained. Instead of appealing, he recommended that I file a petition in bankruptcy immediately.

As soon as Mr. Noble had finished I told the group, "I have rent to the end of the year paid in advance, thirty-nine fine milch cows, and a little more than thirty-six hundred dollars in the bank. If I could work out a deal with the receiver to let me stay on the place, and not to attach my bank account, I'd much rather pay off the judgment than take bankruptcy. Except for a bad loss when the hog market broke so sharply last October, I've been able to do fairly well as a livestock dealer. If I'm left enough capital to carry on the business unhampered, and if I'm not eaten up with interest, I think I could pay that thirteen thousand off in a couple of years. But if I'm stripped right down to the hide, and interest is piling up at the rate of ten per cent, taking bankruptcy would seem the only sensible thing to do."

Then I looked around at Mr. Frickey and added, ". . . unless the Farmers National Bank makes loans to paupers."

I intended it as a joke, but Mr. Frickey asked seriously, "How much working capital would you require to carry on your livestock dealing business unhampered?"

"Three thousand dollars," I told him.

"Could you handle six per cent interest on the judgment?"

"Yes, sir, if I had a three-thousand-dollar working fund."

Mr. Frickey looked toward Mr. Noble and said, "You've had some dealings with the receiver of that bank and found him a rather reasonable man, haven't you, Jake?"

"Just and reasonable," Mr. Noble answered.

"I presume he's still in town," Mr. Frickey said. "Let's see if we can get him over here to discuss this matter."

Then he told me, "Bankers can sometimes work these matters out better among themselves. We'll try to have a talk with the receiver, and will get in touch with you through the Cedar Bluffs telephone exchange when there's anything to report."

When I left the bank I intended going straight home, but news of the judgment had spread, and so many people stopped me on the street that it was an hour before I got out of Oberlin. Until those people told me how badly I'd been wronged I hadn't thought about being sorry for myself. But I made up for it on the way back to Cedar Bluffs, and was still enjoying my sorrow when Effie called from the door of her office, "Good lands! Where have you been for the last hour? I've like to wore out every line in the township trying to run you down. Bones wants you over to his house as quick as ever you can get there."

Bones showed me into his parlor, where the receiver for the Cedar Bluffs bank was waiting. He rose, and as Bones introduced us he put out his hand to shake, saying, "I don't believe we're going to have much trouble doing business together, but your friends have been giving me a rough time this afternoon. Sit down, and let's talk things over."

Within five minutes I knew exactly where I stood with him and the defunct bank, and I liked it. Half an hour later we'd agreed that I would sell my milch cows as soon as practicable and turn the entire receipts over to apply against the judgment. I'd turn over at once all cash in excess of three thousand dollars, and could keep a working fund of that amount in cash or other assets. At the end of each month I was to turn over to the receiver my net earnings, less living expenses. In exchange, interest on the unpaid balance would be 6 per cent, I would continue in possession of the place, and there would be no attachments or interference of any kind in my affairs.

When I left Bones Kennedy's house I couldn't have felt sorry for myself if I'd tried to, and was anxious to put my place back in condition for handling stock as quickly as possible. I drove around to Simons's corral, tossed my saddle and what few clothes I had into the back of the Maxwell, tied Kitten to a door handle, and set out for home. As we passed the telephone office, Effie again called to me, and that time she demanded that I stop and come in. She'd not only found out that I'd lost the case but about the Topeka lawyer trapping Bones, George, and me with catch questions. She was furious, and after storming that the trial had been an outrage to justice from beginning to end, she told me, "I'm going to phone that justice of the peace right now and give him a piece of my mind."

"Don't do it," I told her; "the fault is mine, not his. I got careless after the big profit Bob and I made on the second lot of stock we fed, and maybe we did come pretty close to partnership on the last one. Anyway, it was close enough that Mr. Noble says there would be little chance of winning a reversal if the case were appealed."

After telling her about my meeting with the receiver and the agreement we'd reached, I said, "You know who has each of those milch cows, Effie. It would be a big help if you'd call up and tell them I'm sorry, but that I'll have to have the cows back tomorrow morning. And I'd appreciate it if you'd put out line calls saying that I'll put all thirty-nine cows, along with any calves they've had, up for auction in the afternoon. Tell the folks, will you, that because of the flood there won't be any barbecue at the auction."

"Hummff!" she snorted. "If I know the folks in this township as well as I think I do, you'd be crazy to have a barbecue, and I'll bet a cookie you get the biggest auction crowd there's been anywheres in western Kansas since you sold your horses. Now get on down there and go to cleanin' up your place. I've got work to do."

When I started for home again I was surprised to find that the Oberlin-McCook road across Beaver Valley was already being rebuilt. More than a dozen of my neighbors with plows and scrapers were raising the level of the old roadway, and a crew was pouring concrete foundations for a new and sturdier bridge. They'd heard of my losing the suit, and gathered around the Maxwell, but dropped the subject quickly when they found that I didn't want to talk about it. Instead they told me to let them know if they could lend me a hand in any way. I pointed at the bunkhouse perched atop the barn, grinned, and told them, "As puny as I'm feeling right now, I might have a little trouble getting that bunkhouse down alone. If you'd like to give me a hand with it at quitting time I'd sure appreciate it."

All the windows in the house were broken, the doors had swollen so tightly into the jambs that they couldn't be budged, the paper was soaked off the walls and ceilings, and the floors were six inches deep in a gruel of slimy mud. When I climbed to the barn roof it wasn't difficult to see why the bunkhouse had floated, even though all my furniture was in it. Four big cottonwood logs had been used as a foundation for the sills, the floor was tongue-and-grove fir planking two inches thick, and the cracks between the upright 1-by-10 wall boards were covered by wide batten strips. The two small windows were four feet above the floor, and the heavy plank door was hung to swing outward.

I doubt that Noah's Ark was much more seaworthy than that bunkhouse. No more than three inches of water had leaked into it before the planking and door swelled tight, so the furniture had been damaged very little. When the men came from work they brought four long, heavy timbers salvaged from the old bridge abutment. We made a slideway of them, and had no trouble in skidding the solid little building down.

Fortunately, I had a few hand tools in the bunkhouse when the flood struck. Aside from those, there wasn't a tool, a piece of equipment, a particle of burnable fuel, or a bit of food for either Kitten or me on the place. As soon as the men had gone I drove up to Joe's store for salmon, sauerkraut, eggs, a can of

coal oil, and a lantern. Then I went over to the Miners' for dry
corn cobs and a few forkfuls of hay, and to ask George if he'd
do the auctionering for me next afternoon.

It was the first chance I'd had to talk with George since the
judgment had been rendered, but he left no doubt that Bones
had told him every detail of the meeting in Mr. Frickey's
office, and of the agreement I'd made with the receiver. He
seemed particularly pleased that I'd decided not to file a petition in bankruptcy. As we loaded the Maxwell he told me, "Irregardless of what the doctors down east had to say, if I don't
miss my guess you've got a lot more years ahead of you, and
when you get along to my age the road you took today will be
a heap of comfort to you. I'm not blamin' them that's gone the
other route, you understand—them with families of little children and the likes. Sure I'll auction off the cows if you want
me to. That's about the least a man could do for a neighbor
that's run into the string of bad luck you've struck lately.
Come on in and have a bite of supper with us. Irene'll have it
on the table in next to no time."

I was anxious to start fixing a place to live in until the house
could be put into shape, so thanked George for his kindness
but told him I'd have to hurry along. To get into the bunkhouse I had to break a window; then I set to work scooping
out and mopping up the bilge water. Next I set up the cook
stove, put several pans of water on to heat, and cooked supper. After I'd eaten I scrubbed every inch of the 12-by-20-foot
room—floor, walls, and ceiling—arranged the furniture, and
set up a double bunk with clean bedding and corn-shuck mat-
tresses. By two o'clock in the morning I had myself a snug little home. I'd had to crawl in and out through the window a
dozen or more times for cobs, but kept a roaring fire going,
and though the heat made me sweat like a harvest hand it
dried the door enough that it would open before I went to
bed.

Early next morning I drove to Oberlin for needed tools that
Joe didn't carry in stock. When I got home three divide farm-

ers were waiting for me. They'd not only brought back the borrowed cows, but knowing that we on the valley floor had lost all our feed and fuel, each man had brought whatever he could spare—not as rental for the cows, but in neighborliness and appreciation of the loan. One man had brought fully half a ton of good prairie hay, another twenty bushels of nubbin corn, and the third a heaping wagonload of corn cobs for fuel.

All forenoon there was a steady stream of farmers bringing back milch cows, together with the calves they'd borne while on loan, and no man came without a wagonload of hay, corn, or cobs. There was no possible doubt that the whole thing had been planned, or that Effie had been the planner, though she'd never admit it. When the last wagon had been unloaded I had not only thirty-nine cows, but nineteen calves, a crib of feed corn higher than my head, a stack of hay as big as the barn, and a pile of cobs the size of the bunkhouse.

By noon both sides of the road, from the depot to the temporary bridge across the creek, were lined with wagons, carriages, and automobiles—some of them from as far as twenty miles up or down Beaver Valley. The dooryard was crowded, and a hundred or more men and their wives were looking over the cows and calves. I didn't have to be very bright to know that George and Effie had been in collusion, for at each cow's head stood the man to whom she'd been on loan, telling prospective buyers how good a milker she was. The sad part of it was that no one of those men would be able to buy the cow himself. The terms of my agreement with the bank receiver required that all sales be for cash, and only the more prosperous farmers had any.

George was no spellbinder as an auctioneer, but no other man could have done so fine a job for me. At one o'clock he climbed onto a wagon in the middle of the dooryard and told the crowd the story of the cows: that they were the best among all those taken by the Cedar Bluffs bank through foreclosure, and that they'd been on loan since January, most of

them to their former owners. After explaining that all sales
would have to be for cash, and why, he had a circle cleared
and a cow led in. Certainly not by accident, she was one of
the best in the lot, and her month-old heifer calf was at her
side. The bidding started at $55, moved quickly to $65, and
slowed down as it moved up a half-dollar at a time. At $69.50
it appeared to have reached the limit, and George had called
out, "Going, going . . ." when the last bidder shouted that
he'd make it $70 even.

With the livestock market demoralized, and so soon after a
disastrous flood, that was a tremendous price for an unregis-
tered cow and calf to bring. Since they'd done so well, George
put all the calves up for sale with their mothers, and though
no other pair brought $70, none brought less than $65. One or
two of the cows without calves went for as little as $40, and a
few brought $53 or $54. The bidding moved along so rapidly
that the last cow was gone by four o'clock, and I had checks
for more than two thousand dollars, well above twice what the
cows had originally cost me. That evening I drove to Oberlin
and turned the checks over to the bank receiver. I've seldom
seen a man more surprised, and he seemed as pleased as I was
at the amount. There was still a long way to go, but on the
first day after the trial I had more than 20 per cent of my debt
behind me.

Sunday morning I started work on the house by scooping up
the muck and slime on the floors and shoveling it out the nearest window. Then I set to work scrubbing ceilings, walls,
woodwork, and floors with water as hot as my hands would
endure, using brick after brick of Irene Miner's home-made lye
soap. For the next week my hands were kept so parboiled with
hot soapsuds that they looked like hanks of tripe, but by Saturday night the inside of the house was as clean as if it were
brand new.

I spent Sunday, the third in June, setting window glass and
repairing damage to the outside of the house. And as I worked
I did considerable thinking and planning. The hog market was

still in the doldrums, but I felt confident enough that the upward cycle would set in by early July that I decided to speculate on it to the limit of my trading fund. With long stretches of the railroad through Beaver Valley washed out, I'd have to ship from Oberlin, and it would still be on Saturdays.

Stock shipped on the first Saturday of the month would reach Kansas City on Fourth of July morning, there'd be no auctions, and I'd have to pay yardage and feeding bills to hold the stock over until Tuesday. To save the extra expense, I decided to put off any shipping until July 9, then remembered that the demand for bacon hogs had—for the first time in three months—been greater than the supply on the first market day after Christmas. The reason had been that most feeders and traders had held off from shipping on Christmas Day, so they'd probably avoid having stock arrive at the yards on Fourth of July. If so, it seemed to me that the demand on the fifth might again be greater than the supply, and that it could easily be the turning point that would start the hog cycle on an upward swing. Before the afternoon was over, I'd made up my mind to put 90 per cent of my trading funds into the best 225-pound bacon hogs I could find, and to ship them on July second.

Monday morning I set out on my first buying trip since the flood, but decided to call only upon the most prosperous farmers in Beaver Valley, so as to keep away from the red tape of trying to buy mortgaged stock. When I could pay a reasonable percentage in cash, it was always easier to dicker with a man whose stock was mortgaged than with one who had money in the bank; and I planned to drive close deals, so I knew it would be no easy buying job. The last quotation on bacon hogs to come over the air had been $7.85 at Kansas City, but I made up my mind not to pay over six dollars for top grade hogs delivered to the shipping pens in Oberlin. It took me five days from dawn till dusk, but by Friday evening I'd made deals for two hundred hogs of just the size and type I wanted, all to be delivered, weighed in, and paid for at Oberlin on July second.

16

Horse of a Different Color

ALTHOUGH the house was ready to move into, I was comfortable in the bunkhouse, so stayed there and spent the next week repairing fences, cleaning the platform scales, and getting the place back into working order. On Friday I went to Dr. DeMay for my first checkup since the flood, then had lunch at the hotel and tried to sell a few hogs to the McCook butchers. I was talking to Rudy Schneider when the depot agent came into the shop, fairly bubbling with excitement.

"Here's your chance to make a heap of money," he told Rudy. "The Q is putting its whole construction crew into Beaver Valley at the end of the month. They're going to rebuild the washed-out line and raise the grade of the tracks three feet above the highest flood level. The job'll take four months, and they're inviting bids on a contract for upwards of five hundred pounds of meat a day to feed the crew. You'll have to mail your bid to the chief of commissary operations at Omaha no later than the tenth of July, and there's only three items to bid on: beef steak, pork chops, and pork sausage."

"I wouldn't waste postage on it," Rudy told him. "Every butcher within fifty miles of that job will be asked to bid, and

on a contract of that size they'll all try to undercut the competition. I wouldn't take that contract at less than thirty cents a
pound, but I'd make a bet that leastways half the bids will be
no higher than twenty."

After the agent had gone I said, "I'll sell you overweight
sows and canner cows at a nickel a pound. Can't contracts for
construction-crew meat be filled with cow beef and sow
pork?"

"Sure they can," he told me, "and that's where the butchers
will make their big mistake. They'll think about a dressed-
meat cost of eight to ten cents a pound, and overlook that the
bid is mostly for steak and chops. That crew will get sausage
and eggs for breakfast, chops for dinner, and steak for supper,
so there'll be no more than fifty pounds of sausage to five hundred of chops and steak. If a man gets twenty pounds of chops
out of a three-hundred-pound sow he's doing good, and out of
an eight-hundred-pound canner cow he can't cut more than a
hundred and twenty pounds of steak that's not too tough to
chew. To fill that contract a man will have to butcher two
cows and a dozen hogs a day, and he'll have about a ton and a
half of fat sow pork and tough cow beef left over that he'll be
lucky to get rid of at a nickel a pound. Now do you see why a
butcher has to get high prices on a meat contract like that
one?"

I told him that I saw, but not what I saw, then got out of
there and drove to the Miner place as fast as I could make it
over the roads, still in bad shape from the spring rains. The
temperature was well above 100 degrees, and when I pulled
into the dooryard George was sitting on the vine-covered
porch. "Goin' to be a scorcher," he called out. "Come on in
and sit a spell. I just fetched some ice and lemons home from
Oberlin, and Irene's whackin' up a pitcher of cold lemonade."

"Can't think of anything that would go better on a day like
this," I called back as I climbed out of the old Maxwell and
started up the walk, "It sure won't be a very good weekend for
shipping if this hot spell holds."

"Still aimin' to ship out them two carloads of bacon hogs to-morrow?" he asked.

"I'll just about have to," I told him; "they were all bought for delivery at Oberlin on July second."

"Don't reckon you're makin' no mis——— Sit over here in the shade, son. Irene, she'll fetch another chair. Irregardless of the hot spell, I have a notion you're on the right track. I wouldn't doubt me that the day-after-the-Fourth hog market will be good enough to more'n make up the extra cost and shrinkage. But if I was in your boots I believe I'd go along with my hogs, and I'd put a water barrel in each deck of both cars, so I could heave a bucket or two over their backs whenever I got a chance. A wet hog won't shrink in hot weather half as much as a dry one."

"I was planning to go along with them," I said, "but I sure wouldn't have thought about putting water barrels in the cars. I'll do it, and I'm much obliged to you for the idea."

"I can't claim much credit for it," he told me. "It used to be in the old days that a man wouldn't think of shippin' hogs in the summertime without he went along to market with 'em and took a barrel or two of . . ."

He was interrupted by Irene's coming out of the house, carrying a napkin-covered tray with three or four tall glasses and a big pitcher of lemonade—chunks of ice and slices of lemon floating on top. George held a brimming glassful out to me, lifted his own, and said, "Here's lookin' at you," took a big swallow, and sang out, "Good gosh a'mighty! That stuff's sour enough to make a pig squeal! You didn't make it that way a-purpose, did you Irene?"

"Of course I made it that way a-purpose," she told him. "You know Ralph can't have sugar, but if you'll hold your horses a minute I'll fetch the bowl." As she went for it she sputtered, "My lands, I never seen a man with such a sweet tooth!"

With a wink at me George sputtered back, "Sweet tooth! By jingo, there ain't a tooth in my head—exceptin' only the bought ones—that ain't stingin' like a frost-bit ear."

Then, as he stirred two spoonfuls of sugar into his lemonade, he asked, "Well, son, what did Doc DeMay tell you this mornin'?"

"That sugar's down a bit from what it was a couple of weeks ago," I said, "but he still thinks I'm cheating on my diet. I haven't been, though it doesn't seem to make much difference. But I heard some really good news. On August first the CB&Q is sending its whole construction crew to rebuild the track through Beaver Valley and raise the grade high enough that floods won't wash it out again. They're asking bids for five hundred pounds of meat a day to feed the crew through November."

"Where'd you get hold of that?" he asked. "Over the radio?"

"No," I said. "I was trying to sell Rudy Schneider some hogs when the McCook depot agent came in and told us about it."

"Did Rudy let on what price he aims to bid?" George asked.

"He isn't going to bid," I told him. "He said he wouldn't waste postage to Omaha on it."

George's head came up with a jerk and he demanded, "What's the matter with that bullheaded Dutchman? Five hundred pounds of meat a day for four months is a lot of business to talk about wastin' two cents' worth of postage on."

"He said he'd bet that every other butcher within fifty miles would bid no more than twenty cents a pound, but that he wouldn't touch the contract for less than thirty cents."

"What's wrong with a twenty-cent price when butchers can buy old sows and canner cows for a nickel a pound? That kind of meat's good enough for fillin' a railroad-crew contract."

"The bids are to be for nothing but beefsteak, pork chops, and pork sausage," I told him. "Rudy says that whoever takes the contract will have to butcher a dozen hogs and two cows a day, and will have a ton and a half of leftovers that he'll be lucky to get rid of it any price."

"Well," George said slowly, "that does make it a horse of a

different color, don't it?"

"I think the butchers are figuring on the wrong grade of hogs and cattle," I told him. "I kept books on every animal Bob and I butchered last winter; that's how we found out which grades paid out best. Toward the last we used nothing but eight-hundred-pound hay-fat heifers and top-grade two-hundred-and-a-quarter-pound bacon hogs. The heifers cost only two dollars a hundredweight more than canner cows would have, and the hogs only two and a half more than lardy old sows. Out of the average heifer we got four hundred and forty pounds of beef; three hundred of them good juicy steak, most of it as tender as steer beef. The hogs dressed out to a hundred and forty-five pounds apiece, and out of the shoulders, hams, and loins we could cut seventy pounds of cutlets that were a whale of a lot better eating than sow pork chops. The rest of the carcass was about twenty-five pounds each of lard, sidemeat, and fatback—besides the by-products—but the fatback in those lightweight bacon hogs was lean enough that people were glad to take it as sidemeat.

"If a man used that grade of butchering stock for this contract and could get pork cutlets included, he'd have to kill only one beef and three hogs a day, and he'd have only seventy-five pounds of lard and three hundred of leftovers to get rid of. Don't you think that a butcher with a shop in a city as big as McCook or Oberlin could easily sell that much good-quality stew beef, hamburger, sidemeat, and sausage a day at no less than two pounds for a quarter?"

"I don't reckon he'd have too much trouble," George told me, "leastways not in the summertime when its too hot for farmers to do their own butcherin'. Why? What you drivin' at, son?"

"Most farmer folks like fresh sidemeat better'n smoked bacon," Irene cut in, "and they use a heap of lard in harvest and thrashing time. Besides that, if there's going to be men enough on that railroad job to eat five hundred pounds of meat, it'll take leastways a hundred pounds of lard a day for

making biscuits and pie crusts, and frying patatas and dough-
nuts and the likes of that."

"Well, now, I wouldn't have thought about that," George
told her, "but let's hold on a minute till we hear what kind of
a bee the boy's got buzzin' in his bonnet."

"This may sound crazy," I told them, "but I've been thinking I might try to get some butcher to send in a bid on supplying top-grade pork cutlets and heifer steak, and to give me a
quarter of the net profit—if he got the contract—for showing
him what kind of butchering stock would make the most
money, and for selling it to him at cost. All I could lose would
be a little feed and the time it took to buy and handle the
stock. If he could get close to twenty cents a pound, I'm sure a
lot of money could be made on the contract—that is, if his
overhead wasn't too high and there's no big rise in the price of
cattle and hogs between now and fall. What would you think
about it?"

"Ain't you about fed up on partnerships?" George asked.

"This wouldn't be a partnership," I told him. "The business
would be entirely the butcher's; I'd just be getting a quarter of
the net profit for the idea and finding him the right kind of
butchering livestock."

"How do you reckon a butcher with enough shop trade to
get rid of that much leftovers could keep the income and
outgo on the railroad contract separate from the rest of his
business?"

"He could keep books on it," I said, "the way I did when
Bob and I were butchering."

"Butchers ain't bookkeepers," he told me. "Most of 'em does
well to keep track of what they owe and what's owed to 'em,
and net profit is a tricky figure to get down to. I'd bet a hat
you couldn't figure out what the net profit was on that butcherin' you and Bob done."

"No, I couldn't," I told him, "but only because most of the
meat was traded for corn, chickens, butter, and eggs. I don't
know how much Bivans allowed on the butter and eggs that

were turned in on the grocery bill, and we gave the same amount of meat for every bushel of corn brought in, though the best of it was worth as much as a dime a bushel more than the poorest. But I can tell you what the net profit would have been if we'd sold the steak and cutlets for twenty cents a pound and the rest at two pounds for a quarter. The heifers cost us thirty-five dollars apiece, and the meat would have brought in eighty-seven dollars and a half. A bacon hog cost thirteen-fifty, and the meat would have sold for twenty-three and a half. We didn't have any overhead expenses, except about fifty cents for paper and twine, so the net profit would have been . . ."

"Gosh a'mighty!" George exploded. "That would be eighty-two dollars a day if a man was to butcher one heifer and three hogs, and his overhead hadn't ought to run more'n half that much. By jingo, if I was in your boots, son, I believe I'd mail in a bid on that contract my own self. No I wouldn't neither! I'd go right on down there to Omaha where I could talk to the head man in the buyin' department, and I'd take along some cutlet samples out of a nice lean young bacon hog to show him. They'd keep all right if you packed 'em in a tub of ice. And come to think about it, I have a notion you'd be better to ship your hogs to Omaha anyways. The hog market up there's been runnin' a nickel or more above Kansas City the last few days, and bein' further north the weather hadn't ought to be so hot, so you'd prob'ly have less shrinkage."

"I think you're right about shipping to Omaha," I told him, "but what would I do with the meat contract if I got it? I'm not only broke but up to my ears in debt, and all I know about meat cutting is what little I learned from Bob. To handle a job like that railroad contract a man would need to be a first-class butcher and have a well-equipped shop with a walk-in icebox, and in a city big enough that he could get rid of his left-overs."

"Oh, I don't know about that," George told me. "Around McCook and Oberlin I have a notion you could hire all the

meat cutters you'd have any use for, and at not over five dollars a day. As for you bein' broke, if you was to talk to
Charley Frickey like you just talked to Irene and me—tellin'
him the railroad was askin' for bids on a big meat contract
here in the valley, and what Rudy Schneider had to say about
leftovers, and about the kind of heifers and hogs you and Bob
butchered along towards the last of it, and you keepin' book
on 'em, and what you'd have made at twenty-cent and two-for-
a-quarter prices—it wouldn't surprise me none if he'd lend
you enough so's you could set up to handle the railroad business; that is, of course, if you was to get the contract at a price
anywheres near twenty cents a pound and it called for pork
cutlets instead of chops."

"Big as the contract will be, it's only a four-months' job," I
said. "Wouldn't it cost too much to build and equip a new
butcher shop for that short a time, and after the job is done
would either McCook or Oberlin support another . . ."

"Hold your horse a minute," George broke in. "Why in
tunket would you put a shop in McCook or Oberlin? The job's
goin' to be right here in Beaver Valley, ain't it?"

"Sure it is," I said, "but when it's finished there wouldn't be
enough butcher business in Cedar Bluffs to . . ."

"How much trouble did you and Bob have in gettin' rid of
meat last winter?" he asked.

"None," I said, "but we didn't try to sell it; we traded it for
whatever people could spare—corn and chickens and eggs and
butter."

"And I reckon you'd have taken pigs and calves and cows if
they'd been offered, wouldn't you?"

I nodded.

"Anything wrong about a trader tradin' what he wants to
get rid of for somethin' he can sell?"

I grinned and said, "It worked all right for Bob and me."

"Ever been inside an old-time icehouse?" he asked.

"No," I said, "but I've seen them in New England."

"When I was about your age I helped to build one over by

McCook," George told me; "that was back in the days when we had colder winters than what we have now. The ice would freeze two feet thick on a pond alongside the Republican River, and some winters they'd put up a couple hundred tons of it. Well, what I set out to tell you was that we started off with an old rough-board barn. First we dug the dirt floor down about three feet and filled the hole in with coarse gravel, so's to have good drainage. Then we lined the inside of the old barn with tongue-and-groove sheathing, clean up to the ridgepole, and stuffed the spaces between the studs and rafters tight with straw. Irregardless of how hot the summer was, that straw kept the heat from strikin' through and meltin' the ice."

I had no idea what George was driving at, so just said, "I've heard that straw was real good insulation."

"Best there is," he told me, "if you pack it in good and tight and keep it dry. Well now, this is what's been goin' through my head: That bunkhouse of yours was tight enough to float in the flood, so it's a darn sight better buildin' than the old barn was. If you'd sheath it on the inside and stuff straw between the studs and rafters, and put in an insulated door with gaskets, I have a notion it would make you a plenty good enough icebox. It's big enough that you could keep a ton or more of ice in a crib at one end and still have room to hang up a dozen or more sides of beef and pork. The way you've scrubbed that house, I don't see a reason in the world why you couldn't fix the kitchen up for a butcher shop. Then, bein' right on the railroad line they're goin' to rebuild, you'd have a big edge over any McCook or Oberlin butcher, because in hot weather you could deliver meat still cold out of the icebox.

By the time George stopped I was sitting on the edge of my chair, and asked, "How much do you think it would cost?"

"Oh, not too much, I wouldn't think," he said. "I reckon you'd have to put a sink and runnin' water in the house, but with the windmill right close by the way it is that wouldn't be much of a job. And you might want to run a drain pipe to the creek, so's to keep the dooryard from gettin' muddied up with water from meltin' ice and the sink drain. Of course you could use the barn for a slaughterhouse, but with that much killin' to do every day I have a notion it would get pretty ripe after a while. If I was in your boots I'd build me a slaughterin' shed right on the edge of the creek bank, with a block and tackle for heistin' up critters, and a tight plank floor. Then I'd run a water pipe out there from the windmill so I could hose it down after every killin'. And for makin' deliveries I wouldn't be surprised none if you could get ahold of a repossessed wheat-haulin' truck pretty cheap.

"About all you'd need in the shop, it seems to me, would be three or four butcher's blocks to cut meat on, and a good solid bench, and scales and plenty of hand tools—knives of different kinds and cleavers and bone saws and the likes—and a big kettle for renderin' lard. To grind as much hamburger and sausage as you'll have to, you'd prob'ly ought to have a power grinder. It would be cheaper to buy a gas engine than to hire a man to turn the crank. For a job like that railroad contract I can't see where you'd need much of anything else exceptin' a few buckets and tubs and meat hooks and one thing another. I don't believe the whole shebang would cost much over a thousand dollars. In the big cities there's been a lot of butcher shops close up since the war, and I have a notion you'd find everything you needed in the secondhand stores down to Omaha."

"Even at that, it would run up my overhead two hundred and fifty dollars a month," I said, "because it wouldn't be worth anything when the job is finished. Then too, if more than half the established butchers are likely to bid no higher than twenty cents, do you think I'd have any chance of getting the contract unless I undercut that figure quite a bit?"

We'd all forgotten our lemonade, and for perhaps half a minute George sat with his eyes closed, as he often did when he was thinking. Then he looked up at me and said, "I don't have a notion that too many of 'em will go much under twenty, but to have a chance against butchers a'ready in business I reckon you'd have to undercut their lowest bid by leastways a cent."

"I believe I could make a pretty fair profit on seventeen and a half cents if I kept a tight watch on expenses and there was no rise in livestock prices," I said, "but don't you think it would be kind of risky to bid that low with the hog cycle due for an upward turn at any time now? I'd expect cattle to follow hogs, and a rise of two dollars a hundredweight on bacon hogs and fat heifers would make it an awful tight squeeze."

"The way things are lookin' right now," George answered, "I doubt me that—leastways before spring—you'll see any rise in the cattle market that amounts to a Hannah Cook. If the hog cycle ain't been knocked galley-west along with everything else, a two-dollar rise wouldn't surprise me none, but you've got an ace in the hole against that. All you'd have to do is to put two or three hundred young shoats into that corn field of yours before the price goes up, and without costin' you another penny they'd grow to bacon size on the corn that got buried in the flood. If I was in your boots I'd put a few old sows in there too; they'll root far enough down to turn up the deepest-buried ears, and the shoats'll learn from 'em."

Irene broke in to tell me, "There's lots of corners you could cut if livestock prices was to go up on you. You can't hardly give beef suet away, but you could render it right along with your hog lard and it would make plenty good enough short'nin' for a railroad crew or anybody else. The Kansas City packers generally always put some suet in their bucket lard, and the price is the same as for straight leaf lard out of a barrel, but lots of folks buy it anyways; it makes just as good biscuits and pie crust, and the bucket comes in handy. Suet renders out kind of yellowish, but if you only use one pound to three of hog fat, and simmer raw patata peelings in it a few minutes to clarify it, there can't scarcely anybody notice it. Then again if you could sell enough lard you wouldn't need to use so many high-priced bacon hogs. Sow fatback makes good lard, and a little of it helps hamburger, specially if the beef is real lean and a bit dry."

"In a pinch, fatback and cow beef will make pretty good sausage too," I told her.

Irene only looked skeptical, but George told me, "I'm from Missouri on that one; you'd have to show me. But like I was sayin', if I was in your boots I'd go on over to Oberlin and have a talk with CharleyFrickey. Take along your book so's to show him how you and Bob come out on the bacon hogs and heifers you butchered, and if you have a mind to you can tell him what I figure it'll cost to fix the place up for handlin' the railroad job. He can't no more than turn you down, and if he does you'll be no worse off than what you are now."

I gulped down my lemonade, thanked George and Irene, and headed for Oberlin, stopping at home only long enough to pick up my butchering book.

Mr. Frickey seemed glad to see me and let me tell him the whole story. If he was surprised he didn't show it, but asked, "Would you plan to bid seventeen and a half cents a pound?"

"Yes, sir," I said, "or a shade less if it seemed necessary."

"Don't you think it would be a pretty big undertaking for a boy of your age with no more experience than you've had in the butchering business?" he asked.

"Yes, sir," I answered again, "but from what Rudy Schneider said I don't believe anybody else has figured it out well enough to make a profit on the contract, and George Miner thinks I could hire plenty of good meat cutters at five dollars a day."

Mr. Frickey locked his fingers together behind his neck and rocked his chair back and forth a few times with his face turned up toward the ceiling. Then he looked back at me and said, "Both of you are probably right, but it's still a big undertaking for a boy with your experience. Do you have an idea how much financing it would take to handle that contract?"

"Well," I said, "besides the thousand dollars for fixing up the place and getting a delivery truck, I'd probably need another thousand for butchering stock and meeting payrolls until the checks started coming in from the railroad."

"That's the rub," he told me. "Railroads are mighty slow pay and you could have several thousand dollars on the books before you collected a dime."

"Couldn't I give the bank an assignment of the amounts due me as security for loans?" I asked.

"Because of the judgment against you, that's the only way I could make you a loan of any amount," he said; "that and a mortgage on the equipment and butchering stock. I'll think it over, but in competition with established butchers I really don't believe you'd have much chance of getting that contract anyway. How long before you'd have to mail in your bid?"

"I'm not going to mail one in," I said. "This weekend I'm taking two carloads of hogs to Omaha. If I could get the financing I'd go to see the buyer for the railroad's commissary department on Tuesday and try to make a deal with him. That's why I need to know about the loan this afternoon."

Mr. Frickey rocked and looked at the ceiling another minute or two, then he let his chair come down with a thump and told me, "Go ahead and see what you can do. I doubt you'll get to first base, but it won't cost anything to try, and if you can get that contract at a profitable figure the bank will finance you up to five thousand dollars. That's the best I can do."

I thanked him, hurried to the depot, changed the routing on my cars to Omaha, and wired my agent there that I'd arrive on Fourth of July morning with two hundred prime bacon hogs.

17

Mother's Sausage

MY HOG CARS had been spotted at the shipping pens, so I thought it would be better to put water barrels into them before going home, rather than having to fuss with them next day. Besides, I was anxious to find out if John Bivans was going to bid on the railroad contract, so I drove up to his market for the barrels.

I didn't like to come right out and ask John if he was going to bid, so while he was helping me load the barrels into the Maxwell I said, "I'll sure be glad when I can ship out of Cedar Bluffs again, and it shouldn't be too long now. I hear the railroad's putting its whole construction crew into Beaver Valley next month to rebuild the line."

"That's right," he said, "and they're going to contract locally for steak and chops to feed the crew, but I don't aim to bid. My trade would buy the left-over hams and sidemeat if it wasn't too fat, and farmers will always take sausage if it's good and tasty, but I'd be stuck with tons of fatback and tough cow beef that I couldn't get rid of. I like to gamble as well as any other man, but this is one poker game I'll stay out of."

I'd realized from the start that I'd probably lose the friendship of the butchers who had been my livestock customers if I were to underbid them and get the railroad contract, but John Bivans was the only one I really cared about. It was a big relief to have him tell me he was going to stay out of the game. The Maxwell's gears always clattered before they'd mesh, and she backfired a couple of times when I warmed up the engine for a start. Over the racket I called out, "Thanks for the barrels, John. Mind if I sit in and draw a hand in your place?"

I don't think he understood that I meant to bid on the contract, but as I pulled away he shouted, "Sit right in and have fun, Bud, but don't try to fill any belly straights."

John's saying that farmers would always buy sausage if it was good and tasty set me to recalling my boyhood, and as I lugged water to fill the barrels I found myself going over every detail of the first sausage-making I could remember.

1907 was not only the gold-panic year, but Colorado had a crop failure. The officers at Fort Logan were the only people in our area who had any money to spend, and their wives would buy only the choicest cuts of meat, so our storekeeper couldn't take whole sides of beef or pork from farmers. Like our neighbors, we had to let our grocery bill pile up a little that spring and summer, but in the fall my father butchered our three hogs and turned the loins, hams, and bacon over to the storekeeper to settle our bill. At the same time, our nearest neighbor butchered a young cow and turned the rounds, loins, rib roasts, and shoulder clods in on his bill. His family was left with no meat for the winter except shortribs and stew beef, while we had only pork shoulders, fatback, and trimmings. So that both families might have a little variety, my father traded two pork shoulders for the beef neck. Then my mother did some experimenting.

The neck was tough and dry, and the fatback almost pure fat. Neither was very good eating, but Mother thought it might make fairly good sausage if moistened and highly seasoned. She sent me to Fort Logan for all the stale baker's bread the grocer had, a pound of bulk sage, half a pound of ground black pepper, an ounce of cayenne, and two ounces of ginger. That evening we set to work making sausage, using half fatback and the other half a mixture of beef neck and lean pork trimmings. Each time Father ground a dishpanful Mother soaked a five-cent loaf of bread in water and crumbled it, dripping wet, onto the meat, then added what seemed to me a tremendous amount of sage, salt, and black pepper, along with a generous pinch of cayenne and two of ginger. After she'd mixed the mass thoroughly she had Father put it through the grinder again, using the finest cutting disks we had. My older sister and I shaped the reground meat into patties, fried them, packed them in stone crocks, and covered them with hot fat from the frying, so they'd be sealed airtight and would keep all winter.

I thought that was the best-tasting sausage ever made, and I wasn't alone in thinking so. Before the week was out, every neighbor within miles had been to our house for Mother's recipe. More than a thousand pounds of sausage were made by it that fall, fried, and packed away in fat for the winter.

Since Colorado farmers had liked that kind of sausage, it seemed to me that Kansas farmers might like it too. If they did, and I got the railroad contract, it would not only give me an extra market for beef leftovers but would also make it possible to use a considerably cheaper grade of hogs. By the time the barrels were filled I'd decided to try making some of that sausage myself. Knowing I'd have a lot of experimenting to do, I bought sixty pounds of the same ingredients Mother had used, a meat grinder, scales, large pans, and a big block of ice.

George was doing his evening chores when I passed the Miner place, so I just stopped in the road a minute and called to him that Mr. Frickey would make me a loan if I got the contract, and that I'd be over in the morning to tell him about it. I got home at sunset, and it was nearly dawn before I'd made a batch of sausage that seemed to have the same flavor and texture that my mother's used to have. I'd kept careful records of what I'd put into each batch, right down to an eighth-ounce of salt, so there was no great trick to working out a recipe for making a hundred-pound batch like my best one.

I totaled the exact amount of each ingredient in all the rejects, put them together, and added just enough more of each to make up the amount needed for a fifty-pound batch according to my receipe. After regrinding, the sausage was a bit finer grained than my mother's used to be, but the flavor seemed very close to the same. I divided the batch into packages, according to the family size of each man who would be bringing me hogs that day, then buried them in a tub of chipped ice.

As soon as I'd finished with the sausage I diced three pounds of fatback and one of beef suet, rendered it slowly, and simmered potato peelings in it. Then I strained a quart jar of the hot fat through a clean cloth, and it cooled out nearly as white as leaf lard.

It was sunup by the time I'd set the shortening to cool; too early for Effie to have the switchboard open, but we could reach any other phone on our line by cranking the right combination of rings. I knew that George would already be at his morning chores, and that Irene would be starting to put breakfast on the stove in a few minutes. So would every other farmer's wife up and down Beaver Valley, and every one of them would run to pick up the receiver if anybody else on the line had a phone call, so one had to be careful what he said.

I shaped a dozen sausage patties from the last experimental batch I'd made, put them on to fry slowly, and cranked the Miner's ring combination. Irene was a bit stout and not as fast on her feet as some of the younger women, so I'd heard seven or eight receivers come off the hooks before she answered.

"Had breakfast yet?" I asked.

"Land sakes, no," she exclaimed; "it ain't a quarter to five yet. George won't be in from his chores for another twenty minutes, and I just now put the biscuits in the oven."

"You know, I'm shipping hogs today and won't be back till the middle of next week," I said, "so I didn't get in any groceries. Could I bum a bite of breakfast if I came over?"

"Outside of eggs, I don't know what in the world I've got that you could eat," she told me, "but come right on over. Breakfast will be on the table in twenty minutes, and least-ways there'll be some good hot coffee."

When I came back from the telephone the sausage patties were sizzling in their own fat, the bunkhouse was fragrant with the smell of sage, and the bottoms of the patties were a light golden-brown when I turned them over, just as Mother's used to be. I stowed my jar of shortening and a sample of the raw sausage in the Maxwell, then started the engine and went to feed old Kitten while it warmed up. With everything ready to go, I drained most of the fat from the frying pan, covered it with a clean dishtowel, and drove to the Miner place.

George was washing his face and hands at a basin on the back stoop when I turned into the dooryard, and Irene called to me from the kitchen doorway, "You're right on time; I just now put breakfast on the table."

I climbed out of the Maxwell, reached for the frying pan, and called back, "I'm sure much obliged to you, and I brought along what I could with me."

"There was no need of you doing that," she told me. "There's plenty of eggs and milk, and I warmed up some chicken fricassee left from last night's supper."

As I started up the walk George splashed a double handful of cold water over his face, then straightened up to dry it vigorously with a rough towel. When I passed him he sang out, "By jingo, that sausage smells good, son! Where'd you get it?"

"At Norton," I told him. "I went over there after I'd talked to Mr. Frickey."

Then I passed the frying pan to Irene and said, "I believe I'll use a little of that soap and water myself. Come to think of it, I haven't washed my face yet this morning."

George flung the water out of the basin, rinsed it with more from the bucket, and told me, "Help yourself, and then come on in to breakfast; I'm curious to hear what Charley Frickey had to say to you."

When I went in the table looked more as if it were set for dinner than breakfast. My sausage patties, seven or eight fried eggs, and as many thick strips of bacon were on a big platter at the center. A smaller one was mounded with hashed brown potatoes. Beside them sat a bowl with browned pieces of chicken peeping through creamy yellow gravy. There was a heaping plate of hot biscuits, a bowl of applesauce, a pound or more of butter, a pitcher of milk, another of cream, a jug of syrup, and a half-gallon pot of steaming coffee.

We were no sooner seated than Irene passed me the bowl of chicken, saying, "There was only half of the breast and one thigh left, but along with some eggs and milk maybe you can make out. My lands, I don't know what keeps you from starving to death! Always on the run like there was a fire someplace, and no good solid meat to eat or potatas and biscuits and the likes."

"Don't you worry about me," I told her. I've been on this diet for two and a half years, and I'm a lot stouter now than when I went on it."

While I spooned out the chicken George helped himself to a couple of fried eggs, a couple of sausage cakes, a mound of potatoes, a biscuit, and a wedge of butter. As Irene poured the coffee he cut off a bite-sized piece of sausage, balanced a quarter of a fried egg on top of it, and said, "It didn't surprise me none to hear that Charley Frickey would back you on that railroad contract, but I'm kind of curious to hear what he had to say about it."

I was telling about showing Mr. Frickey my book when George put the forkful into his mouth, but before I could finish the sentence he broke in, "By jingo, I never tasted sausage the likes of this before. Where'd you say you bought it?"

"At the new butcher shop that opened next to the department store over at Norton," I said. "Do you like it?"

"Tain't bad," he said. "Kind of hot tastin' and sagey, but it ain't bad at all. It must be that butcher's Eyetalian, or maybe

Mexican. Both of 'em like their grub spicy."

I didn't make any comment, but went on from where George had interrupted me, repeating almost word for word the conversation I'd had with Mr. Frickey. As I talked both George and Irene finished their first sausage pattie and started on another. George seemed intent on every word I said, but I couldn't help seeing that Irene could hardly wait for me to finish. The moment I did, she told us, "I'd bet a cookie there's chili powder in this sausage, and it seems like I taste a smidgen of ginger in it too."

"I wouldn't doubt me," George told her, then turned back to me and said, "By gosh, I didn't suppose railroads would be slow pay, not the way they make us farmers come through the rye for freight bills almost before a car's unloaded, but Charley wouldn't have told you that without he knew what he was talkin' about. That does make it a horse of a different color, don't it? A bill could pile up awful fast on five hundred pounds of meat a day, and you could find yourself squeezed by that limit of five thousand. The hog cycle bein' where it's at right now, and you havin' all that buried corn over there that's bound to sprout and go to ruin before long, you'd ought to have leastways a thousand dollars that you could put into young shoats right off the bat. Then, like you told Charley, besides what it costs to fix up the place and get a truck, you'd need another thousand for heifers and payrolls and one thing another. But if the railroad's liable to let your bill run up . . . What did Charley say when you told him you might shade that seventeen-and-a-half-cent price if you had to?"

"Nothing," I told him. "He just nodded his head as if he thought it would be all right."

"You're better at doin' sums in your head than what I am," he said. "If you could get the railroad to pay your bills at the end of every week do you reckon you could afford to shade that price as much as a cent?"

"I could if I got all the lard business for the job at a fair price," I said, "and if Kansas farmers would buy the kind of sausage you're eating."

"Of course they'd buy it," he told me just a bit irritably, "but what's that got to do with the railroad contract?"

"Plenty," I said. "That's cow-beef-and-fatback sausage; the kind I told you about yesterday. Irene's right about there being ginger in it, but it's cayenne pepper instead of chili powder that gives it most of the hot taste."

I told them about my mother's inventing that kind of sausage the year Colorado had the crop failure, and of our neighbors liking it so well that they made hundreds of pounds by her recipe. Then I recited the whole conversation I'd had with John Bivans, and said, "It seemed to me that if John's farm customers preferred tasty sausage to hamburger they might like the highly-seasoned kind that Colorado farmers used to like, so I went over to Norton for the makings and spent all night experimenting to find the right combination. If I could sell a fairly good amount of it I could use a cheaper grade of hogs as well as getting rid of my least salable beef leftovers, so I could easily cut the railroad bid a cent, or even more if I could get lard compound included in the contract."

"Lard compound! What's that?" he asked.

Before I could answer, Irene told him, "Land sakes alive, George, you'd ought to know that! It's bucket lard. Some of the buckets have 'Pure Leaf Lard' on 'em in big letters shaped like a rainbow, with a maple leaf inside the arch and 'Beef suet added' printed in little bitsy letters down underneath. Others of 'em have 'Lard Compound' on the bucket and don't mention the suet, but it's all the same thing."

"I've got some out in the Maxwell that I made this morning," I told her. "I'd like to bring it in and have you see if it's good enough to take down to Omaha for a sample." Actually, I was so proud of the shortening I'd made that I was more anxious to show it off than to get her opinion.

As I started to leave the table George told me, "There'll be time enough for that after breakfast. Lard's lard, but if it was me goin' down there I'd take along a bucket of this sausage to show the man."

He put another bite of it into his mouth, chewed thoughtfully a moment or two, and said, "No, by jingo, I wouldn't neither! Sausage is kind of like chuckwagon pudd'n; a man can't tell much about it by the looks; to find out if it's good or not he's got to taste it. I'd take my sample to the man the same way you fetched this over here, hot in the fry pan, so's't he could get a smell of the sage and a taste of the ginger. Like Charley Frickey told you, you'll have an uphill haul to get that contract away from the established butchers, and it's a heap easier to make a deal with a man when he's got a good taste in his mouth."

"Supposing I could get a good taste in his mouth, how low do you think I'd have to bid to make a deal?" I asked.

"Well," he said, "like John Bivans told you, biddin' on this contract is like sittin' in on a poker game. Nobody can tell you what kind of a hand you'll draw, or what to bet on it; every man has to depend on his own judgment in a poker game. So far, you don't know if the railroad would even take a bid from anybody that ain't a'ready got a butcher shop, or if the man that makes the contracts would allow any change from straight pork chops and regulation sausage. It's my guess that you'll find the first fence the highest one to jump, but if you get over it I wouldn't doubt me you could dicker with the man to change the contract any way that's reasonable—that is, if he could save money for the railroad by it. At a right price I don't reckon you'd have a bit of trouble gettin' lard compound included, and I don't believe he'd care a tinker whether it was pork chops or cutlets. There's always lots of Mexicans on railroad gangs, so they'd ought to like this sausage first rate."

"In that case, and if I could get my bills paid every week, I believe I could make a good profit on sixteen cents straight across the board," I told him.

"Wouldn't surprise me none," he said, "but if I was in your boots I'd go over my arithmetic mighty careful before I bid it. But when I was dead-sure of my figures I'd push all my chips out onto the table at one swipe; a good strong bluff's the only way to win a big pot with a weak hand, and yours ain't much better'n two pairs."

George pushed his chair back, got to his feet, and said, "Well, that's about all I know to tell you, son, and with two carloads of hogs to ship today I reckon you want to get an early start; Irene'll look at that lard sample outside."

While Irene looked at the compound, tasted it, asked how I'd got it so white, and questioned me about the proportions I'd used, George opened the sausage sample and examined it carefully. He didn't say anything until I'd cranked the Maxwell, warmed up the engine, and was ready to go. Then he leaned an elbow on the door beside me and said, "Don't know as I'd tell the man—or anybody else—just what all was in my sausage, but in the raw stuff he'll see the beef anyways, so I'd let on about it's bein' there right off the bat, and the reason for it. A man that's smart enough to be at the head of that department is smart enough to know you've got to cut the corners close to make a low bid, and he'll think more of you for comin' right out and sayin' so. Good luck to you, boy."

As soon as I got home I cut what was left of the pork shoulder into inch-thick slices and trimmed out a half dozen cutlets to look as much as possible like chops. After wrapping them in waxed paper I put them in a small tight-lidded bucket, then stowed them in the ice tub with the farmers' packages, a quart jar of raw sausage, and the lard compound sample. I took me until mid-afternoon to clean up after my experimenting, scrub the bunkhouse, shave, and take a bath, so most of the farmers were waiting with their hogs when I got to Oberlin. As each wagon load was weighed in and I paid the man I gave him a package of sausage, simply saying it was the kind my mother used to make when I was a boy.

In making the deals for those hogs I'd taken only what I judged to be 225-pounders, so that two hundred of them would cost about $2700 and leave 10 per cent of my trading fund in the bank. But my judgment had been awfully poor or those hogs had grown like toadstools since I'd seen them; they scaled in at over 49,000 pounds and cost nearly $2950. That, together with the amount I'd spent on the sausage experiment, left my bank balance just a few cents above twenty-one dollars. I couldn't set out to get the railroad contract in blue jeans with absolutely empty pockets, so just before the train pulled out I cashed a check for twenty dollars, filled my tub with fresh ice, and set it in the caboose.

18

Making My Bid

THE STOCK TRAIN on the main line was even shorter than the one on Christmas, and I was the only shipper to travel with his stock, so had the stockmen's caboose to myself. Sunday was hot but the short train made fast time and the stops were long. I refilled my barrels and wet my hogs seven or eight times, and doubt that any one of them drew a panting breath.

I'd brought my butchering book along, and spent most of Saturday night rechecking yield figures. They showed that if I could hold my overhead to 25 per cent and livestock prices remained unchanged, there would be good profit in the contract at an across-the-board price of fifteen cents a pound. Sunday morning I began going over arguments I'd use to convince the commissary chief to award me the contract, and his probable arguments against it. It became almost a game, and I spent every minute I wasn't lugging water and wetting hogs in carrying on both sides of imaginary arguments and dickering with the head of the CB&Q's commissary department.

When the train pulled into the Omaha stockyards on Fourth of July morning my agent, Matt Quinlan, was there to meet it.

He'd arranged for my hogs to be held over the holiday in shaded pens where there'd be a little breeze from the Missouri, and had a man on duty to feed and keep an eye on them.

After we'd unloaded and penned the hogs Matt walked back to the caboose with me, and as we talked I fished my two glass jars and bucket of samples out of the icy water in the tub. He was naturally curious, so I told him the whole story, saying that I'd shipped my hogs to Omaha in hope of getting an interview with the head of the CB&Q's commissary department. I couldn't have picked a better man to tell it to, for Matt knew all about the Q's method of handling meat contracts for their construction crews. He told me that the chief of commissary operations had his office in Chicago, that the man to see in Omaha was Emmet Donovan, a neighbor of his, and that he'd get me an appointment for Tuesday morning. Matt wanted to take me to the doubleheader ball game that afternoon, but I had to get myself some respectable clothes before the appointment, and I wanted to look around the secondhand equipment stores, so I told him I'd take a rain check until my next trip.

When I shipped to Omaha I'd always eaten in a little hole-in-the-wall restaurant near the depot, and the owner, Spiro Gusko, had become my friend. As soon as my hogs had been fed I took my samples to the restaurant and asked Spiro if he'd keep them in his icebox for me until next morning. He sat with me while I ate breakfast, so of course I had to tell him what the samples were for. When I mentioned setting up a butcher shop he became wildly excited, insisting that I must hire his brother Nick. According to Spiro, there was nothing in the world that Nick couldn't do, except to speak good English. Although he was careful not to say so, it was evident that Nick had come to this country to escape service in the Greek army. He'd served out his apprenticeship to one of the largest building contractors in the old country, but because he couldn't speak English the only work he'd been able to get since coming to Omaha was in packing plants, and he'd been laid off when the livestock market collapsed. To calm Spiro I said we'd talk more about it if I got the meat contract.

After taking a room at the stockmen's hotel, I set out to see what could be done with twenty dollars to make me presentable for calling on Mr. Donovan. Most of the pawn shops in the stockyards district were open and I found some real good bargains. For fifteen dollars I got a pair of dress shoes nearly new, a pair of gray wool pants that showed very little wear, a brown jacket that fitted pretty well in the shoulders, a white shirt, a bow tie, a pair of socks, a white handkerchief, and a stiff-brimmed straw hat. I found a tailor who lengthened the pants legs and jacket sleeves for a dollar, and on the way back to the hotel I got a two-bit haircut. When I'd taken a bath and changed clothes I didn't look too bad in my city-slicker outfit.

I'd worn jeans, jumper, and brogans so long that I didn't feel comfortable in city clothes, so wore my new outfit only to go uptown and watch the Fourth of July parade for half an hour. After I'd changed back I set out to hunt secondhand fixture stores where I could buy what I'd need for setting up a shop in case I got the meat contract. The secondhand stores were closed, but in nearly every window there was a heavy-duty meat grinder powered by an electric motor. A man could make as much sausage in an hour with one of those machines as he could make in a week with a hand grinder, but they'd be of no use to me because we had no electricity at Cedar Bluffs. My grinder would have to be powered by a gasoline engine requiring a tricky setup. To protect the meat from dust and flies, the grinder must be inside the house, and to protect the user from carbon monoxide fumes the engine would have to be outside.

It seemed to me that the best way to make the setup would be to run a drive shaft through the wall of the house, but it would have to be perfectly balanced and aligned to eliminate vibration. I couldn't do the job myself, and didn't dare trust it to any blacksmith in Oberlin or McCook. What I needed was an expert machinist who had a well-equipped shop, but whose business was small enough that he'd take such a job at a reasonable price and do it in a reasonable time.

I stumbled onto the right man for the job when taking a shortcut back to the hotel. His shop was in an alley, and except for a space at the front it was crowded with second-hand machines of all sorts. Just inside the window there was a metal lathe and workbench, and a man who looked to be in his late sixties was fitting a bearing to the drive wheel of a band saw. I stood watching him for maybe five minutes, but he was so absorbed in his careful scraping and fitting that he didn't notice me. During the war I'd worked as a carpenter, and was mechanic enough to know an expert when I saw one, so went in to ask if he'd make me the grinding equipment I had in mind, and what he'd charge for it. He didn't pay any attention to me or look up from the bearing until it fitted perfectly, and in the fifteen minutes or so I stood waiting I had a chance to do some thinking.

If the temperature dropped to near zero when Bob and I were butchering, meat froze so stiff that it couldn't be cut with a knife, but it sawed like soft wood. It occurred to me that if carcasses were thoroughly chilled a band saw would cut through meat and bones as easily as through knotty lumber. If so, it would speed up cutting steaks and chops as much as a power grinder would speed up sausage making. The only difficulty I could think of was that it would be almost impossible to push a heavy piece of meat past the blade steadily enough to cut steaks of uniform thickness. That, I believed, could be overcome by a sledlike carrier with runners sliding back and forth in oiled grooves. But the piece would have to be moved forward each time and lined up perfectly straight for the next cut. I was trying to figure out some way of moving and lining it up automatically when the old machinist demanded gruffly, "Vell, vot after you kommt?"

I told him that I might be going into the meat business in a place where there was no electricity, so would have to power my grinder with a gasoline engine outside the house. I'd just started explaining my idea for making the hookup by means of a drive shaft through the wall when the old German cut in, "Nein! Nein! Ver ist de vindow? Ver ist de vindow?" As he spoke he stepped to the workbench, took a pad of yellow paper and a pencil from one of the drawers, and pushed them toward me.

I marked out a rectangle to represent the east wall of the kitchen, and drew diagonal lines from each corner to indicate side walls, floor, and ceiling. More to let him see my skill as a draftsman than for any other reason, I sketched in a big ice-box door at the center of the north wall, the back door near the left side of the east wall, and a window well to the right.

In less than two minutes that gruff old man made my sketching look like a first grader's work. With a few deft strokes of the pencil he drew the corner of the room, sketching the window with broken lines to indicate a transparent outer wall. Butted tightly into the corner he drew a thick-topped workbench, with the front portion extending about three feet out through the window. Atop this outside shelf he drew what was unmistakably the engine hood of a model T Ford, with the crank handle hanging down at the front. Projecting below the shelf he sketched the transmission housing, with the drive shaft extending under the bench to a gear box six feet inside the room.

As if suspended above the bench top, he drew a meat grinder head, also with a gear box, from which a square shank extended downward. In English so strongly spiced with German that I could hardly understand it, he explained that this would permit the grinder to be removed when not in use, or set to discharge onto the bench or into a container on the floor. The controls for the rebuilt Ford engine, he told me, would be just inside the window, so the speed could be regulated easily, the drive shaft disengaged, or its direction reversed.

If the man had been less ingenious I might have gone no

further with the idea of slicing meat with a band saw. But I was almost certain that he could work out a means of moving a large piece of meat past the blade in such a way that uniform slices could be cut semi-automatically. He agreed that a band saw would cut chilled meat and bone without difficulty if a fine-toothed blade were used, and he liked the idea of a carriage mounted on runners, but could think of no way to move the meat up to the blade so as to make uniform slices. Neither could he give me a price on the grinder setup, but said he would have it for me the next afternoon, and that he'd think more about the band saw problem in the meantime.

I didn't go to Spiro's for supper, but stopped by the stockyards to be sure my hogs had been fed, listened to a band concert in the park for an hour or so, and went to bed early. From long habit I woke at dawn, and was in the stockyards by four-thirty, but Matt Quinlan didn't show up until six. He said he'd made me an eight o'clock appointment with Mr. Donovan, but that he already had a nineteen-cent bid, including pork chops.

While waiting for Matt I'd watched every carload of stock that arrived, but there were very few hogs; most of them heavyweights of only fair quality. Certain there would be a shortage of top-grade bacon hogs, I told Matt to hold mine back until the supply was exhausted, then I set out for the hotel at a run. I shaved, took a bath, rigged myself out of my city clothes, and was at Spiro's restaurant by seven-thirty. The place was crowded and Spiro was watching for me. I was barely inside when he rushed from the kitchen, yammering at me about hiring his brother Nick. To keep him quiet I said, "Okay, Spiro. You let me fry some sausage in your kitchen and I'll hire Nick if I get the contract."

At ten minutes of eight I set off for my appointment, carrying a jar of raw sausage and a package of pork cutlets under one arm, a jar of shortening under the other, and a napkin-covered plate of hot sausage patties in my hands. The CB&Q building was little more than a block from the restaurant, and

I had no trouble in finding the right office; the door was marked COMMISSARY DEPARTMENT, and under it in smaller letters, Emmet F. Donovan. It was a rather large office with a dozen or more clerks, a wide aisle between two rows of desks, and a closed door at the far end of it. When I told the nearest clerk my name and that I had an eight o'clock appointment with Mr. Donovan he pointed a thumb over his shoulder and told me, "The door back there. Knock before you go in."

When I knocked a hearty voice called, "Come in."

I'd tucked the stiff brim of my hat under the plate, to hold both with one hand, but when I turned the doorknob with the other the jar of shortening nearly slipped out from under my arm. I made a frantic grab to catch it, lurched against the door and swung it wide open. A big ruddy-faced man was sitting behind a desk at the center of the room, and there was a trace of brogue in the words when he sang out, "Have a care, lad! Looks like you've got both hands full and your britches to hold up."

I knew instantly that I'd found a friend and a man with good solid common sense, so decided to lay my cards face-up on the table right away. "I sure have," I told him as I slid the plate, package, and jars onto his desk, "but no other man ever had his hands so full and his pockets so empty. That's why I've come to see you instead of mailing in a bid. I'm dead broke and in debt up to my ears, with neither a slaughterhouse nor butcher's shop, but I want the meat contract for the Beaver Valley job, and if you'll give me ten minutes of your time I'll bet you a hat you'll give me the contract."

"I could use a hat," he said. "Have a chair."

I took the napkin off the plate, pushed it toward him, and said, "First I'd like you to taste a bite of this sausage if you will. It's the kind my mother used to make when I was a kid on the ranch, and our neighbors liked it better than any other kind. I didn't bring it here to try and fool you. There's some cow beef in it."

He reached for the fork without much enthusiasm, and told me, "a bit of pork helps canner-cow hamburger, but I'm thinking that cow beef would ruin pork sausage."

As he said it, he cut off a scrap from a patty, put it into his mouth, and looked up at me with a surprised expression. "Not bad! Not bad at all, at all," he said. "What's in it besides beef and pork?" Then he reached for a larger bite.

Instead of answering, I told him I was the cattle trader at Cedar Bluffs, that one of the McCook butchers had told me he wasn't going to bid on the contract, and why. "Matt Quinlan tells me you already have a bid of nineteen cents," I said. "If the man who made it has a butcher shop near enough that washout to handle the fresh meat business, the chances are ten to one that he buys livestock from me. At that price I'll make you a bet that he aims to supply you meat from the cheapest old canner cows and worn-out brood sows I can find for him—meat so tough and strong you'd be ashamed to give it to your dog."

Then I explained why I thought the job could be done far more economically by using good-grade stock. "To get the contract, I'll shade the nineteen-cent price considerably," I said, "and guarantee to supply tender meat from young hogs and grass-fat heifers, but the contract will have to call for pork cutlets instead of chops, and for sausage per sample submitted. I'm gambling that the men will like this kind of sausage well enough to eat it at other meals than breakfast. If a quarter of the meat for the job was sausage, and I supplied lard compound like this sample, I could use most of my fatback and beef trimmings, and wouldn't have much left over to get rid of at give-away prices."

Mr. Donovan had sampled a third bite of sausage, reached for another as I was finishing, and told me, "This stuff is kind of like peanuts. It's easy to keep nibbling on, and I don't doubt the men would eat a spate of it. But, lad, I can't give you that contract, much as I'd like to. It's not that the wording couldn't be changed easy enough, and the good Lord knows I'd like to

see the men get first-class meat instead of the junk the other
bidders will deliver. But there's too many strikes against you.
It's a fine kettle of fish I'd be in with the home office if
ptomaine poisoning was to break out on a job where I'd let the
meat contract to a lad with no experience, slaughterhouse,
shop, or sanitary facilities of any kind. And what could you do
with the contract if you got it? By your own word you're dead
broke, and to handle a deal as big as that Beaver Valley contract a man will need at least five thousand in ready cash
along with a well equipped shop.

"Don't forget that railroads pay only once a month, and on
the tenth of the following month at that. If the job takes five
hundred pounds of meat a day—and I figure it will—a man
could easy enough have four thousand dollars due him before
he was paid a cent, and he'd need at least another thousand to
keep plenty of butchering stock on hand. Sorry, lad, but even
if you underbid the lowest established butcher by two or three
cents a pound I couldn't give you the contract."

I grinned and said, "Now that you've told me why you can't
risk giving me the contract, can I have five minutes to show
you why you can't afford not to?"

He grinned back and said, "Six, if you want, but it'll be a
waste of time. I can't let my heart get in the way of my head
on railroad business."

"That's why I think I'll get the contract," I told him. "My
credit's fairly good out Beaver Valley way, so I can raise
whatever cash is needed to handle the deal. But before making any bid I'd like to remind you of something you may have
overlooked. Being a livestock dealer, I know every butcher
within forty miles of that washout, and exactly what he has in
the way of slaughterhouse, shop, refrigeration, and delivery
equipment. Barring John Bivans at Oberlin, who isn't going to
bid, the nearest established butcher will be twenty miles or
more from the job. August and September are hot months out
our way, the roads are in bad condition since the flood, and no
butcher has a covered truck. Has the Q ever collected dam-

ages from a meat contractor due to a case of ptomaine poisoning?"

Mr. Donovan had reached for another bite of sausage, but stopped with it in mid-air and exclaimed, "Louks! Don't even mention ptomaine. Feed a batch of bad meat to a big crew and you'd like as not get fifty cases, and before it was done with—doctors' bills, lost time, and all—it could run up as high as a thousand dollars."

I grinned again and said, "That's all I want to know. Now I'll make my proposition. The place I lease adjoins the railroad's right-of-way at Cedar Bluffs, about as near the center of that construction job as a man could get. There's a good set of buildings on the place, including a vacant five-room house that has just been renovated. If I'm awarded the contract today, these are the preparations I'll make by August first:

"I'll screen the house, put in running water, whatever equipment is needed to handle the business, hire a professional packing-house butcher, and install an icebox as big and cold as any in western Kansas. In addition, I'll deposit a thousand dollars to be forfeited for failure to have adequate and sanitary facilities ready for operation by August first, failure to complete the contract, and for supplying as little as one pound of meat that is contaminated at the time of delivery. To avoid any possibility of ptomaine, I'll provide a covered vehicle, and make two deliveries daily when requested.

"The price a man can reasonably bid on this contract, and the quality of meat he can afford to deliver depend entirely on the amount of business he can be sure of every day and how near he can come to using entire carcasses of both pork and beef. If the contract is written to call for beefsteak, pork cutlets, and sausage as per sample, I'll bid seventeen and a half cents a pound, straight across the board. But if lard compound is included and I'm guaranteed four months' business at a minimum of eighty-five dollars a day, with payment in full at the end of every week, I'll cut my across-the-board price to fifteen cents a pound."

Mr. Donovan put a bite of sausage in his mouth, and asked around it, "Want to give me a bank reference?"

"Yes, sir," I told him. "I'll pay the toll charges if you'll phone C. L. Frickey, president of the Farmers National Bank at Oberlin. I'd appreciate it if you'd tell him which deal you're going to take. It will make considerable difference in the amount I'll have to borrow, and he'll want to know."

"Who said I'd be taking either of 'em?" he asked, then chuckled and told me, "Don't rush me, lad. I've never run into a deal the likes of this before, and I'll have to take the whole thing up with headquarters. If they'll go for the deal there'll have to be a special contract written up by the legal department. But there's no sense going into all that till I've talked to your banker. Write his name down on this pad for me, then get out of here and let me see what I can do for you."

After I'd written the name he reached across the desk, shook hands, and told me, "I'll do the best I can. Come back at noonday, and I'll have the answer for you."

"I'll be here," I told him, "and I'm grateful to you." Then I picked up the sample plate and got out of there.

19

Both Pockets Full of Fish

I STOPPED at the restaurant only long enough to leave the plate and tell Spiro I wouldn't know about the contract till afternoon. It was barely nine-thirty when I reached the stockyards, but my hogs had already been sold, and Matt called out, "We sure guessed right in holding 'em back to the last auction. They were the only prime bacon hogs to come in, and every buyer in town was red hot for 'em. Both cars brought eight eighty-five. How'd you make out with Emmet?"

I'd hoped to get as much as $7.85 a hundredweight for my hogs, but $8.85 was almost unbelievable. For a moment I was so amazed that I didn't comprehend what he meant by asking how I'd made out with Emmet. Then I remembered seeing the name, Emmet F. Donovan, on the office door. "I won't know till noon," I said, "but I have a hunch that I'm going to get that contract if there's any way he can push it through."

"You couldn't have a better man pushing for you," he said. "Come on inside and let's settle up on those hogs."

The figuring didn't take long, and left no doubt about the value of keeping hogs wet during shipment in hot weather. My shrinkage had been very slight, and the net proceeds were

191

nearly four thousand dollars—five hundred more than I'd even hoped for. I stood bemused by my good fortune until Matt asked, "Want a check now, or shall I mail it to the Farmers National at Oberlin?"

With the tide of luck running my way as strongly as it had for the past few days, I felt so confident of getting the meat contract that I told him, "Mail a check for two thousand to the bank for my account, and give me one made out to the CB&Q for a thousand, and I'd like the balance in cash."

Ordinarily, if I'd had no hard work to do and was obliged to wait two or three hours for a decision as important to me as that meat contract, my nerves would have been tighter than fiddle strings, but that forenoon I was completely relaxed. Until eleven-thirty I loafed around the stockyards, visiting with other stockmen, then timed myself to reach Mr. Donovan's office a few minutes before twelve o'clock.

The moment I opened his door I knew the contract was mine. There was a twinkle in the big Irishman's eyes and a broad contagious smile on his face. "Well, lad," he told me, "it's here, but I had to burn up half the wires to Chicago, and it was like pullin' crocodile teeth to get it. They hollered like knaves at the daily minimum and paying every week, but I left them no doubt it was the only way I could come close to a fifteen-cent price, and they finally gave in. By the way, that banker out at Oberlin is a pretty good friend of yours. He even phoned one of the big bosses at Chicago, trying to save you posting the deposit, but the legal department wouldn't stand for it."

I'd thought I might have a lawyer examine the contract, but there was no need of it. The wording was clear and the terms exactly those I proposed. Within half an hour I'd turned the thousand-dollar guarantee check over to Mr. Donovan, and we'd signed two copies of the contract. As I left, Mr. Donovan told me he'd be out to inspect my facilities at the end of July.

The first thing I did was to send George Miner an unsigned telegram saying, "Have corralled the horse of a different color." Then I mailed the contract to Mr. Frickey, so there'd be no chance of losing it, and went to the German machinist's shop.

He'd worked all night on the meat carriage problem, solved it, and made a wooden model that worked perfectly. The platform of the carriage, mounted to slide past the saw blade on parallel rails, was made up of eight rollers studded with rows of sharp brads for holding a large piece of meat firmly in place. A lever-and-ratchet device turned the rollers in unison, moving the meat forward for a uniform cut of any desired thickness. Although I lacked the ingenuity to invent the contraption I knew instantly that it would do exactly what I wanted.

The old machinist had also made new drawings that showed the workbench lengthened to ten feet, with the band saw and sliding carriage at the end farthest from the window. The saw, powered by an extension of the drive shaft, was positioned so that the cutting blade passed through the bench top eighteen inches from the end and midway between front and back. This would permit a cut half the width of the bench and allow space for piling up the slices. The carriage was to be made entirely of metal, and the bench top of three-inch maple. With no haggling we agreed on a price of $385, to include a reconditioned Ford motor and an extra saw blade. In exchange for my paying in advance, he promised to have the setup completed and shipped within fifteen days.

A couple of small packing plants as well as several meat markets had gone out of business in Omaha since the war, and most of the equipment from them was still in secondhand fixture stores. My German friend not only knew where every piece of it was, but what the various dealers had paid, and which ones were the most anxious to sell. He wouldn't go with me or let me use his name, but told me where to go for everything I needed, and what I should pay for it.

By closing time I'd bought enough fixtures, equipment, utensils, hand tools, and plumbing supplies to set up a well equipped butcher's shop and slaughterhouse, and had spent less than three hundred dollars. Among other things I'd been so fortunate as to get all the fittings from a huge icebox—including two four-by-seven-foot insulated doors with their casings, and forty feet of overhead rail with rolling hooks for handling heavy carcasses—a chain hoist with which one man could easily lift a ton, and a fifty-gallon copper rendering vat.

It was late when I got back to Spiro's for supper, and he came running from the kitchen, demanding to know if I'd got the meat contract. When I told him I had he shouted a few words in Greek over his shoulder, then yammered excitedly at me in English, reminding me that I'd promised to hire his brother Nick. In the midst of it Nick, obviously dressed in his Sunday best, came out of the kitchen. He was no more than five-feet-six tall, but outweighed me by at least eighty pounds—brunet as I was blond, red cheeked as compared to my leathery tan, and almost stolid in his movements, while I was inclined to move quickly. Besides, he was as calm and bashful as Spiro was excitable and bold. He had no sooner appeared than Spiro began telling me that he was the finest butcher in Omaha.

My first inkling that Nick understood English came when Spiro assured me that before being laid off his brother had cut all the meat for the best hotel trade in town. The boy's face became fire red, and he blurted in heavily accented English, "No! Skinner. Killing floor."

Up to that moment I'd been hunting some excuse that would let me out of my thoughtless promise, but after Nick spoke I didn't want any excuse. I not only liked his straightforwardness, but knew I'd be able to trust him under any circumstances, and it suddenly occurred to me that I might be lucky he wasn't an expert butcher. Slaughtering had always been revolting to me, but it would be no problem to a man used to working on the killing floor of a packing house. Furthermore, skinning would be a big part of my butchering operation, for there was no reason to scald and scrape hogs when none of the pork would be cured. Then too, with the band saw I'd have no need for an expert meat cutter.

I asked Nick only if he was willing to work as many hours a day as I did, and at any job that needed to be done. He simply nodded, so I shook his hand and told him, "It's a deal. Five dollars a day, starting tomorrow morning. You meet me here at seven o'clock."

Self-conscious because of his poor English, Nick spoke only when necessary. Together with his stolidness, it made him appear a bit stupid, but he was far from it. I soon discovered that he was an excellent and ingenious mechanic, skillful with any hand tool, and although deliberate in his movements he made every one of them count.

As soon as I met him our first morning we set off for the pawnshops, and within a couple of hours had bought full sets of carpenters', plumbers', and masons' tools, together with an old whaleback trunk for shipping them.

We hired a team and wagon from a livery stable, and while Nick collected and packed the tools, Spiro took me to his wholesale grocer and baker. My reason for dealing with an Omaha grocery firm and bakery was not only to get wholesale prices, but to keep local butchers from finding out the ingredients in my sausage. I arranged with the baker to ship me, beginning on July twenty-fifth, a hundred pounds of bone-dry stale white bread each week, instructing him that it was to be packed in flour barrels and expressed to Nickolas Gusko at McCook. From the grocery firm I bought a barrel of rough-rubbed sage, a hundred pounds of ground black pepper, twenty-five of powdered ginger, and fifteen of cayenne, also having the shipment made in Nick's name.

To collect all the materials I'd bought, crate, and deliver them to the express dock, kept Nick and me going at a trot right up till train time that evening. During the whole day I doubt that he'd said more than a dozen words except, "Okay, boss," and I hadn't tried to force him. But it's embarrassing to sit in silence beside a man for any great length of time, and

we'd be sitting together about fifteen hours before reaching
Oberlin. I'd had plenty of proof all through the day that he
could understand almost anything said to him in English if I
spoke slowly and was careful to use simple words. Besides, I'd
noticed that people who were inclined to be self-conscious became more so if questioned, but usually forgot all about it if
intently interested in a project or story.

I waited until our train was well out of Omaha, then told
Nick about the flood, that I thought there should be a good
profit in the meat contract if we could avoid wastage, how I
intended to handle it, and of my plans for rebuilding the
kitchen and bunkhouse into a little butchering plant.

Haltingly, and often pausing to hunt through his memory
for English words, he told me of his apprenticeship in Greece,
of Spiro's insistence that he come to America, and of his being
unable to find work except as a skinner in the packing plants.
To relieve him from the strain of talking, I told a story or two
of my boyhood on Colorado cattle ranches, and he told a bit
about his boyhood in Larissa, his home in Greece. By the time
the conductor came through to turn down the lights for the
night, Nick and I were good friends, and he was never again
self-conscious unless there were strangers with us. We never
talked much, but there isn't much need for talking when two
men understand and like each other.

I didn't sleep well on the train, but did considerable thinking about the hog market cycle and the buried corn on my
place. Stocker pigs and heavyweight sows were still a drug on
the market, but the price my bacon hogs had 'brought made
me almost certain that George was right. It was, of course, too
early to be at all sure, but I believed the upward cycle had already begun. When we reached Oberlin I set Nick to loading
our baggage into the Maxwell while I went to see Mr.
Frickey. He rose and held out his hand to shake, saying, "Congratulations, boy! I didn't think you had a chance of getting
that contract. With the railroad paying weekly, how much
financing will you need?"

"I could squeeze by on three thousand dollars," I said, "but it would take another two to buy as big an inventory of butchering stock as I'd like to carry."

"We're somewhat reluctant to make livestock loans at this time unless it's absolutely necessary," he told me.

"I couldn't say that what I have in mind is absolutely necessary," I said, "but I think it would be awfully good insurance for the success of the business, and so does George Miner."

"Sit down," he said, "and tell me about it."

I told him of the astonishingly high price my hogs had brought, and that I thought it was due not only to the holiday but to the beginning of an upward cycle in the hog market. Then I explained George Miner's theory of a nine-month cycle and said that the downward trend appeared to have ended when hog prices fell to their five-year low on June fifteenth.

"You say this is George Miner's theory?" he asked.

"Yes, sir," I told him, "and I believe he's right. I've checked the hog market back for several years, and it has moved up and down in alternate periods of roughly nine months."

Mr. Frickey excused himself and left his desk for a few minutes. When he came back he said, "That theory of cycles seems to have some merit. What did you have in mind?"

I first pointed out that with a fifteen-cent meat contract I could be badly hurt if obliged to buy hogs from week to week on a sharply rising market. Then I told him of the buried corn on my place, though most Beaver Valley farmers had lost their corn in the flood but saved their hogs. Next I mentioned that no mortgaged hogs had been shipped out of Beaver Township since the bank closing, that most of the valley farmers were overstocked with spring pigs and heavyweights, and that their alfalfa fields were being ruined by excessive hog pasturing.

"I'd like to buy those surplus hogs and pigs," I told him, "and turn them into my field to salvage the buried corn before it rots. By the end of the month I believe I'd have a good profit in the hogs, and the pigs would supply me with plenty of cheap pork to complete the contract. If our bank were still

open and Mr. Kennedy had control of it there'd be no problem. I have enough money in my trading account to take care
of the equities, but with the bank in receivership I can't have
the mortgage balances transferred from the seller's account to
mine. The extra two thousand I'd like to borrow would take
care of those balances, and I'd pay them off as I butchered or
shipped the hogs."

Mr. Frickey listened without comment until I'd finished,
then asked, "Have you talked with the receiver about this?"

"No, sir," I said, "but I thought a receiver"s job was to
liquidate loans, not make them."

"It is," he said, "but what you have in mind would be a
form of liquidation. If necessary, the Farmers National will
finance you to the extent of five thousand dollars in the contract venture, as I told you Friday. If you wish, you may use
half the amount for buying hogs, but I'd suggest you talk with
the receiver before doing anything else. He's at the bank now,
and phoned me less than half an hour ago. If you'd like I'll
call back and tell him you're on the way."

After I'd thanked Mr. Frickey he walked to the door with
me, saying, "If you don't work out something over there, come
back to see me, but as I said before, we're somewhat reluctant
to make livestock loans at this time."

Nick was waiting patiently in the Maxwell when I went
back to the depot. So there'd be something for him to eat besides canned salmon and sauerkraut, I stopped at Bivans's
store for meat and groceries, but didn't mention having got
the contract. When we reached Cedar Bluffs I didn't stop at
the bank, but drove right home, set Nick to unloading the
Maxwell, flipped onto Kitten bareback, and rode over to the
Miner place for a talk to George before going to see the receiver.

As Kitten slid to a stop in the dooryard Irene came out to
the porch laughing, and told me, "I wish you could have seen
how tickled George was with that telegram. The Oberlin
depot agent phoned it at a quarter to one Tuesday noontime,

right when everybody was in from the fields for dinner. I'd bet a cookie there was somebody listenin' in on every phone up and down the valley, and I never in all my born days seen folks so curious. There's been leastways a dozen of 'em stopped by to try a little pump priming, and Effie's fit to be tied, but George won't let on that he knows who sent the telegram or has any notion what it means. He went to an auction over to Norcatur this afternoon and I don't look for him home till chore time. Anything you want me to tell him?"

"Just tell him I've come out of the creek again with both pockets full of fish," I said, "and that I'll be over to see him after supper." Then I gave Kitten her head and we streaked for home at a dead run.

20

Sweet Music

I STOPPED at home just long enough to put Kitten in the corral and tell Nick I'd be back as soon as I could, then drove up to the closed bank. The receiver was apparently waiting for me. I'd barely knocked when he opened the door, said he was glad to see me, and that Mr. Frickey had phoned saying I was on the way from Oberlin. As we walked back to the desk that used to be Bones Kennedy's he said, "I've spent the whole forenoon going over the bank's outstanding loans, and it seems to me that you and I could be of considerable help to each other."

When we were seated I said, "That's what I came to talk to you about. I'm sure you've heard that although the Beaver Valley farmers were able to save most of their livestock at the time of the flood they lost nearly all their corn."

"Yes," he said, "I know, and it makes me reluctant to press them on past-due loans before another crop is harvested."

"It was just the opposite with Bob Wilson and me," I told him. "We lost every hog we had, but I doubt that the flood washed away an ear of our corn. As near as I can tell by digging, there's about three thousand bushels of it buried under five or six inches of silt in that field adjoining the railroad. It will rot if it's left there till fall, but if I could put a couple of hundred stocker pigs in that field, along with some old sows to do the rooting, I'd be able to save every ear of it. On the other hand, no mortgaged livestock has been shipped out of this township since the bank closed, and with Wilson and me no longer in the feeding business there's no market for stocker pigs here. As a result, most of the valley farms are way overstocked with shoats, and what were good bacon hogs a couple of months ago have grown into rangy heavyweights that are almost a drug on the market. With no corn to feed their hogs, the farmers have had to overpasture their alfalfa fields, and if the hogs are left on them till fall a good many of those fields will be ruined."

"I didn't realize the situation was that bad," he said, "but if you have the corn and the farmers have the hogs we should be able to find a way of getting them together."

"There is if you're willing and this is something a bank receiver can do," I said. "Before the new bankers came here Mr. Kennedy used to give me an up-to-date list every month showing what percentage of equity each borrower had in his livestock. When I bought mortgaged animals I paid the seller his equity in cash, we both reported the sale to the bank, the unpaid balance was transferred to my loan account, and I signed a mortgage note for it. If I can make the same arrangement with you I'll agree to buy all the mortgaged hogs the farmers in this township want to sell at a dollar and a half a hundredweight below today's Kansas City market quotation, with George Miner doing the grading. Each hog will be numbered for identification as it is weighed in, I'll pay the seller in cash whatever percentage you'll allow him, take over the mortgage obligation for the balance, and pay it off when the hog is shipped or disposed of otherwise."

He listened intently until I'd finished, then said, "That sounds to me like a fine idea for all parties concerned. Such transactions come well within the scope of a bank receiver's authority, and I'm more than willing to enter into the agreement you've outlined. I'll type out a list of equity percentages and bring it to you before I go back to Oberlin this evening."

I thanked him and while we were walking to the door he told me, "I hear you've acquired a contract to supply all the meat for the railroad reconstruction job. You're to be congratulated for having the initiative to go after it, and I want you to know that I'll help in any way I can within the scope of my receivership."

"I'll need every bit of help I can get," I said. "The initiative was all George Miner's, and I've done little more than to follow his advice."

"You're still to be congratulated," he said as he let me out; "I'll bring that list to you as soon as it's ready."

It was all too evident that he'd been convinced to make the agreement with me before I'd ever reached the bank, so I was sure that Mr. Frickey had told him over the phone about my getting the meat contract. But I didn't know how many of the details he might have given, and there were some of them that I didn't want broadcast. With a direct wire between the Oberlin and Cedar Bluffs telephone offices, and with Bones and the bank both on one-party lines, no one except the switchboard operators could have eavesdropped on the conversation, but I was sure that Effie had listened to every word. To find out how much she knew, and in hope that I could head her off before she'd broadcast it to the whole township, I went right from the bank to the telephone office, directly across the street.

I found Effie absorbed in a half-whispered phone conversation, but I'd no sooner stepped inside her office than she yanked the line plug out, sprang from her chair, threw both arms around my neck, and nearly smothered me against her bulging bosom. Then she stood me away at arm's length and chortled, "So it was you sent George that telegram about corrallin' a horse of a different color! If I was your own mother I couldn't be happier about the whole thing, and I'd ought to have guessed who sent that telegram right off the reel, but I thought you was in Kansas City. Wasn't that where you told the depot agent to route your hog cars when you ordered 'em?"

"That's what you get for eavesdropping," I told her. "But I'd have been tempted to do a little of it myself if I'd been sitting in your chair this . . ."

"It would'a been sweet music to your ears if you had of," she cut in. "My land o' Goshen, if you had Charley Frickey and Bones Kennedy pullin' for you as hard down to Omaha as they've been at it here to home this afternoon it's no wonder you got that meat contract. To hear 'em braggin' you up to this bank receiver a body'd think you was smarter'n horseradish and cleverer'n a kitten.

"Charley told him all about the big profit you got out of your hogs by shippin' 'em over the Fourth, and what a good contract you made with the railroad, and about one of the big bosses phonin' him up from Omaha, and that the Farmers National had guaranteed to finance you up to five thousand dollars, and about you going to fix your place over into a slaughterhouse and butcher shop. Then Bones come on the wire and told him the only way he could hope to collect past-due livestock loans this fall was to leave you buy all the mortgaged cattle and hogs you could handle, and to transfer the debts on 'em to you till the critters got butchered or shipped."

"How did he seem to take it?" I asked.

"Well," she told me, "he was kind of standoffish at first, but it sounded like he was comin' around pretty good by the time they got done with him. Why don't you go on over and see him? He knows you're on the way from Oberlin and it would sure be a godsend to lots of folks in this township if they could get a little cash money out of their mortgaged cattle and hogs."

"If you hadn't been listening in on that line like a coyote at a gopher hole you'd have seen me go through town half an hour ago," I told her, "and you'd have seen me go into the bank ten minutes later if you hadn't been so busy broadcasting what you'd heard."

"Honest to John, I didn't peep a word to a soul," she told me. "When you come in I was just gossipin' a little with some of the women folks down the valley about that new hired girl of Russy Redfern's . . . the redheaded one."

Effie was so serious about it that I kissed a finger, touched it to the tip of her nose, and told her, "I was only joshing you, sweetheart. I'd like to have you tell the folks about my getting the contract, but it might cause hard feelings if the butchers I've been selling livestock found out how low I bid to get it, and I don't believe it would help my trading business to have the farmers know how much I made on those hogs I shipped. Another thing you could tell the folks if you'd like to is that the bank receiver is going to let me buy mortgaged livestock the same way Bones used to. I can't handle cattle right now, but I've told him I'd take all the mortgaged hogs and stocker pigs offered me at a dollar fifty a hundred below today's Kansas City radio quotation. The price includes delivery to Oberlin, and I may not ship till August, but anybody willing to rehaul later on can deliver stock to my place tomorrow and pick up a check for his equity."

Tears welled suddenly into Effie's eyes. She engulfed me in another bear hug for a moment, then turned me loose and scolded, "Now get out of here! Get out before I go to bawlin' like a little kid! I've got work to do."

She hurried back to her switchboard and was cranking the 4-4-4 line-call ring when the screen door banged behind me. As I climbed into the Maxwell I heard a half-sobbing, half-joyful voice sing out, "Line call! Line call, folks! Here's the best news I've had to tell you in a month of Sundays."

When I got home I decided to move into the house, believing Nick would feel more comfortable in a room by himself. We set up a kitchen in what had been the dining room, a living room in the old parlor, and divided the remaining furniture between the two bedrooms. Then we moved my radio bench into the barn, leaving the bunkhouse and former kitchen clear for remodeling into an icebox and butcher's shop.

Just before sunset the receiver brought the percentage list, and asked what plans I'd made for handling the railroad contract. I told him I'd hired a professional packing-house butcher while I was in Omaha, and that I'd bought secondhand, or was having built, all the fixtures and equipment I'd need. Then I explained how I was going to fit the old kitchen up for a butcher shop with a semiautomatic slicing maching and power grinder, showed him the bunkhouse, and said, "I plan to attach it to the north side of what used to be the kitchen, insulate it with straw, and convert it into an icebox big and cold enough to keep two tons of meat thoroughly chilled. There will be a large door at each end; one directly into the shop, and the other opening to the outside for bringing in ice and dressed carcasses from the slaughterhouse. To have running water I'll mount a small tank about halfway up the windmill tower, and to keep the yard from getting muddy I'll run a drain pipe from the shop and icebox to the creek."

He didn't seem much interested in my plumbing plans, but asked, "Where will you do your slaughtering?"

"Right here," I told him. "Most of the butchers I sell livestock to do theirs in some old shed well away from town, where a few flies are no great nuisance and coyotes clean up the offal. My slaughtering will be much more sanitary. Back there at the edge of the creek gorge I'm going to build a little screened-in slaughterhouse with a solid plank floor. I bought enough nearly-new water pipe to run a line back there, so we can scrub down after every slaughtering and do away with any possibility of a bad odor."

He told me it sounded as though my plans had been well made, and as we walked back to his car he asked, "When do you plan to start buying those hogs we were talking about?"

"Tomorrow morning," I told him.

"Mind if I drop over?" he asked. "It would give me a good chance to get better acquainted with the farmers, and maybe I could be of some help to you with the paper work."

"I'd be glad to have you," I told him, "and I could certainly use the help. I have an idea the first loads will come in right after sunrise. They usually do."

As he started his car he told me jovially, "That's pretty early for a banker, but I'll be here," then drove away.

Nick had hidden away in his room when the receiver drove into the yard. After he'd gone I took the boy around the place, telling him the plans I had in mind, and scratching lines on the ground to show him the locations of icebox, slaughter-house, and where I planned to run the drain line to the creek. He made no comments, and except for the animation of his face I might have thought him unable to understand what I was trying to explain. During supper he seemed completely lost in his own thoughts, so I made no attempt at conversation. After we'd eaten I left him to wash the dishes while I went over to tell George Miner all that had happened since I'd last seen him, and to ask if he'd act as grader of the hogs that were brought in next day.

George and Irene were sitting on the front porch when I rode Kitten up to the gate. "Glad to see you back, son," George called. "From what Irene tells me about Effie's line call this afternoon, I take it you're still rarin' at things whole-hog-or-none. Ain't promisin' to buy all the hogs anybody wants to sell kind of like proposin' marriage to a widow woman before askin' how many youngsters she's got? Come on in and sit a spell."

I visited with the Miners until nearly ten o'clock and told them the whole story step by step.

Although George would take no credit for any of my good fortune, he left no doubt as to how happy it made him. When I left he walked out to the gate with one hand on my shoulder, and told me. "There's no two ways about it, son, you're doin' some awful risky gamblin' all the way along the line, but with that judgment agin you you've a'ready got a pretty big stake in the game, and a man don't win big pots by playin' his cards close to his belly. Of course you'll have to watch every card that's dealt or throwed away, and you'll have to keep your chew right square in the middle of your mouth; a man with his mouth tight shut ain't very likely to tip his hand." At the gate he slapped my shoulder and told me, "Get on home and get some sleep, boy. I'll be over about sunup."

When I got home Nick was in his room with the door closed and a lamp lighted. And, strangely, the plaid oilcloth was missing from the kitchen table.

The next morning we were up by four o'clock, ate breakfast by lamplight, and in the first gray of dawn began fencing a runway from the scales to the field where the corn was buried. When at sunrise George and the bank receiver arrived, Nick looked bewildered, almost like a frightened child who wanted to run and hide. I realized that it would be an ordeal for him to meet as many strangers as would be coming to the place that day, so sent him to take the tools to the house, and said I'd come for him if he was needed. A little later I caught a glimpse of him behind the house, but for the rest of the day I was too busy to think of him again.

Before seven o'clock that morning one might have thought a county fair was being held at my place. The dooryard and driveway were clogged with wagonloads of hogs and several more were lined up along the McCook-Oberlin road. It seldom took longer than ten minutes to unload a wagon, grade and number the hogs, weigh them, and write out the bill of sale. While another farmer was backing his wagon into place at the unloading chute, the man before him signed his bill of sale, I gave him a check for the amount payable in cash, and the receiver charged my mortgage account with the balance.

I never found out exactly what Effie had said when making the line calls, but she certainly jarred loose an avalanche of hogs—not only from those whose stock was mortgaged, but from almost every farmer in Beaver Township. And no man

pulled away without telling me he'd furnish hauling to Oberlin whenever I wanted it.

When, just before sunset, the last wagon pulled away there
were 561 hogs—including every imaginable color, shape, and
size—rooting corn out of the silt in my hog pasture. I'd
written checks for more than 'two thousand dollars and signed
a mortgage for nearly forty-six hundred, although I'd intended
to invest no more than half that amount in hogs. Not only was
the number far greater than I'd figured on, but the stocker
pigs averaged to weigh nearly double what I'd expected them
to, and many of the sows scaled well above three hundred
pounds.

As soon as George and I were alone I said, "I didn't plan to
get in more than half this deep, but with the hog cycle due for
an upward turn I don't intend to sell a single porker until the
market rises considerable. Do you think I'm on the right
track?"

"That all depends on how far you aim to ride," he told me.
"I'd prob'ly light down before you'll want to, but I'm more'n
double your age, and a man grows cautious as he grows older.
It's lucky the Almighty made us that way, elsewise nobody'd
get married and have a family till he'd built up a good parcel
of property, and the race would soon die out."

"Will you tell me when to light down?" I asked.

"No, I wouldn't do that," he said. "No man ought to tell
another what to do in marriage or politics or religion or business. But I'll let you know when I'd light down if it was
me."

I reached out my hand to shake, and George squeezed it
hard enough to hurt. Then he spoke almost in a whisper,
"It's a pity a man can't stay young and full of vinegar longer."
Without another word he strode off toward the creek and
home.

21

Ready for Business

UNTIL twilight deepened I stood watching the hogs at their contented rooting; then a lamp was lighted at the house, so I went in to cook supper. When I opened the door Nick sat hunched over the kitchen table, so absorbed in what he was doing that he didn't hear me. He still hadn't heard me when I came close enough to see over his shoulder, and I couldn't have been more surprised if I'd found him dissecting a cadaver. He'd turned the oilcloth over and completely covered the white underside with drawings. They were so clear and detailed as to leave no doubt that he'd understood every word I'd told him about my plans—or that he'd improved on them tremendously. I should have known that his apprenticeship to a building contractor in Greece included training in layout and drafting, but it had never occurred to me.

Nick's plan showed the bunkhouse converted to a refrigerator with solid concrete foundation and floor, the walls and ceiling thickly insulated and metal lined, the entire loft a heavily beamed ice chamber, a large door opening into the shop, and another directly into the adjoining slaughterhouse. It also had concrete foundations and floor, the walls were metal sheathed, and at one side there was a sink with hot and cold water lines. An overhead rail extended above the connecting door, so that sides of beef or pork could be rolled from the slaughterhouse into the refrigerator without lifting.

The drawings showed what was unmistakably the big watering tank from the feed lot—the only one not swept away by the flood—to be mounted high above the slaughterhouse. The four great timbers forming the tower also served as corner posts for the building, and were undoubtedly those the road crew had used to get the bunkhouse down from the barn roof. On the dooryard side of the building there was a brick furnace, with hot-water tank mounted above the firebox and the rendering vat beyond, so that fat would not be scorched by too direct heat. Near the brink of the creek, with lines running to it from the shop, refrigerator, and slaughterhouse, was what looked to be a pit full of broken stone.

Nick was so intent on preparing material lists that I studied his drawing for fully ten minutes without attracting his attention. When, at last, I leaned over his shoulder, pointed to the pit, and asked, "What for?" he jumped as if he'd been hurt, then seemed lost for English words.

After a few moments he told me, "For wash-up water, so flies no come 'round."

I would have recognized the rock-filled pit as a cesspool if I'd had any experience with them, but I hadn't. When I'd lived in cities the drains were connected to sewers, and on the farms waste water was simply thrown out on the ground— with care not to make a mud puddle near the back door.

Nick's plans would have been fine if we'd had three months before the start of the railroad contract, or if I could afford a whole crew of carpenters, plumbers, masons, teams, and drivers. But for two of us to do any such job in twenty-three days was impossible, and to hire it done for a four-months business would be reckless extravagance. "That's a wonderful set of plans, Nick," I told him, "but you and I couldn't come within a mile of building such a layout by the first of August. I'm afraid we'll have to get along without the concrete floors and hot-water system and cesspool and . . ."

Nick looked up at me pleadingly, apparently on the verge of tears, and said hesitantly, "I work hard, boss . . . lots hours . . . fast I can."

I'd always heard that the sensibilities of any man who had worked on the killing floor of a packing plant became so numbed that he was incapable of being stirred by emotions. Maybe that's why the shock of Nick's nearly tipping over affected me as it did. I put a hand on his shoulder and told him, "Let's stop and get some supper now, Nick, then I'll try to figure out how much of it we can possibly do."

I said it more to comfort him than because I thought there was much we could do beyond my original plans. Then, when I was putting supper on the table, the depot agent at Oberlin phoned that my express shipment had arrived. I knew there'd be more than a wagon load of it, so I'd have to find a couple of haulers, and trying to think who I might get gave me an idea about our building plans. Almost every farmer in Beaver Township was a jack-at-all-trades, the more skillful could handle any work required by Nick's plans, and most of them owed me hog hauling, some of which I'd have no need for.

As soon as we'd eaten I told Nick to go on with his material listing, then I took another look at the hogs in the pasture, and went on to town for a visit with Effie. I spent nearly an hour telling her about Nick, his training in Greece, and every detail of the plans he'd drawn; stressing the hot and cold running water, the sanitary drain lines and cesspool, and the concrete floors. "There's a day or two of hog hauling due me from almost every man in this township," I told her. "If some of them would as soon haul material, or dig ditches and pound nails, I have an idea the whole layout the boy has planned could be built in three weeks."

"When do you aim to get started on it?" she asked.

"I'd start in the morning if I had a team or two for hauling," I told her.

"Great Jehoshaphat!" Effie exploded. "Here it is ha'past nine o'clock at night! Why in the wide world didn't you let on what you wanted when you first come in here, 'stead of pussyfootin' 'round like a lovesick lummox till time for all respectable folks to be abed. Now get out of here! Skedaddle and leave me elbowroom to try some line calls! If I rouse anybody I'll ring you up before I close the switchboard."

The moonlight was so bright that when I crossed the railroad track on the way home I could see hogs still rooting up corn all around my pasture. I climbed the fence and spent maybe half an hour walking around among them, making sure the big sows weren't driving the smaller shoats away from corn that had been turned up.

When I'd circled the field as far as the scale runway I became conscious that the phone was ringing my combination, 3-2-3, over and over. I sprinted across the dooryard, rushed into the house, and snatched the receiver off the hook, not more than four feet from where Nick sat hunched over the kitchen table. I was blowing like a wind-broken nag, and before I could catch my breath enough to speak Effie shouted, "Land sakes alive! Where on this green earth have you been at for the last hour?"

"I stopped to see how the hogs were doing," I told her, "but it wasn't more than . . ."

"Well, what's the matter with that Eyetalian you was braggin' so much about? Don't he know enough to answer a phone, or is he deefer'n a post? I been ringin' steady for leastways twenty minutes."

There was no point in telling her again that Nick was Greek, not Italian, and her voice was so loud that I was afraid he might hear and understand what she was saying. I held the receiver tight against my cheek to muffle her voice, and to cool her down I said, "It's my fault, Effie; I forgot to tell him that three-two-three was my ring."

"What odds does that make when a phone's ringin' fit to tear itself off the wall?" she demanded stridently. "He'd ought to had sense enough to take down the receiver and find out what was goin' on. Everybody else on that line did."

"He doesn't speak very good English," I told her, "and with everbody here a stranger to him he's a bit bashful."

"Bashful! Sounds to me more like he's scared to death of folks. So that's why there didn't nobody see hide nor hair of him when they hauled hogs to your place today? Oh well, it don't make no never-minds anyways. What I called for was to tell you you'd have plenty of help in the morning. My lands, it seems like everybody in the township wants to get a finger into the pie. I didn't bother to set down any names, but told 'em the more the merrier, and not to forget to fetch along their tools. Well, I'd best to ring off now so's the both of us can get some sleep. I didn't aim to be so cussed ornery when I called, but it sets my blood to boilin' when I know there's somebody to home and they won't answer." Then she broke the connection before I could thank her for her help.

It was past midnight before Nick completed his lists and we'd translated them into English. Before dawn we were out with lanterns, taking measurements and driving stakes to mark the corners of the refrigerator, slaughterhouse, and cesspool, and to string up twine marking where ditches were to be dug. By six o'clock a dozen wagons had rolled into the yard, so I started three of them with four-horse hitches off for Oberlin, telling the drivers I'd meet them there with the material lists.

Every man had a plow, a scraper, or a box of tools in his wagon, and several had brought along a son or two to help with the work. As I was sure he would be, George Miner was among the first to arrive, though he owed me no hauling. I asked him to take charge of the cesspool and ditch digging while I went to Oberlin for materials. Then I set Bill Justice, who was quiet, careful, and a good carpenter, to work with Nick on the foundation forms for the refrigerator and slaughterhouse.

Halfway to Oberlin I passed the three wagons I'd sent ahead, the horses stepping along at a brisk trot. By the time they reached town I'd found and bought all the materials on Nick's lists. A few minutes after nine o'clock the wagons were pulling out for home, heavily loaded with lumber, cement, bricks, an additional three hundred feet of drain and water pipe, hardware, other building materials, and the express shipment from Omaha.

Between material and hog buying I'd drained my trading fund down to almost nothing, so I borrowed a thousand dollars as soon as the Farmers National opened. Mr. Frickey told me that the receiver of the Cedar Bluffs bank had phoned him of our agreement and of the number of hogs I'd bought. He said they both were pleased and thought I'd made a good investment.

When I left the Farmers National I stopped at the drug store and bought Effie the biggest box of candy in Oberlin. Then I went to Bivans' store for fifty pounds of steak and a load of groceries, but I didn't look forward with any great joy to meeting John. He'd not only know about my having got the railroad contract, but that I'd have to cut deeply into his farm trade to get rid of my leftovers, and I was afraid he might be sore about it.

There were no customers in the store when I got there; John was alone behind the grocery counter, and he didn't look overly cordial when I went in. It seemed to me that the best way to avoid unpleasantness was by coming straight to the point, so I said, "As you must know, I've bid in the railroad meat contract, so I'll have lots of leftovers to get rid of. I aim to go after all the farm trade I can get, but I won't cut prices to less than a dime a pound. Anything except by-products that I can't get that much for I'll feed back to my hogs. Is that fair enough?"

Bivans looked surprised, stuck his hand across the counter to shake, and told me, "Fair enough! What the McCook butchers and I have been scared of was that you'd go to dumping stuff at a nickel or less. That could come mighty close to putting some of us out of business, but a dime for the grade of stuff you'll have left over from that railroad contract is all right. Any butcher that can't stand that kind of competition ought to be out of business. You go right ahead and get all the farm trade you can, and there's none of us will begrudge it to you so long as you don't cut under a dime a pound."

I couldn't see any reason for telling him that the meat I'd have left over would be of better grade than most of the Mc-Cook butchers were selling their farm trade, so kept the conversation on something else until he finished putting up my order. He didn't ask what price I'd bid to get the contract, and of course I didn't tell him.

A few miles out of town I passed the heavily loaded wagons, then stopped at Cedar Bluffs only long enough to take the box of candy in to Effie. As always, she scolded at me for bringing it, and said that if I didn't quit I'd have her fatter than any hog in Beaver Township, but she had the top off the box before I could get out of her office.

When I got home I found the whole place a beehive of activity. The hogs were spread out over the entire forty-acre field, rooting deep into the silt, and every one of them was champing on an ear of corn. The ditches and cesspool pit had been dug, the floor had been removed from the bunkhouse, and forms for the foundations were nearly completed.

My neighbors were as used to saw and hammer as to plow and harrow, and when one of them built a new house or barn the others always pitched in to help. Sometimes a boss carpenter was hired to lay out the framing, but there were never any drawn plans, so Nick's oilcloth was a source of amazement. While the potatoes boiled I explained it to George Miner and Dave Goodenberger, then let them take it outside to show the other men.

As I fried steak and sliced bread I could hear Dave's voice in the dooryard: "Come look at these pi'tures the Eyetalian boy drawed of the layout Bud aims to build. That there brick thing? Why that's the firebox for makin' hot water. Don't you see the lines runnin' all abouts where we've been diggin' ditches this mornin'? Them's water and drain pipes. Yes, sirree, boys! Hot and cold runnin' water all over the place, jest like the Brown Palace Hotel up to Denver. Don't reckon I'll let on about this to the old lady—leastways, not till I get the mortgage on my place paid off."

By quitting time we'd laid all the drain and underground water lines, erected the tower, mounted the water tank on it, filled the cesspool pit with limestone and the foundation forms with concrete. On Sunday evening there was many a cow milked late in Beaver Township. No man would leave the job until the water system had been completed, the heavy carpentry on the refrigerator and slaughterhouse finished, and concrete floors laid. Five hundred dollars wouldn't have paid for the work my neighbors had done for me in those two days, but no man would take a penny or the cancellation of his hog-hauling obligation.

With the start we'd been given, two men could easily have slapped the rest of the job together in three weeks. But Nick didn't slap anything together, and I'd have been ashamed to do it when working with him. Every board had to be planed to a perfect fit, every nail set, and his solder joints looked more like those of a jeweler than a tinsmith.

In his drive for perfection Nick always had me up before daylight, and sometimes he wouldn't quit until nearly midnight. In trying to match his pace and endurance I found myself constantly running out of steam on my salmon, sauerkraut, and gluten bread diet. After four days of nearly starving, I ate a breakfast of half a dozen hot biscuits, a big heap of fried potatoes, a pound of steak, and a pint of coffee with cream and sugar.

With a belly full of meat, potatoes, and biscuits, I had no trouble in keeping pace with Nick, and abandoned my diet completely. I couldn't help feeling guilty about it, though, so mailed Dr. DeMay a specimen at the end of the week. On Tuesday I received a postal card from him with only five words on it: "Good specimen. Sugar slightly down."

The next morning I changed our menu a little: we had pancakes with our steak and potatoes instead of hot biscuits. For the rest of the summer and fall that was about as much as our meals ever varied, but I didn't send any more specimens to Dr. DeMay.

From the day I'd bought my hogs the market had been moving up steadily, at an average daily rate of about ten cents a hundred. As mid-July approached I began avoiding George a bit for fear he'd tell me that if he were in my boots he'd ship his excess hogs. With the market still going up, I dropped over for a visit with him on the evening of the twentieth, but he didn't mention hogs or the market, so I didn't either.

On Monday, the twenty-fifth, the special fixtures arrived from the German machinist, the white butchers' coats and aprons came from Sears Roebuck, and that day's mail brought a letter from Mr. Donovan. He wrote that he'd come to Cedar Bluffs on Friday, the twenty-ninth, and that if my facilities passed inspection, I should be prepared to make my initial delivery on the thirty-first.

From then until midnight on the twenty-seventh I was too busy to think about hogs or pay any attention to what the market was doing. By that time our building job was finished and we were ready to go into the butchering business. Nick had converted the old Maxwell into a dust-tight little delivery truck by cutting away the body behind the front seat and replacing it with what looked like a large canvas-covered cupboard. We'd lined the refrigerator with galvanized iron sheeting—every joint soldered airtight—and I'd had two tons of ice hauled to fill the cribs. We'd given every inch of the house, inside and out, at least one coat of white paint, had screened every door and window, installed all the equipment, and finished up by scrubbing every floor with scalding water and lye soap.

Next morning we slept until six o'clock, and right after breakfast George dropped over. As he came up from the creek he called out cheerily, "Don't know if it's women folks' gossip, but Irene tells me the chief cook and bottle washer for the railroad will be here for inspection tomorrow. Reckoned I'd mosey over to see if I could be of help anywheres along the line."

Thursday was the last day I could order cars for shipping hogs on Saturday, so I had an idea that George's visit was an invitation for me to ask his advice about selling, but I didn't want to appear too anxious, so called back, "This time the women made a good guess, but we're as ready for him as I know how to get. Come on inside and take a look at the place."

When George saw that we'd scrubbed the floors until they were bleached almost white he wouldn't step a foot inside without pulling off his boots. As we padded around in our stockings he reminded me of a little boy at a circus, and when I'd shown him through the workroom, refrigerator, and slaughterhouse, he told me, "By jiggers, the Lord must be lookin' after somebody besides fools and drunkards this season, elseways He'd never have led you to that boy Nick. Was I you, I'd be danged careful I didn't lose him till this whole shenanigan was all wound up and over with. It looks to me like you've got a heap of kettles on the fire and all of 'em comin' to a boil at the same time."

"Then you think I'd better sell whatever hogs I won't be needing for the railroad contract?" I asked.

"Well now," he said slowly, "I wouldn't say you'd better. Nobody could say that without he knew if the market was going down, and I don't know that. Don't know at all that I'd ship this next Saturday if I was you . . . and your age. Hog market is still movin' right along, steady as a trottin' horse, up a dime to fifteen cents every day."

"What would you do if these hogs were yours and you were your age?" I asked.

"I'd sell 'em," he said without a moment's hesitation. "Cycle or no cycle, pork's gettin' mighty high alongside the price of prime beef and veal and chicken, and the bosses at the stockyard auctions are the women folks that buy meat in the butcher shops all over this country. If they switch away from pork the price can't help but go down. By ginger, I'd best to get on home before Irene comes huntin' me with a broom handle, but don't you go and ship just because I would, son. You know I'm gettin' old and cautious; kind of like an old saddle pony that's been wire cut a few times."

As he started off toward the creek I called after him, "Come over Saturday morning, will you, and bring old Jack along." Jack was the best dog in Beaver Valley for rounding up and sorting hogs, so I didn't need to tell George that I was going to ship my excess.

He was certainly right about my having a heap of kettles coming to a boil all at the same time. To have meat chilled firm enough for band-saw slicing by Saturday, we'd have to butcher right away, but I'd had no time to buy cattle. Then too, I'd need hay for them, and the buried corn must be nearly gone after 561 hogs had lived on it for three weeks. Before the day was over I'd have to order cars, line up thirty wagons for hauling hogs on Saturday, pick up my shipment of spices and stale bread at the McCook express office, and buy cattle, hay, corn, and wrapping materials.

As soon as George had gone Nick and I rounded up a couple of the best bacon hogs in the pasture for him to slaughter and dress while I went to get some of the other kettles off the fire. The latest Kansas City radio quotation on top grade grass-fat heifers was six fifty a hundredweight, making their local value five dollars. I could well afford to pay that much if most of my beef leftovers could be sold at fifteen cents a pound, and I believed they could be if the quality was high. As insurance against a rising market, I decided to buy enough top grade heifers to fill my contract for at least a month.

Since I'd bought the larger part of my hogs from valley farmers, it seemed only fair to give the divide farmers first chance to sell the heifers. There was no corn to be had in Beaver Valley, but the tenants on the divide never had enough stock to clean up their nubbins. They'd make good feed for my pasture hogs, and I could pay the full price in cash because the bank receiver had written off all nubbin piles as worthless. Then too, the poorer of the tenant farmers up there had only a couple or three hogs to sell when I'd been buying, but every one of them had promised to haul a full load to Oberlin when I shipped, and several had come down to help us with the building.

Most of the farmers on the divide seemed to feel that I'd done them a favor by not shipping until they'd finished their harvesting, and I had no trouble in finding plenty of hog haulers. If a wheat farmer had a few grass-fat heifers to sell I looked them over and dickered for any that were top quality, but held the corn and hay business back for the poorer tenants who had no wheat to harvest and no fat cattle to sell. By noon I'd bought twenty-seven excellent heifers, ten tons of good prairie hay, and fifty tons of nubbins.

From the divide I drove to Oberlin, ordered cars for Saturday, and bought wrapping paper, twine, and order pads with carbon, so I'd be able to keep track of credit sales. I hadn't expected to be in town more than fifteen minutes, but so many people wanted to congratulate me on getting the railroad contract—or try to pump me about the price I'd bid to get it—that I didn't get away for more than an hour.

22

Effie to the Rescue

I HADN'T planned to stop in Cedar Bluffs on my way home, but as I was passing the telephone office Effie flung the screen door open, looking as ruffled as a setting hen that's just been tossed off her nest. "Where in the name of common sense have you been at for the last couple of hours?" she called irritably. "I've been wearin' out the wires hunting you all over Beaver Township."

"Oberlin," I called back as I braked the Maxwell to a stop in a cloud of dust.

"Well, come in here!" she demanded, went back inside, and slammed the door behind her.

I climbed out of the Maxwell, followed her inside, and asked, "What's all the shooting about, Honeybunch?"

"Don't you honeybunch me!" she flared. "I'll swear to goodness the women folks in this township have like to drove me out my head with questions I couldn't answer about your butcher business. The gossip's out that you're aimin' to sell meat on credit and will take your pay in nubbin corn. Have you gone clean out of your senses?"

"Maybe so," I said, "but anybody in the township can have

a charge account with me if he'll agree to settle no later than Thanksgiving in livestock, corn, or cash. I'll take nubbins only from the tenant farmers on the divide."

Effie cooled down a little before I'd finished, sniffed, and asked, "What kind of sausage did you give the folks that sold you hogs the last time you shipped?"

"The kind my mother used to make when I was a kid" I told her.

"Aim to make any of it to sell?"

"As much as anybody'll buy," I answered.

"What prices you goin' to charge for your stuff: sausage and pork chops and beefsteak and the likes?"

For a moment I didn't know what to say. I'd hoped to get fifteen cents a pound for the best of my leftovers, and I'd given Bivans my word that I wouldn't sell anything but by-products for less than a dime. But it occurred to me that, regardless of price, getting rid of my leftovers would depend on how much line-call help I got from Effie, and that she'd be more enthusiastic if she had some part in the planning and felt that I was holding nothing back from her. I'd never asked her what details of my contract she'd learned when she listened in on the conversation between Mr. Frickey and the bank receiver, and she'd never told me. But, gossip monger that she was, she'd never told anyone else, or people wouldn't still be trying to pump me for information, so I decided to talk freely.

"I've been too busy to think much about prices," I told her, "and I wish you'd help me with it. I suppose you know that the railroad asked for bids on nothing but beefsteak, pork chops, and pork sausage. For that reason all the butchers who bid less than twenty cents a pound were going to use the cheapest old cows and worn-out brood sows they could buy, and to sell their leftovers to the farm trade for whatever they could get. George and I thought they were making a mistake, because there would be more than a ton of leftovers a day, most of it so rank and tough you'd be ashamed to throw it out to the coyotes. We figured that if pork cutlets could be substituted for chops the job could be done better and cheaper by using top grade heifers and bacon hogs, because there wouldn't be a quarter as much leftovers and it would all be good tender meat."

Effie had forgotten her peevishness, and asked, "Is that why you shipped your hogs to Omaha and went along with 'em?"

"That's right," I told her. "I wouldn't have stood a chance of getting the contract unless I'd been where I could find out what substitutions could be made and how low I'd have to bid. To get some other terms I needed, I had to cut my price to fifteen cents a pound, straight across the board, but I got pork cutlets and lard compound included in the contract, and the kind of sausage I gave the folks here. The price is awfully low for beefsteak and pork chops, but it's okay for cutlets and high for that kind of sausage and lard compound, so they'll average out fairly well. I should make a good profit on the contract if I can sell all my leftovers and get reasonable prices for them."

"What if you can't?" Effie asked.

I grinned, shrugged my shoulders, and told her, "It might be better for me than all the doctors in the world; I'd be so deep in debt that I'd need a long lifetime to dig my way out."

"Don't talk nonsense!" she snapped. "I'll sell the stuff for you if the price is reasonable. What'll you have to get?"

"I'd like to average twelve and a half cents a pound," I told her. "If I could get fifteen cents for stew beef, hamburger, sidemeat, and leaf lard, I could afford to sell short ribs, sausage, and lard compound as low as a dime. What would you think about that?"

She turned down the corners of her mouth and told me, "I'd think the loco weed had got to you! Lard compound's eighty-five cents for a five-pound bucket in all the stores over to McCook, and why in heaven's name would you sell sausage for a dime a pound when folks are hollerin' to get it without askin' the price?"

"I wouldn't like the word to get out," I said, "but the kind of sausage I'm going to make—the kind I gave the folks when I went to Omaha—is mostly hog fatback and beef trimmings, and my compound will be all fatback and beef suet rendered together. The suet wouldn't bring a dollar a ton in any other way, and Rudy Schneider told me a man would be lucky to get a nickel a pound for as much hog fatback as would be left over from the railroad contract. My aim is to get rid of my fatback by pricing compound and sausage low enough that I'll sell a lot of them."

Hmfff!" Effie sniffed. "You aim like a drunken harvest hand! For the past three or four hours I've been pestered to death by folks with the notion that your sausage is the best they every tasted, and them that's got the price would pay two bits a pound for it with no questions asked. But if you go and price it at a dime you wouldn't sell enough to wad a shotgun, and I couldn't sell it for you, 'cause everybody'd know there was something wrong with it. And it would be the same way with your lard compound."

"Well," I said, "as near as I can figure, leftover fatback is going to make all the difference between a good profit and a big loss on this railroad contract, and unless I can find some way to get rid of mine at a reasonable price I'll be licked."

"All you got to do is use your head," she told me. "Why on this green earth do you reckon farmer women buy lard compound at eight-five cents for a five pound bucket when they can get straight leaf lard for sixteen cents a pound?"

"Irene Miner says it's because the bucket comes in handy."

"Of course it is, you ninny," Effie told me, "but them buckets ain't worth a nickel apiece; they're too flimsy for anything besides a school lunch bucket, and not big enough for anything else. What farm women want is a good stout galvanized bucket; one that's big enough for gatherin' the eggs or milkin' a cow, but not so big it'll be too heavy to lug when it's full. Unless a woman's got a cream separator—and there's precious few in this township that's got 'em—she has to set her milk in pans to raise the cream for butter. What them women like best is a pan about three times as wide across the top as it is deep, made out of bright tin that won't rust easy, and that's thick enough the bottom won't buckle every time she lifts a panful.

"If I was you I'd put the stuff I wanted to sell the most of into pans and buckets. Most of the women in these parts set their milk in gallon and half-gallon pans, but I'd put my sausage in two-and-a-half-quart and five-quart pans. That way they'd hold five or ten pounds apiece, 'cause a pint's a pound the world around. Then I'd put my lard compound and short ribs and stuff like that in ten-quart buckets, so's to sell 'em twenty pounds at a crack."

"I wouldn't think there'd be many people who'd want to buy as much as ten pounds of sausage or twenty pounds of shortening at a time," I said.

"Didn't you say you aimed to leave 'em have credit?" she asked.

"That's right," I said.

"Then I guess you don't know farm women as good as a butcher had ought to," she said. "What with thrashing season commencin' any day now, and the fall plowing and sowing to be done, and the corn to be shucked as soon as frost hits, there'll be a heap of hired hands to feed between now and Thanksgivin' time, and these women folks'll buy whatever they have to to get a pan that catches their eye or a good milk bucket the right size—that is, they will if they think the bucket or the pan is free and they don't have to pay cash for the stuff they buy."

"How much would you charge for sausage you sold in pans, and lard compound by the bucket?" I asked.

"Different prices only make it harder for women folks to make up their minds," she told me. "The more of a thing I wanted to sell the better the pan or bucket or dish I'd put it into, but I wouldn't have more than two prices: one for steak and chops and roasts, and another for everything else."

"Then I'll have only one price," I said, "because with a contract like mine I won't have any steaks or chops or roasts to sell."

"Don't be a jackass!" Effie scolded. "You're not fool enough to think these folks will come to you for the stuff you want to get rid of when they have to drive to McCook or Oberlin for the rest of their meat, do you? If you want their trade you'll have to sell 'em the stuff they want right along with the stuff you want to get shut of."

"I can see what you mean," I told her, "but I can't see where it would do me any good. A hog is less than one quarter ham steaks and chops, and for every pound of those I sell I'll be stuck with two pounds of fatback to get rid . . ."

"Oh, fiddlesticks!" she broke in. "If you butcher top grade bacon hogs, like you said you was going to, the backs'll be lean enough that most farmer folks will buy 'em for sidemeat, and if you charge twenty cents a pound for steak and chops and the likes you'll head the folks off from buyin' too much of them things."

"Don't you think twenty cents is pretty high, considering that I'm going to get only fifteen from the railroad?" I asked.

"The folks couldn't do no better in McCook or Oberlin, could they?" she asked in reply.

"Well, maybe not for the same grade of meat," I said, "but . . ."

"Buttin's for billy goats!" she snapped. "Now skedaddle out of here and see what kind of milk buckets and pans you can find in McCook that look real nice but don't cost too much. Get leastways ten dozen pans of both sizes and five dozen buckets; I've got a hunch we're goin' to need 'em. I won't put out line calls till you get back, so don't stop to tell no long stories."

That "we're goin' to need 'em" took a lot of worry off my mind, and I headed for McCook as fast as the old Maxwell would go.

In the department store I found sturdy, brightly tinned 2½-

and 5-quart pans, and 10-quart galvanized buckets that were light in weight but not flimsy, with good stout bails. Rubber stamped in purple ink on the bottom of the larger pans was a big 25¢, on the smaller ones 15¢, and on the buckets 40¢. After a little haggling the store manager agreed to give me a 25 per cent discount if I'd take two gross of pans and half a gross of buckets. Then he gave me the same discount on a dozen galvanized wash tubs we needed for storing cut meat, sausage, and hamburger in the refrigerator.

By the time I'd picked up my shipment of spices and stale bread at the express office the old Maxwell was loaded so full there was barely room for me to squeeze in behind the wheel, and I had to drive slowly on the way home. I stopped there just long enough to unload, then took a bucket and a pan of each size up to show Effie. As I pulled to a stop in front of her office she stepped into the doorway and called, "Land sakes alive, what took you so long? These women folks haven't let up on me for a blessed minute. What luck did you have?"

"Pretty good," I called back, and held up a bucket so she'd be sure to see the 40¢ mark on the bottom.

"Jumpin' Jehoshaphat!" she exclaimed. "Have you took leave of your senses altogether? You can't afford that kind of stuff in place of paper and twine."

"Sure I can," I said, holding up the pans with the price marks toward her. "I bought six dozen buckets and twenty-four dozen pans like these."

"You didn't go and pay fifteen cents and a quarter apiece for them pans, did you?" she demanded. "Good lands, I'd ought to had better sense than to leave you go alone. Well, fetch 'em in here so's't I can see how bad you got stuck. I'll swear to goodness every line on the switchboard has been buzzin' like a bee in a bottle ever since you left."

When I went into the little office every light on the switchboard was blinking, a sure sign that impatient women were jiggling receivers on every line in the township, and with each blink of a light a buzzer stuttered and whined. Effie had plugged the cord of her headset into one of the line jacks and was saying irritably, "Yes, Matty, I know he's back from McCook, but there's nothin' I can tell you yet. Soon as ever there is I'll put out line calls, like I've been sayin' for the past two hours."

She broke the connection with a yank of the cord, stripped off her headset, and told me "A body can't hardly hear herself think with all this racket goin' on. Pull the switch on that battery, will you, Bud, so's't we can get down to business in peace."

The whole Beaver Township telephone system was powered by a single brine battery, so when I pulled the switch the lights on the switchboard stopped blinking and the buzzers became mute. Effie blew out her breath in a long "whissssht" and mopped the sweat off her forehead. "Well," she said, "I hope there don't nobody's buildin's catch afire while I've got them lines killed, but if I'd had to of listened to that hullabaloo for another five minutes it would have drove me stark starin' crazy. Now let me have a look at them buckets and pans you bought."

After she'd examined each piece thoroughly and tested its weight by bouncing it on her hand, she looked up at me and said, "They're mighty nice stuff, all right, and I wouldn't mind havin' a set of 'em my own self, but they're a lot too costive to give away with sausage and lard compound and the likes of that."

"No, they're not," I told her. "I got a 25 per cent discount by taking them in gross and half-gross lots, so the buckets were only thirty cents apiece, and that's just a cent and a half a pound on twenty pounds of shortening."

"What'll it come to on stuff in the pans?" she asked.

"Two and a quarter cents a pound in the small ones," I said, "but less than two cents in the big ones."

"Lucky it wasn't the other way abouts," she said, looking back at the pans again. "No woman with more'n one or two cows wants to mess around settin' milk to rise in a whole raft of little pans if she can get good big ones by just buyin' twice as much sausage or whatever at one time—that is, if she's buyin' on credit—and the more of anything a woman's got in her larder the more of it she's bound to use. If it was me doin' it, I wouldn't put up shortenin' in nothing but buckets, or wrapped in paper if somebody wanted less'n twenty pounds. And I wouldn't put nothing but sausage in pans—that is . . . Hold your horse a minute! Didn't you tell me you was goin' to render out most of the fatback you didn't make into sausage?"

"That's right," I said.

"Then you'll have cracklin's till you can't rest, won't you?"

"I suppose I will," I said, "but they'll make awfully good hog feed."

"Hog feed! Fiddlesticks!" she sputtered. "Why don't you use your head a bit before you go to throwin' stuff out to the hogs? Don't you know that almost everybody likes to make a batch of cracklin' bread once in a while? And some folks salt cracklin's and nibble on 'em of an evenin' like they was peanuts—don't let me forget to say somethin' about that when I make the line calls—and it's a cinch that everybody'll want all the free pans and buckets they can get. If I was you I'd sell one of them big pans heapin' full o' cracklin's for fifty cents, or a bucketful for a dollar. And, you know, there's lots of German folks hereabouts, and they make sausage out of critters' heads and insides. Why don't you sell the whole works from a hog or a heifer—liver, lights, head, heart, and kidneys— bucket and all for a dollar. Elsewise you'll have to give that kind of stuff away or throw it out."

"How about pigs' feet and ham hocks?" I asked. "Would you put those in pans or buckets?"

"I'd wrap 'em in paper," she told me. "You can get a nickel apiece for pigs' feet and a dime for hocks, anyways, and you couldn't get a penny more if you was to put 'em in a thirty-cent bucket. It's women folks that buys the meat, and if you aim to make any money doin' business with 'em you'll have to learn to use your head."

"I've never had much experience doing business with women," I said, "and it's a little late for me to start learning to use my head. What I need is you for a partner."

"Hmmfff!" she jeered. "And I need a partner that's a'ready up to his neck in debt like I need a broken leg." Then she turned serious again and told me, "I was only joshin' you, Bud, and didn't aim to poke you on the hurt place. You don't need a partner no more'n a cat needs two tails, but I'll tell you what I'll do; I'll put out line calls and take phone orders for you, and you can keep Guy and me in fresh meat if you have a mind to. Is that a deal?"

"You bet your boots it's a deal," I told her, kissed a finger, and touched it to the end of her nose.

"Well then," she said as she picked up her headset, "switch that battery back on and get out of here. I'll put out line calls right away, and give you a ring as soon as ever I get all the orders in. What time on Sunday should I tell the folks they can come for their stuff?"

"Oh, it doesn't matter," I said. "I'll be around the place all day and all evening."

"Don't be a fool!" she told me. "If we don't stop 'em right at the start, some of these women folks will devil you to death—comin' by any time from sunup till midnight for a pound of spareribs or a bone for the dog. That Eyetalian bein' scared of his own shadow the way he is, how do you reckon you'd get away to do any trading? I'm goin' to tell the folks that the only hours you'll be open for meat business are from six to eight on weekday evenin's, and ten to one o'clock on Sundays. That way they'll have a chance to come after supper, and them that goes to church can stop by on their way home. It'll save time for all hands, and you won't sell a nickel's worth less than you would the other way. Now get out of here."

Most of the heifers I'd bought were to be delivered when the sellers came to haul hogs on Saturday, but I'd arranged to have four delivered that afternoon. As soon as they arrived we picked out the fattest one and butchered her right away. Actually, Nick did most of the work. He was an expert at it and, as always, the sight and smell of slaughtering nauseated me. After the job was finished he stayed to scrub down the slaughterhouse while I went to start supper. The telephone was ringing wildly, and when I picked up the receiver Effie's voice came over the wire irritably, "Where in the name of common sense have you been for the past hour? I was just about to send Guy over to find out if that Eyetalian had cut your throat, or if the both of you was froze to death in the icebox."

"I've been out to the slaughterhouse," I said. "We had to do some butchering so we'd be ready for Sunday's business."

"Well, I hope to goodness you done a plenty of it," she told me proudly. "I've got orders enough here to choke a billy goat. Nelly Moss wants a bucket of that shortenin' and a big pan of sausage and five pounds of beefsteak and . . ."

"Hold it, Effie!" I broke in. "All I need to know right now is how much sausage and shortening to get ready. Will you add up the totals and call me back? I'll bring you up some pork chops after supper and pick up the separate orders then."

I barely had the fire started when she called back, "Well, here's your totals," she told me, "but land knows how long they'll be good for. There's still orders comin' in faster'n I can write 'em down. Let's see, it's eleven big pans of sausage and six little ones, and eighteen buckets of shortenin'."

"Whewwww," I whistled, "that'll be a hundred and forty pounds of sausage and three hundred and sixty of shortening."

"I told you what would happen if you put the stuff into free milk pans and buckets, didn't I?" she gloated. "There's more calls comin' in, so I got to ring off now, but listen Bud, when you come up for the orders bring a little liver for my cat, will you? She's crazy about it."

As soon as we'd eaten supper Nick and I rounded up our three biggest hogs and had driven them to the slaughterhouse when he stepped in front of me and said, "I take now."

With my squeamish stomach I was glad enough to have him take over the slaughtering. The pork he'd butchered that morning was thoroughly chilled, so I cut half a dozen thick loin chops, wrapped a pound of liver, packed them in one of the buckets, and drove up to the telephone office.

It was hard to tell whether Effie was more pleased with the bucket, the chops, the liver for her cat, or the orders she'd taken. "I'm a'ready up to my neck in orders," she told me, "and there's more still dribblin' in. Besides, there's forty things I've got to find out from you. First off, can folks outside the township have charge accounts if they've been doing livestock business with you? It seems like the news has leaked out and they're callin' in from all over."

"Anybody with good credit can have a charge account if he'll agree to settle up by Thanksgiving," I told her.

"Well then," she told me happily, "I've got orders for eighty pounds more sausage and five buckets of shortening, along with four hundred and fifty-one pounds of other stuff."

I was too astonished to speak for a moment, but as soon as I'd collected my wits I asked, "For heaven's sake, Effie, did you blackmail people into giving you orders? I didn't think there was this much meat business in Decatur County."

"You didn't do much thinkin' then," she told me smugly. "Farmers won't do their own butcherin', leastways in summer, if they can buy meat on credit for fifteen cents a pound with free buckets and pans throwed in. But how you're goin' to make a profit on it—the price hogs have gone to—is more than I can figure out. Accordin' to the six o'clock broadcast, top grade hogs brought eleven-fifty at Kansas City this morning."

I reminded her that I'd bought my hogs before the market went up, and told her I'd come out all right on my prices if she kept on getting me shortening orders the way she'd started out. Then I hurried home and got back to work. By the time Nick had finished dressing the three hogs and scrubbed down the slaughterhouse, I'd broken down the pork carcasses from the refrigerator, ready for cutting into chops and cutlets, side-meat slabs, spareribs, and scraps for making sausage.

It was past ten o'clock before we'd scrubbed the cutting room and gone to bed, but we were up, had eaten breakfast, and were back at work by four the next morning. In doing it we established a pattern that we seldom broke, for the hours from four to seven were the coolest of the day. Meat could safely be kept out of the refrigerator longer, remained firmer during the processing, and the work went faster.

The band saw with its semiautomatic carriage made cutting steaks, chops, and cutlets a simple matter, and the closer to the time of sale they were cut the fresher they would appear. As we broke down the carcasses of the hogs slaughtered the day before we hung the hams, shoulders, loins, and sidemeat slabs back in the refrigerator. Then Nick diced fatback for rendering while I boned leftovers for sausage. Boning a neck is rather tricky business for an inexpert butcher, but I soon discovered that it required little skill if I first cut it into inch-thick slices with the saw.

By eight o'clock we had the hog carcasses processed except for sawing chops and cutlets. But Effie had taken orders for so much shortening and sausage that we'd have to kill another beef and two more big hogs before we could fill the expected railroad order. We'd driven two enormous sows into the slaughterhouse chute when Nick again stepped in front of me and said, "I take now." There was a certain finality in his voice, as much as to say, "This is my end of the business. You stay out of it." From that time on I never went into the slaughterhouse except to show it to visitors when it wasn't in use, and I always found it scrubbed spotlessly clean.

I returned to the cutting room, put on my white coat and apron, and had started breaking down a beef forequarter when the McCook taxi clattered into the yard. Although I hadn't expected him so early, I knew it would be Mr. Donovan, so went out to meet him. He was cordial and friendly, but seemed embarrassed at having come to make the inspection. His only purpose, he told me, was to make sure the premises were clean enough and the refrigeration sufficient that there would be no danger of ptomaine. I told him I was glad he'd come, then led the way to the cutting room door and flung it open. For a moment or two he stood looking into the room with his mouth half open. Then he said, almost reverently, "Glory be . . ."

The inspection took no more than ten minutes, with Mr. Donovan exclaiming over almost everything I showed him. When we'd finished the round he told me, "I'm that sorry, lad! I should have told you right at the outset that you didn't need a fancy layout the likes of this. It's a shame you've gone to so much expense, and for only a four-months' business. Tell me, what ever will you do with it when the job is finished and done with? You can't move a refrigerator like that one, or a slaughterhouse that's cemented tight to the ground."

There was no reason for telling him that the whole setup had cost only a shade more than a thousand dollars, or that it looked as though the farmer business would considerably exceed the railroad contract, so I said, "If my luck holds out until Thanksgiving the way it's been running for the past month, I have an idea the setup will have paid for itself so I'm not going to worry about it."

After the inspection Mr. Donovan asked if I'd mind driving him to Danbury, Nebraska, ten miles down Beaver Valley and beyond the railroad washout. On the way he told me that the equipment and commissary train had arrived, and that the work train would bring the construction crew Sunday forenoon. He said the camp would be mobile, always at railhead as the track was reconstructed westward, and it was there that I would make my deliveries. As we neared Danbury I could see that the shipping pens were crowded with horses and mules. A dozen carloads of grading and track-laying equipment were lined up on the siding, and beyond them stood three kitchen and bakery cars.

At one of the kitchens Mr. Donovan introduced me to the chief steward, an enormous, good natured Irishman named Tim. When I asked if he could give me his meat order for the first three meals he told me, "Surest thing you know! The lads'll get here with their bellies as empty as their pockets, and for a couple o' days they'll eat a pound or more of meat at a meal. I'll be needing two hundred pound o' pork chops for Sunday dinner, the same o' beefsteak for supper, and for Monday's breakfast you'd best to make it a hundred and fifty pounds of pork chops and fifty o' sausage. Fetch it Sunday mornin' and bring a hundred pounds of lard for the bakers."

I was worried by the proportion of pork to beef, and by Tim's ordering chops and lard. But before I could say anything Mr. Donovan explained that the contract called for cutlets rather than chops, and shortening instead of lard. Then he said that my sausage was the tastiest he'd ever eaten, and suggested that Tim increase his order to a hundred pounds. Breathing more easily, I thanked Mr. Donovan for his kindness and Tim for his order, then got away as soon as I could.

23

My Boyhood Sweetheart

NICK and I were by no means expert meat cutters, but I'd used a band saw a good deal while working as a carpenter during the war, and the piece of equipment made by the old German machinist was a lifesaver for us. While Nick finished his slaughtering and scrubbing that Friday forenoon I broke down and processed the first beef carcass, going at it more like a sawyer than a meat cutter. I first sawed out what ordinarily would be the rib roasts, the thick shoulder clods and rolls, the loins, rumps, and rounds, then hung them back in the refrigerator to be sliced into steak. The brisket and lower half of the ribs I sawed into three-inch strips, cut the best portions into short-rib chunks, and boned the rest of the leftovers for stew meat, hamburger, and sausage scraps.

That afternoon and evening Nick rendered shortening while I processed the second beef, then weighed out and ground meat for four one-hundred-pound batches of sausage. Worried as I'd been about getting rid of fatback if we used heavy hogs, Nick needed all we had for shortening, so I had to use largely sidemeat for pork fat in the sausage. For each batch I weighed the salt and seasoning carefully and mixed it with the meat before grinding, but held back the bread and water for the second grinding, to be made just before the sausage was sold.

We quit at nine o'clock, to get our cleaning done and be in bed by ten, but were back on the job by four Saturday morning. Soon after sunrise George Miner came over with Jack at his heels. I told Nick I'd be busy with the shipping till evening, and that he was to go ahead with the rendering until he had six hundred pounds of shortening, even though he had to use partly leaf lard to make up the weight.

In little more than an hour, and with only a few arm or whistle signals from George, Jack rounded up every hog on the place and brought them into the sorting pens. Until then I had no idea what tremendous growth they'd made in the twenty-three days since their diet had been changed from silted alfalfa pasturage to all the corn they could hold. As near as George and I could estimate, the whole herd had gained about a third in weight; the smallest shoats taking on about twenty-five pounds apiece, and some of the biggest sows nearly a hundred.

If I'd shipped two days earlier, I'd have sent every one of those heavyweights to market, but considering the way shortening and sausage had sold to the farm trade I thought best to hold onto them, and George agreed with me. We cut out and turned back to pasture all hogs weighing under 210 pounds or over 285, together with any others that showed a blemish, were too fat for their length, or too runty for their age. By noon we'd culled them down to four pens of sixty hogs each; one lot weighing between 210 and 235 pounds, two that scaled between 235 and 260, and the fourth from 260 to 285. Allowing for a ten-pound shipping shrinkage, those divisions would hit the three highest priced grades squarely on the button.

Hauling fat hogs more than a few miles on a hot July day is hazardous business, but exercise, excitement, or crowding will overheat and kill them more quickly than hot sunshine. We loaded no wagon until they had all arrived, then assigned each man his place in line—those with the slowest horses at the front, and those with the fastest at the rear. With no more than an occasional word or signal from George, old Jack did the loading all by himself, and no hog tried to turn back, squealed, or took a hurried step. One after another the wagons were backed up to the loading chute; eight or nine hogs waddled aboard like portly commuters getting onto a streetcar, the tailgate was closed, and the wagon pulled away. In less than an hour all twenty-eight wagons were on the road to Oberlin, and they arrived well before train time without a single casualty.

Getting the hogs off the wagons and into the cars was no more difficult than loading them at home had been. I'd had one of the farmers from whom I bought nubbins take a load to Oberlin, divide it between the four decks of my cars, and see that the watering troughs in the shipping pens were filled. As wagons were backed to the chutes the thirsty hogs unloaded themselves, drank their fill, and with a little urging by old Jack trudged up the ramps and aboard the cars.

As soon as the bills of lading had been made out I wired my Omaha agent, giving him the car numbers. I asked him to wire me the results of the sale, to send a check for $4600 to the receiver of the Cedar Bluffs bank, and the balance of the net receipts to the Farmers National. I didn't wait for the train to pull out, but drove George and old Jack home, and was back in my white coat and apron by six o'clock.

Nick had completed rendering thirty buckets of shortening, processed the hogs he'd slaughtered the previous evening, and packed all the by-products. We stopped only to wolf down a cold supper, then set to work cutting steaks, chops, and cutlets. Since I was charging my farm trade twenty cents a pound it seemed only fair that they should have the best cuts, so we sorted out the center-cut pork chops and the sirloin, porterhouse, T-bone, and rib steaks. In packing cutlets for the railroad order we cut the ham and shoulder slices into roughly three pieces to the pound. Anything smaller, or that was more than a third bone, we threw into the sausage scraps. We didn't cut the steaks to any particular size, but trimmed away any excessive fat or bone, stripped out the heavy sinews, and threw aside for stew or hamburger any pieces that weren't cut reasonably straight across the grain of the meat. To make up the full two hundred pounds that had been ordered, we used mostly chuck and neck, then filled out with the poorer cuts from the rumps and rounds.

It was eleven o'clock before we finished, and midnight by the time we'd scrubbed up and gone to bed. At three-thirty Nick woke me by rattling the stove lids as he cooked breakfast. By four o'clock we were back on the job, the Ford engine that powered the grinder and saw backfiring in its indignation at being put to work so early. From our trimming we'd accumulated enough scraps for another hundred-pound batch of sausage, so I decided to make it—partly to teach Nick the formula, but more in hope that Effie might scare up more sausage business.

I had Nick weigh the various ingredients, mix the seasoning with the meat, grind it together to distribute the flavor, then add the water-soaked bread and regrind the batch with our finest cutting disk. While he added soaked bread and reground the batches I'd started the night before, I washed and dried tin pans, filled them with sausage, weighed and wrapped orders for the farm trade, and packed them away in the icebox. The last hundred pounds of sausage we packed in a tub for the railroad order, and by seven thirty I was on my way to Danbury.

I felt rather guilty about having held out all the best steaks and chops for my farm trade, and for having butchered mostly heavyweight sows when I'd told Mr. Donovan I planned to use bacon hogs. I got all over the guilty feeling two minutes after reaching the railroad camp. Mr. Donovan had gone back to Omaha, but Tim came to inspect the meat—and almost gloated over it. As he jabbed a finger into one piece after another he called to the head cook, "Come take a look at the meat we've got here. It's that tender you can poke a finger clean through it, and trimmed as good as you'd find at the best market."

When I unloaded the tub of sausage he turned the paper back and said, "So that's the sa'sage the boss was doin' all the talkin' about!" He scooped up a couple of ounces, sniffed it, and told the cook, "B'dad, there's a tasty smell about it. Fry up a bit and let's see what it's like."

He turned to me, pointed a thumb toward the next car, and said, "Take the lard yonder to the head baker. Get his tomorrow's order, and I'll have mine ready when you come back."

The baker was new on the job and didn't know how much shortening to order, so I told him I'd bring plenty every morning and leave as many full buckets as he had empty ones to return. When I went back to the kitchen Tim was as enthusiastic about the sausage as Mr. Donovan had been. His order for the next morning—and for most of the days until Thanksgiving—was for two hundred pounds of steak and one hundred and fifty pounds each of sausage and pork cutlets.

While I was making the delivery Nick finished grinding the hamburger, cutting stew beef, and scrubbing the refrigerator shelves and floor. Weighing and wrapping orders, cleaning equipment, washing utensils, and scrubbing the cutting room tables, sink, and floor kept us busy until nine forty five. Toward the end of the cleaning Nick watched the clock nervously, and the moment we finished he asked, "Okay, boss, I slaughter now?"

Thereafter he did his slaughtering between six and eight o'clock on weekday evenings, and from nine thirty Sunday mornings until the last customer had gone in the afternoon. Of the hundreds who came to the place, I doubt that more than two or three—except the men who helped us with our first two days of building—ever caught a glimpse of him. Most people spoke of him as The Eyetalian, but George called him The Prairie Dog, for a prairie dog dives into his hole at sight of a stranger. If we were alone Nick would work at the rendering vat or help me round up hogs, but if anyone turned in at the driveway he'd duck for cover. The cutting room was his burrow, but the slaughterhouse—completely hidden from the road, the dooryard, and the house—became his sanctuary.

That Sunday morning we rounded up a couple of hogs and a heifer for butchering, and I'd just changed into a clean white coat when customers began driving into the dooryard. From then on there was no letup. Fully a third of those who came had phoned in no order and were from surrounding townships. A good many were on their way to or from church, but others had probably come out of curiosity. By ten thirty the shop was so crowded that I could barely get through to the refrigerator.

Fortunately, George and Irene Miner came over when I was so swamped I hardly knew which way to turn. Irene was good at figures, her writing looked like a schoolteacher's and she knew everybody within twenty miles of Cedar Bluffs. When George saw the mess I was in he sent her to write charge slips for me, then called to the crowd, "Let's get outside and give the boy a chance to work. He can take care of you twice as fast if there's only two or three in here at a time."

With room to work, and the meat all cut and processed, I had no difficulty in taking care of the trade. If some of the folks were skeptical when they came, they got over it by the time George had shown them through the refrigerator and cutting room. Buckets and pans proved as popular with the women who hadn't placed orders as with those who had. I sold every spare pan of sausage and cracklings, every bucket of shortening and by-products, and could have sold double the number if I'd had them.

Although Effie had set my Sunday hours as being from ten to one, they didn't work out that way. It was past three o'clock when my last customer drove away, and there was then nothing left in the icebox except five hundred pounds of steaks, cutlets, and sausage that I'd held back for filling the railroad order next morning. I'd had dozens of compliments on the cleanliness of the shop, and everyone had been happy with the quality of the meat, the prices, and the charge accounts. Before leaving, nearly every man told me he'd have a hog, a calf, a cow, or a load of corn to turn in on his bill whenever I wanted it.

Nick and I hadn't eaten since three-thirty that morning, so when George and Irene left I started a fire and put a kettle of potatoes on to boil. After I'd washed up I put on a pot of coffee and whacked up a big batch of biscuits. While they were baking I set the big iron skillet on to get smoking hot, picked out the two biggest steaks in the icebox, laid them on the skillet to broil, and shouted for Nick to come and get it.

The pork and beef he'd dressed that forenoon wouldn't be chilled enough for cutting with the saw before morning, but we needed shortening for delivery with the railroad order. To have it cooled out and ready, Nick rendered that afternoon, stripping the leaf and fatback from the pork carcasses and suet from the beef. It was a one-man job, so I washed the dishes, posted the charge slips in the ledger, and brought the books up to date.

During the whole day I hadn't taken in a nickel, but the charge slips for the farm trade totaled $217.85, the railroad delivery had amounted to $112.50, the meat still in the icebox was worth $52.50, and the two cowhides would bring the total up to $390. As near as I could figure, the seven hogs we'd butchered had cost $90, the heifers $70, pans and buckets $11, ice $16, and bread, seasoning, etc., $3, leaving a profit of $200 before allowing for Nick's wages or investment writeoff. I had sense enough to know I'd never have another day so profitable, and that I'd probably lose 3 or 4 percent on my charge accounts. But I was reasonably sure that I hadn't set my prices too low, and that the venture wouldn't end in failure.

Effie always scolded at me for working too hard, but my roughest times were those when I had no work to do. Since the Wilsons left I'd been too busy to be lonely, and had little time for fretting and worrying. But when I finished my bookkeeping that Sunday afternoon I was stuck. No meat cutting could be done until the carcasses were thoroughly chilled, and there was nothing I could do to help Nick with the rendering. I got out the little Bible that had been my father's and tried to read, but couldn't keep my mind on it. When I found myself thinking about the folks back home I realized that I was lonely, and the one I thought most about was Edna Hudgins.

Edna's folks moved to Medford, the Massachusetts city where our family lived, while I was farming with my grandfather in Maine. She went to our church, sang in the choir with my sister Grace, and they became close friends. When I came home on my sixteenth birthday Grace fixed up a date for me, and Edna became my girl. When we were seventeen I asked her if she'd marry me when we were old enough, and she said she would, but our engagement broke up in a quarrel about the ring. It was a quarter-carat blue-white diamond, and it took me more than a year to save the twenty-five dollars that it cost.

Edna was graduating from high school in the class I'd have been in if I could have gone on from grammar school, and it seemed to me that it would be almost the same as having made the grade myself if my girl were there, wearing my engagement ring. For months I'd saved every penny that wasn't needed in the family, got the twenty-five dollars together just in time, and bought the ring the day before graduation. That evening I took Edna to choir practice, but didn't mention the ring until we were on the way back to her house. Then I showed it to her under an arc light at the corner of a little park, slipped it onto her finger, and told her I wanted her to wear it to the graduation exercises. For some reason, she didn't want to start wearing it until afterward. Having set my heart on it as I had, my feelings were hurt, and I didn't have any better sense than to tell her that if she didn't love me enough to wear my ring to the graduation she didn't love me enough to marry me.

I could never remember who said what after that, except that Edna told me not to get the idea that ring was a slave bracelet, stripped it off her finger, and held it out toward me. That was before I'd learned to control my temper, and it was the best lesson I ever had. I snatched the ring and threw it as hard as I could toward a shrubbery patch, then walked her home and left without either of us saying another word.

Next morning I was up before sunrise, and crawled through that shrubbery on my hands and knees for more than three hours, but I didn't find the ring. I wasn't man enough to go and tell her how ashamed and sorry I was for having made a fool of myself, so she wasn't my girl when I went away to work in the munitions plant during the war. But I didn't want any other girl. When I came home after the armistice it was discovered that I had diabetes and might live only six months, so it would have been senseless for me to try patching up our engagement then. I went to see her, though, before starting West. We didn't mention love or our engagement, or that I might not live very long, but we were both a bit chokey when I left.

In the nearly three years I'd been away I'd never written to Edna, nor she to me, but I couldn't get her out of my mind that evening. After trying to read but losing my place half a dozen times, I went to my trunk, got out paper and envelope, and wrote her a long letter. I'd never told the family about my losses, but had written often about being in the livestock trading business. I knew Grace would have told Edna of it, so started my letter by telling about the hogs I'd shipped on Saturday, of the flood having washed out the railroad, and that I'd been fortunate enough to get the meat contract for the reconstruction job. I wrote a couple of pages about fixing up the place to handle the meat business, and ended by telling her my health was so much improved that I was no longer on a diet—but not that I'd quit it without my doctor's knowledge.

When Nick finished the rendering we went to bed, but it was a long while before I could go to sleep, and most of that time I was building or tearing down air castles. Since I'd started eating three square meals of meat, potatoes, and biscuits a day I'd been able to work as hard and as many hours a day without tiring as any man I knew, including Nick. And even though I was deep in debt I was far from licked, for I'd made nearly two hundred dollars in that one day.

As I lay there in the dark I almost convinced myself that I was cured of diabetes, and that I'd not only be out of debt before the railroad contract was completed, but would have made back what I'd lost on the last stock Bob and I had fed. By that time land and livestock values should have become stable, so I'd buy the place and go back into the feeding business. I'd also continue my butcher business with the farmers and keep on with my livestock trading and shipping. That should make me one of the most prosperous men in Beaver Valley. I'd build a big house on the place, with an inside bathroom, and buy the best diamond ring in Kansas City. Then I'd go back to Medford and tell Edna how ashamed I was of myself for the way I'd acted, and ask her to forgive me and be my wife.

It was a beautiful air castle, but ordinary common sense made me tear it down. Every doctor I'd been to had told me there was no cure for diabetes. Even though I'd managed to outlive the specialists' prediction by a couple of years, I could never have a wife and family. Then too, the fabulous profits were no more than a pipe dream. I'd made a huge profit that day only because—with Effie's help and by throwing in a few tin pans and buckets—I'd unloaded every scrap of leftovers from the railroad contract on my neighbors. When the hot weather was past the farmers would do their own butchering, as they'd always done, and without a market for my leftovers I'd do well to break even on the railroad contract. As for the hogs on their way to market, I'd be lucky if they made five hundred dollars.

I have no idea how long I lay awake, but by four thirty Nick and I were at work in the cutting room, and at half past seven I left with the railroad order. Tim was still enthusiastic about the quality of the meat, gave me the same five-hundred-

pound order for the next morning, and the baker had four
empty shortening buckets to be replaced with full ones. On
my way home Effie yoo-hooed from the doorway of the telephone office. As I braked to a squealing stop she called, "Telegram for you. The station agent over to Oberlin phoned it not
more'n five minutes ago. It sure sounds like good news."

It was good news. The wire was from my Omaha agent, and
read: "CONGRATULATIONS THREE LOTS TOPPED
MARKET NET PROCEEDS SIXTY-THREE FIFTY-SEVEN
EIGHTY-FIVE." For a moment I couldn't comprehend it, for
that was within $215 of what I'd paid for all the hogs I'd
bought, and I still had 314 in the pasture.

Emotionally, I must have been put together backward. I'd
taken it fairly well when the bottom dropped out of the livestock market in December, when the flood cleaned us out, and
when the judge ruled against me on the partnership, but when
I read that telegram my nerves went all haywire for a few seconds. My knees felt wobbly, my hands trembled, and I
couldn't keep tears from coming into my eyes.

Some people said that Effie Simons was coarse and rough,
but that was because they didn't know her very well. She understood what ailed me instantly, and a lot better than I could
have explained it. There were half a dozen men on the street,
and their attention had been attracted when she called out
that there was a telegram for me. But before anyone had a
chance to notice that I was having trouble she stepped back
inside her office and pulled me with her.

Out of sight from the street, she hugged me against her, but
only for a second. If it had been longer I'd have broken down
and blubbered like a baby, but she knew that too, turned me
loose, and gave me a good solid slap on the back. "The kind of
lickin's you've run into this past year are mighty tough for a
kid your age to take," she told me, "and don't forget that the
folks hereabouts know it. That's why some of us are so scared
you've gone and set your meat prices way too cheap."

That slap on the back pulled me together as nothing else

could have. "Without the farm trade, I'd be licked again," I told her. "But if I can hold onto it and get rid of all my leftovers I can make a good profit at these prices."

"You don't need to fret about the farm trade," she told me. "As long as you give the folks the kind of stuff you've turned out so far, along with the price and credit and free pans and buckets, you couldn't drive 'em away. I don't suppose you've made sweethearts out of the butchers over to McCook and Oberlin, but you've sure made a heap of friends up and down this valley and on both divides. Now you trot along home and give me a chance to get line calls out or it'll be noontime before I have today's orders ready for you."

I didn't let myself build any more air castles, but I've seldom been happier than when I left Effie's office. Thanks to George Miner's hog cycle theory, my only cost for enough pork to fill the railroad contract and an equal amount of farm business would be for corn to feed the hogs still in my pasture. If, as Effie believed it would, my farm trade held up, there seemed a reasonably good chance that I might work my way out of debt by the end of the year.

From that day our butcher business settled into a routine. Nick and I were up at four o'clock, by seven I pulled away with the railroad delivery, and by eight I was back with Effie's sheaf of farm orders. Some days I worked in the cutting room with Nick until noon, and sometimes for only a couple of hours, depending on the size of the orders. Then I had the rest of the day to take care of my trading business, haul ice, take hides to the buyer at McCook and bring back our express shipments, or run other necessary errands. I was always home in time to have supper on the table at five thirty, and at six Nick retired to the slaughterhouse to replenish our meat supply. While waiting for customers to pick up their orders I posted the books, and by nine o'clock we were in our bunks.

Seldom more than a dozen farmers came of an evening, each picking up packages for his neighbors. But Sundays were a different matter. Every town along Beaver Valley had its own little nonsectarian church, but people who attended a church of any particular denomination had to drive to McCook or Oberlin. Then too, farm people like to visit with their neighbors, and in western Kansas anyone living within ten miles is a neighbor, but those who went to separate churches had no meeting place to gather and visit. My place, being on the McCook-Oberlin road, was easy for those going to church in either city to drive past, and soon became the meeting and visiting place for not only churchgoers but the whole community.

They'd begin arriving before ten o'clock, and it was often after four when the last one drove away. Few stayed more than an hour, but whenever I found a chance to glance outside, the yard was full of flivvers, carriages, buckboards, and spring wagons. The men always gathered in a single group by the windmill to discuss crops, the reasons for the depressed grain and livestock markets, and the sins of the government.

The women never gathered in a single group, but in knots of four or five, or visited with one another in flivvers and carriages—and it might be that a little gossip was exchanged. But few wives went home without a bucket of shortening, a pan of sausage, or a bundle of meat the size of a watermelon. We got few advance orders for Sundays. To get ready for the big rush Nick and I scaled out and wrapped all such items as stew beef, hamburger, shortribs, and sidemeat in five-pound packages, and no farmer's wife asked to have one broken.

After the first week we cut few steaks and chops ahead, for most of the women preferred to select a particular round, loin, ham, or set of ribs from the refrigerator, tell me how thick they liked the slices, and watch as I cut them with the saw. I never could have handled so much cut-to-order business if Irene and George Miner hadn't "happened over" every Sunday; she to help with the wrapping and billing, and he to fetch and carry between the saw and refrigerator.

The railroad business soon settled down to about fifty pounds of shortening and five hundred of meat a day. Although slightly less in poundage, the farm trade nearly equalled the railroad business in dollars, and by occasionally switching from tin pans and buckets to enamelware kettles and bowls I had no trouble in selling every scrap of leftovers and by-products. Then too, the meat business helped my livestock trading. As I made my trading rounds, one man after another would say, "How about taking this hog (or it might be a calf, cow, or steer) in on my meat bill? I'll fetch it down the next time I come for meat, and you can credit me with whatever's right."

I never made a profit on those animals, but allowed within a cent a pound of the latest radio quotation. When I bought mortgaged stock from a customer he always had me take the amount of his bill out of the percentage the bank would allow me to pay him in cash. From August 7 until Thanksgiving, there was never a Saturday when I didn't ship at least one carload of stock, and from among the cattle I bought I always picked out the best heifers for butchering.

Although I made a fair profit on all but two or three of the carloads I shipped that fall, I made money faster than ever before or since in my life on a couple of carloads that I didn't ship. One Saturday in mid-October I drove two carloads of fat steers to Oberlin. When I got them there the largest shipping pens were filled with sheep and lambs, the gate between them was open, and two double-decked stock cars were spotted on the siding. There were still a couple of hours till train time, but a man with two teen-aged boys and four nondescript dogs was trying unsuccessfully to drive the sheep into the cars. Though obviously a farmer, the man was a stranger to me, and it was evident that he was no stockman. I wanted to be friendly, so went over to tell him that the easy way to load sheep was to tie a bleating lamb at the far end of each deck, then stand aside to close the doors when the curious ewes went in to investigate.

I should have known better, because the man was angry, but I climbed onto the gate, waited for a lull in his swearing, and called, "Can I lend you a hand, mister?"

He glared up at me and shouted, "You tend to your own business and leave me tend to mine! Now get out of here!"

I got out, penned and watered the steers, and went uptown for supper. On the way back an hour later I heard what sounded like a riot at the shipping pens. Dogs were barking wildly, sheep bleating in terror, men hooting, and above the bedlam a booming voice yelling curses insanely.

When I reached the siding the fence around the sheep pens was crowded with other traders and stockmen—laughing, hooting, and enjoying the ill-tempered stranger's predicament. The pens looked like a two-ring circus in the midst of the grand finale. In each of them bewildered, frightened sheep were racing in a circle, two snarling dogs snapping at their heels while a frustrated boy shrieked wildly and flailed them with a bullwhip. The man, his face purple with rage, stood in the gateway between the pens like a tormented bull at bay. Just as I climbed onto the fence he looked up and shouted, "Who'll give me a bid on these blasted sheep?"

I had no idea as to the value of sheep, but he was glaring right into my face and I wanted to start the bidding plenty low, so I called out, "Four dollars a head!"

"Sold!" he bellowed.

In a split second another trader shouted, "Five dollars a head."

"SOLD!" I yelled, right in unison with the irate man in the gateway. He tried his best to run a bluff that he'd never sold to me, but there were too many witnesses present, and I had a lot of good friends among them.

Given ten minutes of quiet, the sheep forgot their panic and loaded easily. The count was 258, and though I'd been a sheep owner for less than two seconds my profit was a good one. On the way home I tried to figure out in my head the amount a man would make in an eight-hour day at $129 a second, but lost track after passing three million.

24

Dr. DeMay's Discovery

FROM the time I quit my diet and went onto beefsteak, potatoes, and hot biscuits three times a day I'd been putting on weight at about the same rate as the hogs in my pasture. I'd never once gone to see Dr. DeMay, and might have stayed away months longer if it hadn't been for the sheep deal and so few people coming to pick up meat packages on weekday evenings.

Nick always retreated to his sanctuary right after supper and never came out until he was sure there'd be no more customers. That left me alone from six till eight thirty with only a few interruptions when someone came for packages. I'd gradually fallen into the habit of writing to Edna every evening, and she'd always answered. Ours weren't love letters—just more or less visiting on paper—but each one added fuel to my rekindled affection for her. I'd been careful to keep it from showing in my letters, but by mid-October I longed for her more than anything I'd ever wanted in my life.

Tuesdays were my paydays. The mail always brought my weekly meat check from the railroad and my agent's check for the livestock I'd shipped on Saturday. In August I'd paid off my loan to the Farmers National and my hog mortgage to the receiver of the Cedar Bluffs bank. Since then I'd been whittling away at my debt by turning over to him each Tuesday the balance of my account in excess of three thousand dollars.

The reduction had been slow, however, for the accounts on my books had increased from week to week, and the payments had all been in nubbin corn or livestock of almost every type and description. It ranged from weanling calves and 50-pound pigs to 400-pound sows and 1000-pound dry cows. The only thing I could do was to put them in the pasture, feed them, and let them accumulate until I had enough of some particular type to ship a carload—and the market slipped steadily downward.

A few days after I sold my two carloads of bacon hogs at the end of July the market fell off sharply. By the end of September hog prices had dropped four dollars a hundred, but I'd been hurt very little by it. Almost invariably, it was shoats or overweight sows that were turned in on the meat accounts. I used the sows for butchering, so had no shipping expense on them, and the shoats I turned into the pasture. For every sixty I took in, I shipped out a carload that had grown from shoats to bacon hogs since I bought them.

By early September I'd taken in more nubbin corn than my hogs could eat, so put sixty good steers in the feed lot. They'd done extremely well and were the ones I'd been shipping when I became a sheep owner for two seconds. The sheep windfall was $258, the steers made a profit of nearly $400, my railroad business that week was larger than usual, and when the checks came in on Tuesday I was able to take the first big slice off my debt.

On the fifteenth of October George Miner helped me round up, inventory, and set a value on every head of livestock in my pasture. The first thing after supper I went over the accounts on my books, adding them up and making allowances for any that I had the least doubt of collecting. To my amazement, I found that my assets, conservatively valued, were within approximately eighteen hundred dollars of my debts. And there were still six weeks until the end of the railroad contract. Unless there was another flood or the place burned down, I was certain to be out of debt before the end of the year.

I was so happy that I couldn't keep it to myself, and that evening I wrote Edna a dozen pages, telling her about all my financial ups and downs since coming to Kansas. I told her of my big hauling, trading, and feeding profits, and of losing everything when the livestock market collapsed in the fall of 1920; of gaining back during the winter and spring of 1921, only to be cleaned out by the flood in June; of thinking I was hopelessly ruined when the court ruled that I was liable for Bob's debts; and about the streak of good luck I'd been riding ever since. I wound the letter up by bragging that I'd made more than a thousand dollars in the past week, would be completely out of debt before Thanksgiving, had gained sixty pounds, and was never healthier in my life. Then I read the letter over, threw it in the stove, and set a match to it.

The next morning I saved the first specimen after getting up—the one doctors always wanted for testing—took it with me when I made the railroad delivery, and drove straight to McCook. I was waiting outside Dr. DeMay's office when he arrived, but he didn't recognize me until I spoke, and then seemed as startled as if he'd seen a ghost. For more than a minute he stood looking me over from head to foot and back again. "Well, son," he said at last, "I've been wondering why you quit me, but I don't wonder any more. Whoever your physician is now, don't leave him. I never saw anything like it in my life."

He looked even more astonished when I told him that I hadn't been to any other doctor, and that I'd been living on beefsteak, potatoes, and hot biscuits for three months. "Hmff!" the old doctor snorted. "There's something here that doesn't gee. Did you bring along a specimen?"

"Yes, sir," I told him, "the first one this morning."

He snatched the bottle from me and ran up the stairs to his

office as though he were sixteen instead of in his sixties, calling back over his shoulder, "This is the most curious thing I've heard of in medical practice. Take a chair by my desk while I run a couple of tests. If anybody else comes, tell 'em to wait outside."

For twenty minutes the only sounds were the tinkle of glass or an occasional snort from the doctor's laboratory room. He didn't say a word when he came out, but sat down at the desk and thumbed back through the book in which he'd always made notes after testing my specimens. Suddenly he whirled his swivel-chair around and began firing questions at me as though he were a lawyer cross-examining a key witness in a murder trial. After a dozen or more that I don't remember, he asked, "How many analyses of your urine had been made before the first one in which sugar was discovered?"

"None," I told him. "There was never anything wrong with me before that except a leaky heart and a few broken bones."

"How many carbuncles did you have last spring?"

"Thirty-nine," I said.

He ran a finger under an entry in the journal and said, "Kind of petered out toward the end, didn't they?"

"Yes, sir," I said. "The last few were only cat boils."

He hummed as if pleased with the answer and said, "Now tell me, how much have you been worrying of late?"

"None," I said with a grin. "I haven't had much to worry about for the past couple of months."

A smile flickered at the corners of his mouth and he said, "So I hear," then drew his brows together in a frown and asked, "Didn't you think your health was something to worry about . . . after quitting your diet without medical advice?"

"I haven't had much time for worrying since then," I told him. "Besides, I've gained nearly a pound a day and never felt better or stronger in my life."

Dr. DeMay sat for a minute, staring down at his desk and tapping it with a stubby forefinger, then looked up and told me, "As I said before, this is the most curious case I've come across in medical practice. There isn't one iota's variation in the sugar content of the specimen I just tested and the one you brought me when you first came in here two years ago."

For another minute the white-thatched doctor sat tapping his desk, then swung toward me and rested his elbows on his knees. "Within the past few months a synthetic insulin has been developed and is now in the experimental stage," he told me. "A little of it injected into the blood stream has been found to give temporary relief from diabetes—retarding the breakdown of proteins and enabling the body to utilize fats and sugars—but there's no known cure for the disease and I never heard of its curing itself. Still and all, you've made a miraculous recovery—that is, if you were ever in bad enough shape to justify that Boston prognosis, and the more I think about it the more I doubt it.

"Now you understand, I'm no specialist at diabetes, and what I'm going to tell you is simply a country doctor's opinion, but it's the only way I can make sense or reason out of this thing. First off, though I don't hold too much with Christian Science, I do believe that a lot of physical ills are brought on and aggravated by state of mind. When you first came to me you'd just made a lot of money hauling wheat, hadn't you, and didn't have a worry in the world—outside of the sentence those Boston specialists had dished out to you?"

"That's right," I said.

"Your specimen showed little more than a trace of sugar then, and remained about the same until last December, then the content doubled. Wasn't that when the livestock market broke, and from then till after the time you saw me in June weren't you worrying yourself about half sick?"

"I had plenty to worry about," I told him.

"Now, when did you quit worrying," he asked, "before or after you quit your diet?"

"At about the same time," I said.

"Thought so! I'm not saying there's any connection, but there just might be. And there's another 'might be.' When I was a boy the old-time country doctors used to say a carbuncle was worth ten dollars to a man—boiled the poison out of his system and purified his blood. I never found scientific proof of it, but those oldtimers got results with lots of remedies that have never been approved by modern science. If there's anything to the theory, your blood sure got a purging at about the time of the flood. I'm not saying that had anything to do with your improvement, but I'm not ruling it out either.

"Then there's a third possibility, and that's the one I'm inclined towards. Though I've never run into a case, there is such a thing as incipient diabetes. As I recall, it has all the symptoms of true diabetes, but is more a malfunction than a disease. In true diabetes the pancreas fails to secrete insulin, the substance that enables the human body to absorb and make use of fats and sugars. In incipient diabetes the insulin is secreted, the body absorbs and utilizes fats in the normal manner, but just as the valve in your heart malfunctions to let a little blood past, the kidneys . . ."

Dr. DeMay broke off in mid-sentence, clasped both hands behind his head, and sat gazing at the ceiling for two or three minutes. Then, as though a spring had suddenly been released, he sprang to his feet and demanded, "Were you in the war?"

"No, sir, I was rejected because of a leaky heart," I said.

"What were you doing when your health failed?" he snapped.

"I was a carpenter at a munitions plant when I began losing weight," I told him, "but I wasn't really sick."

"How much did you lose?"

"About sixty pounds."

"In how short a time?"

"About four months."

The old doctor clasped his hands across his rotund belly and paced back and forth across the little office. "Did you eat three good square meals a day?" he asked.

"Not always. The summer of 1918 was hot in Delaware, and I wasn't always hungry at mealtime."

"Get in much overtime?"

"Quite a bit," I told him. "I wanted to save as much money as I could while the big pay lasted."

Dr. DeMay stopped pacing, whirled, and demanded sharply, "How many days a week were you working?"

"Seven."

"How many hours a week?"

"Sometimes as few as seventy, and occasionally ninety. Usually about eighty-four."

"Now, we're getting somewhere!" he sang out. "Exhaustion! Exhaustion and malnutrition! There's our answer!"

Dr. DeMay sat down again, leaned forward, and told me, "Somewhere in the back of my head I had a recollection that incipient diabetes was the result of exhaustion and malnutrition, but was stumped for any authority until I remembered a lecture I attended during my internship. This lecturer—and I can't tell you who he was now—argued that when the system is debilitated, as by exhaustion or malnutrition, the tissues of the kidneys in some individuals have a tendency to become flaccid, permitting sugar to seep past. I don't know that his theory was ever proved, but it sounds reasonable, and if there's anything to it, it might explain your case.

"A boy nineteen years of age working eighty to ninety hours a week at carpentry would be constantly on the verge of exhaustion, particularly if he was starving himself so as to save every dollar he could lay his hands on. My guess is that you never had true diabetes, but abused your kidneys until the tissues became flabby enough to leak sugar by the gram, producing symptoms of the true disease at a dangerously advanced stage. Your loss of weight could have been as attributable to malnutrition as to loss of sugar, probably more so."

"I hope you're right," I told him, "but I haven't been overworking or starving myself since I came to Kansas, and I'm still passing sugar. Why would that be?"

"Hmmf! Hmmf!" he snorted irritably. "From the day you first came to me, I've never seen you when you weren't tearing into something or other as if you were fighting fire, and that diet you were on kept you undernourished all the while. No wonder you couldn't gain a pound on it. Furthermore, you can't expect vital organs to function perfectly after they've been badly abused. I'll be surprised if you don't pass a little sugar for the rest of your days. Now here's what I want you to do for me: get out of here and run. I don't care where or how fast, but don't come back until you're plumb tuckered out."

Dr. DeMay was waiting for me when I came back two hours later, and seemed delighted that I was so fagged I could hardly keep my balance. He took my blood pressure and listened to my heart and lungs with a stethoscope, then told me, "Well, that didn't do you any harm. Can't see for the life of me why the Army turned you down for a leaky heart. There's a slight regurgitation there, but there isn't one man in forty that has a heart muscle with the strength of that one. And if you don't abuse those lungs they'll carry you a long, long ways. Now go in the back room there and leave me a specimen. I'll be surprised if it doesn't have a tale to tell."

I'd done as he told me, and had been waiting beside his desk five or six minutes when I heard him chuckling in the back room. After another minute or two he came out, still chuckling, sat down, and slapped me on the knee. "Just as I expected," he told me. "Highest sugar content since I've been treating you."

He leaned forward, looked me full in the eyes, and said, "I'd like to tell you right now that—in my opinion, you understand—you're no more likely to die of diabetes than I am, but before I do it I want to make one more experiment. This next week I want you to work just as hard as you worked last week. For the first three days you're to stick rigidly to the diet the Boston specialists put you on. For the last three you're to eat as you have been for the past three months. I'm going to give you half a dozen large sample bottles in mailing tubes, and I want you to mail me your entire first specimen every morning. Then, today a week, I want you back here after so completely exhausting yourself that you can barely make it up the stairs. Now run along and let me get to work. I've got forty calls to make before bedtime."

One of the most difficult things I ever had to do was to get out of McCook without first sending telegrams off to Edna and the folks back home, telling them it had all been a mistake, that I'd never really had diabetes, and that my chances of living to old age were fully as good as the average man's. But it would have been senseless to do anything of the kind before Dr. DeMay was thoroughly satisfied that his diagnosis was correct. To avoid temptation I stayed in McCook only long enough to buy a dozen cans of salmon, a gallon of sauerkraut, and five pounds of gluten flour. Then I headed for Cedar Bluffs as fast as I could drive.

I didn't even tell Effie or the Miners what Dr. DeMay believed he had discovered, but pitched into the work as hard as I could go. The last heifer Nick had butchered was one of the first I'd bought. She'd been on a corn and alfalfa diet only ten weeks but had gained nearly two hundred pounds. The beef from any animal fattened that rapidly is bound to be as tender and juicy as squab. When I started cutting the forequarters that afternoon I noticed that the fat was white as Carrara marble, and the lean looked as though it were flecked with snowflakes, a sure sign of tenderness and delicious flavor.

Probably because I couldn't keep the folks at home out of my mind, I got the idea of sending them one of the loins from that heifer. The weather was cool, perishable express should reach Boston in three days, and there was little risk that a large piece of prechilled meat would spoil in that length of time. I wrapped the thirty-pound loin in clean, loosely woven burlap, tagged it with my mother's name and address, raced back to McCook, and got it aboard the eastbound express train.

That evening I wrote to Edna but found it hard to hold

back the news I wanted most to tell her. To keep from it I wrote nearly two pages about George Miner and Effie Simons, saying that George had been a second father to me and that Effie, old enough to be my mother, had taken me under her wing as if I were an orphan chick. Then I told her about my having been in the cattle and hog feeding business, and that I'd gone somewhat in debt when the livestock market broke, but that with advice and help from George and Effie I was getting myself pulled out of the hole. To fill out the page I wrote that I'd expressed home the beef loin, and asked if she'd drop by and tell my mother that the outside of the piece might become slimy and ill-smelling in shipment, but to trim away an inch all around and the rest would be as sweet and tender as a ripe pear. To avoid mentioning love, I closed my letter, "Ever and ever, Ralph."

The morning I went back to Dr. DeMay I exhausted myself so completely by running that I was staggering when I reached his office. He tested and retested a sample of my urine, then slouched down into his big leather swivel-chair, clasped his hands behind his head, and rocked contentedly.

"Son," he told me, "I've seen many a time when there was a blizzard blowing and I had to make a dozen calls way out on the divides to treat nothing more serious than bellyaches, and knew I'd be lucky to collect two dollars for the day's work. Those times a country doctor feels like cussing himself for having gone into the medical profession, but it takes only one case like yours to make up for all the rest of it, over and over again. I'm only a general practitioner, and from a school those Boston specialists would probably look down their noses at, but I'd stake my life that they were as wrong in their diagnosis as in their prognosis that you could live no more than six months.

"You have incipient diabetes, and probably always will have, but I predict that you'll live to dandle many a grandbaby on your knee. Go on home and live a normal life like any other man, but don't ever forget this: the good God that gave you that body gave you the responsibility of caring for it. No reasonable amount of work will hurt you so long as you balance it with proper nourishment and rest, but another abusing such as you gave yourself during the war could be fatal. You'll have to avoid exhaustion, and for the rest of your life you should never go more than three months without a thorough physical examination. Now run along and take care of yourself. Or better still, get a good wife to take care of you. You're at the stage in life where you ought to have a home and family."

"That's just what I intend to do," I told him, thanked him for all he'd done for me, and ran down the stairs two at a time. I kept right on running to the depot, intending to send telegrams to Edna and my mother. I had the one to Edna half written when I changed my mind. Her letters had never been more than friendly, and our engagement had been broken because I got hot-headed and threw the ring away, not because my health had failed. I'd been away nearly three years, and the chances were ten to one that she was in love with someone else if not already engaged to him. Before I made a complete jackass of myself, I'd better write my sister Grace and find out how matters stood.

When I got home there were two letters in the mailbox: a thick one from my mother and a thin one from Edna. I ripped the envelope off the thin one and found the letter almost formal, the way people sometimes talk when they're self-conscious.

Edna started her letter by telling me she'd been up to my mother's house, that everyone was well, and that the loin of beef had arrived safely. As I had anticipated, it required only a little trimming to remove the shipping damage. My mother had insisted that she take home a big steak, and her parents agreed with her that I was to be congratulated for producing such fine beef. I was most fortunate to have such loyal friends as Mr. Miner and Mrs. Simons. She was glad I'd found a second father in Mr. Miner, and knew how gratified I must be at having recovered from my financial reverses. After another paragraph or two about happenings at the church she closed her letter, as always, "Sincerely, Edna."

I was so disappointed that I stuffed both letters into my pocket, and for the rest of the day I kept too busy to think about anything but the work I was doing. Nick had gone to the slaughterhouse and I'd finished washing the supper dishes before I thought of my mother's letter again, sat down on the back steps, and opened it. *"Dear Son,"* she wrote:

I have a shameful confession to make. This afternoon the expressman rapped at my back door, saying he had a shipment of meat addressed to me from Kansas, but that it had spoiled in transit. From where I stood I could see that the burlap was slimy, and the stench was appalling. I marched straight out to the garbage can, took the cover off, and said, "You may deliver it right in there if you will."

He hadn't been gone twenty minutes when Edna came—the first time she's been to our house since she graduated from high school. She said you'd written her that you had sent home a loin of beef, and that the outside might become slightly tainted in shipment, making a little trimming necessary. I told her the meat had arrived, but in a hopelessly putrid condition, and where I'd had the expressman deliver it.

Son, I have never seen such unquestioning confidence and loyalty in my life. She told me firmly, but without a trace of rudeness, "I can't believe he'd have sent it, or written as he did, unless he'd been sure it would come through all right. Do you mind if I look at it, and would you lend me a butcher knife?"

Of course, I wouldn't let her do such a thing alone, so when I couldn't persuade her against it we hauled the ill-smelling bundle out of the garbage can, unwrapped it, and found—just as you expected—that only the surface was the least bit spoiled.

In the next two or three paragraphs Mother told how good the meat was, which of the neighbors she'd given steaks from

it, and that she'd insisted upon Edna's taking home a big sirloin. Then she wrote, "*I'm sure that her affection for you has
never wavered since you were childhood sweethearts, and
Gracie tells me that she has never had another steady beau. I
pray God for the day when your health has improved enough
that you can again ask her to be your wife.*"

I don't remember just what I said to Edna in the letter I
wrote her that evening—and we've lost it somewhere during
the forty-odd years we've been married—but it did the job I
wanted it to do. Her only objection was that she didn't want
to bring up our children in Beaver Valley, but in a city with
fine schools and other cultural advantages.

I wanted her so much that I'd have gone anywhere or done
anything to make her happy, but the West and horses and cattle had been in my blood from boyhood, and I didn't want the
city to be Boston. I tried to write it to her, but couldn't find a
way to put it on paper without seeming to be bossy, so drove
to McCook and called her on long distance telephone. She understood perfectly, and we compromised on Kansas City, the
gateway between East and West, and settled on January 25,
1922, as our wedding day.

25

The End of My Run

WITH the date set, I began drawing the reins tighter into my hands, as any horseman does when nearing the end of his run. I started by putting a little pressure on the slowest of my meat customers, asking them to turn in whatever livestock was necessary to square their accounts. Then, by shipping out a carload of fat heifers, one of mixed cattle, and two of bacon hogs, I cut my pasture stock down to what I'd need for butchering until the end of the railroad contract. The check for the shipment came in on the fifteenth of November and, using all but two hundred dollars of my trading account, I paid off the last dime of my debt.

I'd known since late October that I had enough accounts on my books and livestock in my pasture to get me entirely out of the hole, and planned to have a celebration dinner for the Miners and Simonses on the day I paid off my debt. Then, when Dr. DeMay made his discovery and Edna wrote that she'd marry me, I thought it would be best to celebrate all my good fortune at one time, so I kept quiet although I wanted to shout the news to everyone.

As soon as I'd made my final payment to the receiver of the

Cedar Bluffs bank I crossed the street to the telephone office, and found Effie in a decidedly testy mood. "Do you think you could find somebody to tend the switchboard this evening so you could get away early?" I asked.

She looked perplexed, frowned, and told me, "Reckon I prob'ly could, but I sure don't aim to. What's goin' on anyways, a shivaree? Whatever it is, it can't amount to a tinker or I'd of heard somethin' about it over the wires."

"You couldn't have heard about this," I said, "because I'm the only one who knows about it."

"Hmmfff!" she sniffed, "then I don't reckon it amounts to enough to lose sleep over. What is it?"

"Nothing much," I said. "I was planning to have a little dinner party over at the Keystone Hotel for a half a dozen of my best friends, and hoped you and Guy could be there."

Effie got over her belligerency in a hurry, but asked, "Why don't you wait till Sunday night when I'll be closin' the switchboard early anyways, and when everybody won't be wore out with a day's work? Why in the name of common sense do you want to have a party in the middle of a week?"

"Because I thought this would be a good day for celebrating," I said. "Ten minutes ago I paid off the last dime of my . . ."

Before I could finish the sentence Effie came off her chair like a charging grizzly, both arms spread wide, and wailing, "God love you, boy!"

After she'd nearly smothered me, she held me at arm's length with one hand, wiped tears off her cheeks with the back of the other, and told me, "I knew all the time you could do it, but I never in this wide world guessed you could do it this soon."

"It would have taken me forever if it hadn't been for the help that you and George Miner gave me," I said.

"Fiddlesticks!" she scoffed. "I didn't do nothin' but put out a few line calls and take down some orders, and you've more'n made up for that in meat you fetched up here."

"Don't try to feed me that stuff," I told her. "If you'd let me price leftovers the way I intended to I'd never have got out of the hole, and if you hadn't given me the idea of selling shortening and sausage in buckets and pans I'd have been buried under tons of fatback months ago." Then I cupped a hand around the back of her neck, drew her to me, and kissed her full on the mouth.

Effie didn't do any resisting until I'd planted a good solid smack, then she pulled away and sputtered, "My Land o' Goshen, what would folks think if somebody was to happen past and see us carryin' on like a pair of moon-struck sweethearts?" As she backed away a step or two she put both hands to her head and scolded, "You've gone and rumpled my hair up till it feels like a magpie's nest, and my curlin' tongs are over to the house, and Guy won't be back from his mail route for another hour. Look, Bud, run over and fetch 'em for me, will you, or I won't look fit to show my head at a dog fight this evenin', leave alone a dinner party in the Keystone Hotel. They're in the top right-hand drawer of the bedroom dresser, wrapped up in a piece of white tissue paper. And fetch along the tall chimbly off'n the lamp in the kitchen; the ones on both these office lamps are so short they leave the end of the tongs touch the wick flame and get all sooted up."

When I got back with the chimney and tongs Effie was talking to Mrs. Lincoln on the phone, saying she had to attend a dinner party at McCook that evening, and asking if Lucy would come and tend the switchboard for her. She cupped a hand over the mouthpiece, turned her head, and told me in a stage whisper, "Leave 'em right there on the lamp table, Bud. What time did you say the party was goin' to commence?"

I hadn't said, or thought about it, but whispered back, "Seven o'clock," and tiptoed out.

I'd have liked to include Nick in the party, but knew that going would be torture for him, so I stopped at home just long enough to tell him the good news and what I was planning for a celebration, then drove on to the Miner's.

I found George on the sunny side of the granary, sorting out the best ears from a freshly harvested load of corn, braiding the husks together, and hanging them up to dry for seed. "How'd you make out with them four carloads you shipped Saturday?" he called as I climbed out of the Maxwell.

"The best I ever made out with any shipment in my life," I called back.

"George looked at me in a puzzled, unbelieving way and said, "By jiggers, I didn't think that stuff you shipped was so fancy; there must'a been somethin' goin' on in the livestock market that I ain't heard about."

As I walked toward him I took from my pocket the receipt-in-full the bank receiver had given me, unfolded it, and said, "I doubt it, but here's what I got out of that shipment," then held the paper out to him.

Still with a puzzled expression, George glanced down at the receipt, then looked up at me with his eyes shining. He held out a hand to shake, squeezed mine so hard it hurt, and told me, "I never misdoubted you could do it, son, but I reckoned—times bein' as hard as what they are now—it would take you leastways four or five years."

"It would have taken me half a lifetime if it hadn't been for your advice and the help Irene and Effie have given me," I told him.

George picked up a couple of corn ears, looked down at them as he started braiding the husks together, and said slowly. "I ain't takin' a thing away from the girls, but I don't recollect givin' you no advice. Of late years I've been kind of leery 'bout passin' it out. If it's good the folks that take it generally always come to believe the notion was theirs in the first place, but if it turns out to be wrong they never forget where it come from, and it can stir up hard feelin's. Of course, there's been times when I've sort of honed to stick my finger into somebody else's business, but . . ."

George broke off quickly, looked up at me, and asked, "Now ain't you proud you took the trail you did when the judgment went ag'in you?"

"I haven't anything to be proud about," I told him. "I took that trail only because I thought it would be better business than taking bankruptcy."

"Then you can leave the proud end of it to me," he said, "but what you done will be a comfort to you as long as you live. You know, son, them heifers I held back when I sold the herd have been doin' awful good, and it still ain't too late in the fall to breed 'em for summer calves. What you aimin' to get into when the railroad contract peters out on you? With the bank closed and all, there won't be enough shippin' business in this valley to keep you out of mischief, and I don't reckon you want to stay in the butcher business the rest of your life."

"No, I said, "I'll have to find me another horse of a different color to ride from now on, and if you're willing we might talk about it this evening. I'm going to have a little celebration dinner over at the Keystone Hotel at about seven o'clock, and I'd sure like it if you and Irene would come."

"We'd be there if we had to crawl on our hands and knees," he told me, "and you and I'll talk some more about them heifers. The way the market's been actin' of late I wouldn't misdoubt me this might be a pretty good time for a young man to start buildin' a breedin'-stock herd, so's't the new crop of young bulls would be ready to sell in about three years."

As he spoke, George hung up the hank of ears he'd just braided together, then reached for his jacket and said, "If that dinner's goin' to commence at seven o'clock I'd best to make an early start on my chores; I ain't as spry as what I used to be a few years back."

He walked to the Maxwell with me, and Irene came out onto the porch to wave as I drove out of the dooryard. Above the backfiring of the engine I heard George call to her, "Get your glad rags on, old girl; the boy's havin' a celebration dinner over to McCook this evenin' and we've got an invite."

I drove straight to McCook, went to Dr. DeMay's office; and

was fortunate enough to find him without any patients there. When we'd talked about my health recovery for a few minutes I told him that I'd taken his advice all the way and was going to be married in January. Then I went on to tell him it had been because of George Miner's encouragement that I'd gone after the railroad meat contract, and that largely because of Effie Simons's advice and help I'd done so well with my farm trade that I'd been able to pay off the last dollar of the judgment against me that afternoon. I said that I wanted to celebrate with a little dinner that evening for the people who had been responsible for my good fortune, and hoped he and Mrs. DeMay would come.

Dr. DeMay seemed as happy about my getting out of debt as he had been at his discovery that my diabetes was incipient, and said that he and his wife would be delighted to come to the dinner. I told him then that George and Effie knew about my having paid off my debt, but that I'd kept his discovery and my coming marriage a secret from them as a surprise for the dinner. When I asked if he'd spring the surprise he said he'd handle the diabetes end of it, but that I'd have to do my own talking about getting married.

I stopped at the hotel just long enough to tell the manager that I wanted a table for seven at seven o'clock, with the finest steak dinner and trimmings his kitchen could turn out. Then I headed for the best clothing store in town. My only city clothes were the secondhand ones I'd bought in Omaha when I went to see Mr. Donovan about the meat contract, but I'd need a complete new outfit for getting married, so it seemed to me that I might as well buy it in time to wear to the dinner. I chose a blue serge suit because I thought it would be more appropriate than anything else for a wedding, but the only one in the store that fitted me in the shoulders was at least six inches too big around the middle. It took a tailor until seven o'clock to make the necessary alterations, and I'd been out of practice long enough that I had a little trouble with the stiff collar and bow tie, so I was late in getting to the hotel.

The dinner was a fine one, and by keeping Effie stirred up a bit on the latest Beaver Township gossip I was able to avoid talking heifers with George. Then, as soon as we'd finished the dessert, I told the Miners and Simonses that Dr. DeMay had a surprise for them. He began his story with my first visit to him in the summer of 1919, took it step by step through the more than two years I'd been his patient, told of his exhaustion experiments, and explained why they proved that my malady was not true diabetes. Then he ended his talk by saying, "I've told him there's no reason on earth that he can't live a long and normal life if he takes reasonably good care of his health, but to make assurance doubly sure I've advised him to find a good wife to watch over him."

After George had nearly broken my hand while congratulating me, and Effie had called upon God to love me as she wiped away the tears of happiness, I said that I'd been following my doctor's advice to the very best of my ability. Then I told the whole story of Edna and me, right through from the time she first became my girl until the telephone call in which we'd agreed on the twenty-fifth of January as our wedding date, and Kansas City as the place we'd begin our married life. Of course I didn't say that Edna was unwilling to bring up a family in Cedar Bluffs, but spoke of her being raised in Boston, and said I thought a move to western Kansas might be too big a change to make right away.

Dr. and Mrs. DeMay congratulated me and said they thought we'd made a wise decision in choosing Kansas City. Guy and Irene added their congratulations, but said they thought I was making a mistake by not bringing my wife home to Cedar Bluffs. Effie wept until her nose was red and her cheeks streaked, partly in happiness that I'd regained my health and was going to marry my boyhood sweetheart, and partly in disappointment that we weren't going to make our home in Cedar Bluffs. George was quiet, and stood back while the others were congratulating me. He laid a hand on my shoulder as we left the hotel, and told me, "I guess you know how glad I am for you, son, and it don't surprise me none that you aim to live in the city, but if you should come to change your mind them heifers will be right there in the pasture for leastways a couple of years."

The day before Thanksgiving the railroad job was finished and the crews moved out of Beaver Valley, but I was paid the daily minimum under my contract through the end of November, and my thousand-dollar forfeit deposit was returned.

So that my farm customers would have plenty of time to do their own butchering for the winter, I asked Effie to put out line calls saying that I'd be going out of the meat business on the tenth of December. I didn't tell her not to spread the news about my personal life, but I don't think it would have made much difference anyway. After she'd made the announcement on each line she told the listeners that I'd paid off the last dime of my debts, had fully regained my health, and was leaving Beaver Valley in the middle of December to marry my childhood sweetheart. Then she urged everyone who owed me an account to bring in enough livestock to pay it off.

All the next week wagon after wagon rolled into my yard, each bringing a hog, a calf, a cow, or a steer. By Saturday, December 10, the balance on my books was down to less than a hundred dollars, and I shipped out four of the most widely mixed carloads of livestock ever to roll over the rebuilt St. Francis branch of the CB&Q. With Kitten the only animal left on the place, our butchering business ended with that shipment. On Sunday it was simply a matter of giving away what little meat remained in the refrigerator, visiting with friends who dropped in to say goodbye, and telling them that before the winter was over I'd bring my wife out to get acquainted with the most beautiful valley and the friendliest people on earth.

Monday and Tuesday Nick and I scrubbed and polished till the place shone like a new penny, then on Wednesday I had an auction. Including my household furnishings, it brought in as much as my entire investment in the butchering business, although there was little from the slaughterhouse that could be sold.

Thursday morning I went to Oberlin to say goodbye to Mr. Frickey, John Bivans, and my other friends there, then stopped at Cedar Bluffs for a visit with Bones on my way home. In the afternoon Nick set off for Omaha, driving the Maxwell and carrying a check for fifteen hundred dollars in his pocket. That evening I went up to see Effie, took her a little present, and told her she'd always be my second-best girl. Then I rode over to spend the night with the Miners and turn old Kitten out to graze away her remaining days along the banks of Beaver Creek.

The next morning—my twenty-third birthday—George drove me to McCook, and with my roving days behind me I swung aboard the eastbound express. I had a fair-sized roll in my pocket, and a couple of thousand dollars in my account at the Farmers National in Oberlin. It wasn't as much as I'd had when I first went into the livestock business, but I was sure it would be enough, for I believed I could make a living for a wife and family wherever other men could.